THE
SEXUAL
LIBERALS
AND THE
ATTACK
ON
FEMINISM

EDITED BY

Dorchen Leidholdt and Janice G. Raymond

PERGAMON PRESS
Member of Maxwell Macmillan Pergamon Publishing Corporation
New York Oxford Beijing Frankfurt São Paulo Sydney Tokyo Toronto

Pergamon Press Offices:

U.S.A.	Pergamon Press, Inc., Maxwell House, Fairview Park, Elmsford, New York 10523, U.S.A.
U.K.	Pergamon Press plc, Headington Hill Hall, Oxford OX3 0BW, England
PEOPLE'S REPUBLIC OF CHINA	Pergamon Press, Room 4037, Qianmen Hotel, Beijing, People's Republic of China
FEDERAL REPUBLIC OF GERMANY	Pergamon Press GmbH, Hammerweg 6, D-6242 Kronberg, Federal Republic of Germany
BRAZIL	Pergamon Editora Ltda, Rua Eça de Queiros, 346, CEP 04011, Paraiso, São Paulo, Brazil
AUSTRALIA	Pergamon Press Australia Pty Ltd., P.O. Box 544, Potts Point, NSW 2011, Australia
JAPAN	Pergamon Press, 8th Floor, Matsuoka Central Building, 1-7-1 Nishishinjuku, Shinjuku-ku, Tokyo 160, Japan
CANADA	Pergamon Press Canada Ltd., Suite 271, 253 College Street, Toronto, Ontario M5T 1R5, Canada

---

First edition 1990

Library of Congress Cataloging in Publication Data

The Sexual liberals and the attack on feminism / edited by Dorchen
  Leidholdt and Janice G. Raymond. -- 1st ed.
    p.   cm. -- (The Athene series)
  Essays which originated as speeches and panel presentations at a
conference on April 6, 1987, at the New York University Law School.
  Includes index.
  ISBN 0-08-037458-1   ISBN 0-08-037457-3 (pbk.)
  1. Feminism--United States--Congresses. 2. Women's rights--United
States--Congresses. 3. Sexual ethics--United States--Congresses.
4. Pornography--Social aspects--United States--Congresses.
I. Leidholdt, Dorchen. II. Raymond, Janice G. III. Series.
HQ1403.S49   1989
305.4′2′0973--dc20   89-32594
                                                                      CIP

Printed in the United States of America

The paper used in this publication meets the minumum requirements of
American National Standard for Information Sciences -- Permanence of
Paper for Printed Library Materials, ANSI Z39.48-1984

THE
SEXUAL
LIBERALS
AND THE
ATTACK
ON
FEMINISM

Related Journals

(Free sample copies available upon request.)

ISSUES IN REPRODUCTIVE AND GENETIC
 ENGINEERING: Journal of International Feminist Analysis
WOMEN'S STUDIES INTERNATIONAL FORUM

The ATHENE Series

General Editors	Consulting Editor
Gloria Bowles	**Dale Spender**
Renate Klein	
Janice Raymond	

The Athene Series assumes that all those who are concerned with formulating explanations of the way the world works need to know and appreciate the significance of basic feminist principles.

The growth of feminist research has challenged almost all aspects of social organization in our culture. The Athene Series focuses on the construction of knowledge and the exclusion of women from the process—both as theorists and subjects of study—and offers innovative studies that challenge established theories and research.

On Athene—When Metis, goddess of wisdom who presided over all knowledge was pregnant with Athene, she was swallowed up by Zeus who then gave birth to Athene from his head. The original Athene is thus the parthenogenetic daughter of a strong mother and as the feminist myth goes, at the "third birth" of Athene she stops being Zeus' obedient mouthpiece and returns to her real source: the science and wisdom of womankind.

Contents

Acknowledgments

Without the help of many individuals and organizations, this book and the conference that gave birth to it would not have been possible. First of all, we would like to express our deepest appreciation to the dedicated activists who helped organize the conference: Dolores Alexander, Sue Batkin, Jillouise Breslauer, Zesara Chan, Michael Christian, Amy Elman, Evelina Giobbe-Kane, Ralph Hummel, Annie McCombs, Maura Maguire, Kristen Reilly, Leslie Rimmel, Evelyn Rivera Radinson, Norma Ramos, David Satz, and Dorothy Teer. Lorelei Pettigrew, Catharine MacKinnon, and Twiss Butler provided invaluable advice during the planning of the conference. Lettie Cottin Pogrebin and Gloria Steinem together gave a statement and show of support that heartened both the organizers and the audience. New York University Law School's Law Women deserve a vote of thanks for their sponsorship, as does the NYU Law School administration for providing funding for sign language interpreters. Words are inadequate to express our gratitude to the individuals and foundations who provided necessary moral and financial support: Laura Lederer and the L. J. Skaggs and Mary C. Skaggs Foundation, the Butler Family Foundation, and Helen Hauben and the Joe and Emily Lowe Foundation. Finally, our thanks to Susan Matula, who painstakingly typed and edited the transcripts of the conference presentations.

Introduction

Dorchen Leidholdt

Most of the essays in this volume began as speeches and panel presentations at a conference that, although all but ignored by the mainstream media, reverberated throughout the women's movement. On April 6, 1987, eight hundred people packed an auditorium at New York University Law School, while hundreds more sat riveted to television monitors outside. They came to hear many of the major feminist writers, thinkers, and leaders address an ideology and a program that, they asserted, was undermining feminism in the guise of being its best friend.

The subject of the conference was liberalism or, to use British feminist historian Sheila Jeffreys' more precise terminology, "sexual liberalism": a set of political beliefs and practices rooted in the assumption that sexual expression is inherently liberating and must be permitted to flourish unchecked, even when it entails the exploitation or brutalization of others.[1] To sexual liberals, sexuality is not a construct of culture that reflects and reinforces a culture's values including its devaluation of women, as feminists contend, but an icon of nature, so fragile that any analysis, criticism, or attempt at change threatens not only the existence of human sexuality but everyone's freedom.

Conflict between feminists and sexual liberals is nothing new. Indeed, the two groups have been at odds from the beginning of the second wave of feminism in the 1960s, if not before. The early consciousness-raising groups and the activism and publications they generated squarely confronted the sexual attitudes and mores of liberal and left-wing men. In *Notes from the First Year*, for example, a collection of essays published by New York Radical Women in 1968, Shulamith Firestone identified and then dissected what she called "the seeming freedoms" for women championed by so-called progressive men. At the top of her list was sexuality:

---

[1] The title of the conference and this volume—"The Sexual Liberals and the Attack on Feminism"—is the inspiration of Sheila Jeffreys.

> As for sex itself, I would argue that any changes were as a result of male interests and not female. . . . A relaxing of mores concerning female sexual behavior was to his advantage; there was a greater sexual supply at a lower or nonexistent cost. But his attitudes haven't changed much.[2]

One participant in a late sixties consciousness-raising group anticipated the analysis that antipornography feminists would make two decades later: "A man's sense of personal worth comes through his cocksmanship, in the Playboy mystique. It's the old business of raising your self-image by lowering someone else."[3]

By 1970, Dana Densmore and others in a Boston-based radical feminist group called Cell 16 made male supremacist sexual values the focus of their theorizing. Densmore argued that the image of the sexually liberated woman extolled by sexually liberal men was nothing more than a repackaged version of the oldest and most dehumanized conception of women:

> People seem to believe that sexual freedom (even when it is only the freedom to actively offer oneself as a willing object) is freedom. When men say to us, "But aren't you already liberated?" what they mean is, "We said it was okay to let us fuck you . . . What more could you want?" The unarticulated assumption behind this misunderstanding is that women are purely sexual beings, bodies and sensuality, fucking machines. Therefore freedom for women can only mean sexual freedom.[4]

As the 1970s progressed, activism often loomed larger than theorizing, as feminists organized against rape, battery, sexual harassment, and child sexual abuse, and protested beauty pageants and sexist ads. Each new phase of feminist work was greeted with fierce and unrelenting opposition by sexually liberal men. Male academicians and social commentators reacted to speakouts by women who had survived rape with disdain and hostility. Although professing to be against rape, these men defined it in the narrowest terms possible, as forced penetration of a sexually inexperienced woman by a stranger, and they defended the mindset underlying rape—that sex is conquest—as natural and inevitable. Sexual liberals argued that "sexual harassment" was a misnomer; that what feminists were misguidedly calling sexual abuse in the workplace or on the street was merely the natural expression of males' sexual attraction to females. With growing vehemence, sexual

---

[2]Shulamith Firestone, "The Women's Rights Movement in the U.S.," in New York Radical Women (ed.), *Notes from the First Year*, June 1968, p. 6 (published privately).
[3]"Women Rap About Sex," *Ibid.*, p. 10.
[4]Dana Densmore, "Independence from the Sexual Revolution," in New York Radical Women (ed.), *Notes from the Third Year: Women's Liberation*, 1971 (published privately).

liberals insisted that feminists were mistaking attraction and affection for hostility and violence and grossly exaggerating the incidence of sexual violence against women and children. This in spite of the growing body of testimony of women who had survived this violence and the consensus among social scientists that sexual violence is far more pervasive than anyone had realized—that one out of four girls is sexually molested and a third of all adult females are raped.[5]

The backlash became even more vociferous when feminists began actively organizing against pornography in the late 1970s. Although feminists had criticized pornography from the start of the contemporary women's movement,[6] now they began to mobilize against it, organizing meetings, marches, picket lines, and press conferences. This new phase of activism reflected the effort of feminists, who had spent a decade fighting to better the lot of victims of sexual violence, to stop the violence at its source. Whereas liberals and conservatives both believed that male sexual violence was innate and thus inevitable, feminists argued that it was learned and that pornographic materials, which eroticize sexual violence and inequality, were a central component of that education. The feminists' targets were not confined to the so-called hardcore materials that at least putatively were prohibited under obscenity laws but also included the "softcore" pornography that sexual liberals like Hugh Hefner had made socially acceptable. For feminists, the issue was not morals, taste, or aesthetics but the attitudes about women that pornography inculcated, the acts of sexual brutality engendered by those attitudes, and the exploitation of real women in the manufacture of pornographic materials.

Pornographers and civil libertarians immediately banded together to defend pornography. Well aware that it would be hard to enter the arena of public debate making a case for pornography, they adopted another, safer strategy: attacking the feminist critics of pornography by evoking long-standing and antiwoman stereotypes. While the pornographers conducted a no-holds-barred character assassination campaign, smearing their feminist opponents as castrating man haters and prudes,

---

[5]Diana E. H. Russell, *Sexual Exploitation*. New York: Macmillan, 1984.
[6]To radical feminists at the beginning of the Second Wave, pornography was nothing more or less than the codification of a male supremacist value system and the reification of male sexual power over women:

> Pornography rests on the accurate assumption that sexual "pleasure" is equal to power and dominance for the man. It expresses a masculine ideology of male power over females, and it cuts across class lines. (Roxanne Dunbar, " 'Sexual Liberation': More of the Same Thing," in *More Fun and Games: A Journal of Female Liberation*, Issue 3, November 1969 [published privately].)

civil libertarians waged a more gentlemanly attack, denouncing anti-pornography feminists as repressive and censorious.[7]

It was not inevitable that civil libertarians would embrace sexual liberalism and do everything in their power to stamp out the feminist movement against pornography; some civil libertarians refused to join the ranks of the sexual liberals. There were several factors, however, that propelled many, if not most, civil libertarians into sexual liberalism.

To start, there was the civil libertarians' philosophy, which considers the state the principal and often the sole threat to human freedom—a good that flourishes as long as the power of the state over the individual is kept in check. In this analysis, freedom is distinct from social and political equality. Although this philosophy accurately describes the situation of white men in this country, it has never been applicable to the situation of minorities and women. For members of these groups, social and political equality is a precondition of freedom. Moreover, for minorities and women, the state is no greater an obstacle to equality than many nongovernmental institutions and organizations.

In addition, there was the history of the civil liberties movement. In the 1950s and 1960s, civil libertarians joined pornographers to fight antiobscenity laws. The pornographers who started out as the clients of civil liberties lawyers soon became their funders and friends. By the end of the 1970s, a symbiotic relationship existed between civil libertarians and pornographers that could not be ignored: the San Diego chapter of the American Civil Liberties Union (ACLU) showed pornographic films as fundraisers in a theater loaned by a local pornographer; the Minnesota chapter (the MCLU) was donated free office space by midwest pornography kingpins; the ACLU's reproductive rights project received substantial funding from the Playboy Foundation; and each year the ACLU's national office helped arrange and judge the Hugh M. Hefner First Amendment Awards, a Playboy public relations effort. (Not surprisingly, recipients of the awards were frequently ACLU officials.)

---

[7]The "anti-sex" label was also foisted on early radical feminists. In "Who Claims Men Are the Enemy," Dana Densmore analyzed this reaction:

Another ploy, a little more subtle, is "Why do you want to get rid of sex?" Again, this may be a smear, a bid for attention, or an honest fear.

When it is an honestly felt fear, what he means is: "I cannot conceive of sex, cannot be sexually interested in a woman, unless I am in a superior-to-inferior, active-to-passive, aggressor-to-victim relationship with her. If you are going to insist that we must approach each other as equals you will have destroyed sex and you might as well demand celibacy." (From *Females and Liberation: A Collection of Articles by Dana Densmore*, 1970 [published privately].)

The contradictions embedded in the philosophy and history of civil libertarians are evident in their reaction to a law, passed by the New York State legislature in the late 1970s, that criminalized the production, distribution, and sale of child pornography. Never even considering the harm of child pornography to the civil liberties of children—in particular, the right of children to live in society free from the threat of sexual exploitation and abuse—the ACLU adopted unquestioningly the domino theory offered as a defense by the child pornographers prosecuted under the statute: prohibition of child pornography would trigger a process that would end in the censorship of masterpieces of literature. The ACLU, along with two other civil libertarian groups (the Media Coalition and American Booksellers Association), fought the child pornography statute all the way to the Supreme Court. Although the Supreme Court unanimously upheld the New York law, which became the model for a federal statute, the domino theory did not become reality. *Huckleberry Finn* and *Ulysses* remained on the bookshelves. This fact, however, did not stop the ACLU from evoking this specious argument against subsequent feminist legal efforts.

Also underlying the alliance of civil libertarians with pornographers and with sexual liberalism is the fact that these organizations were established and have always been controlled by white men. As a consequence, the philosophy and political agenda of civil libertarians have always reflected and furthered white male interests. Although civil libertarian leaders are not necessarily sex industry consumers, it is clear that they do not experience the reduction of women to sexual commodities as demeaning or exploitative. Their domino theory is never applied to the other side of the question: whether the legitimization and proliferation of pornography and prostitution destroy the civil liberties of women. The few women who have risen to positions of importance within the ACLU have shared the values of their male colleagues—indeed, it was the female director of the ACLU's San Diego chapter who arranged to have an X-rated "classic" that featured a coerced and brutalized pornography "model" shown to its members to educate them about the innocuousness of pornography.

The most inescapable evidence of the embracing of sexual liberalism by civil libertarians is the fact that civil libertarians began to mobilize against antipornography feminists almost a decade before feminists began to support any legislative remedies holding the pornographers accountable for pornography's harm. At one of the first feminist conferences on pornography, held in New York City in 1978, prominent civil libertarian men shouted down feminists attempting to discuss the relationship between pornography and sexual violence. One noted New York University law professor, who sat on a panel with Andrea Dworkin, Phyllis Chesler, Florence Rush, and other feminist writers, became so enraged at the feminist presentations that he began stamping his feet and waving his arms in what could only be described as a temper tantrum. Clearly it was not state sanctions against pornography that incurred his wrath but mere feminist speech against pornography. The inescapable conclusion was that continued access to pornography was a cherished privilege of many civil libertarian men.

In the mid-1980s there were two developments that prompted sexual liberals to step up their attacks against feminists. The first was an amendment to a municipal human rights ordinance that defined pornography as a practice of sex discrimination and gave women injured in its production and dissemination a cause of action to sue pornographers. The ordinance, authored by Catharine MacKinnon and Andrea Dworkin, represented a significant break with legal tradition. Unlike antiobscenity laws that frame the harm of pornography in moralistic and aesthetic terms, as the offense that pictures and words that arouse some people's prurient interests do to other people's sensibilities, the ordinance identified pornography's harm in feminist political terms, as its damage to the status and safety of women. Unlike antiobscenity laws, which empower the state's prosecutors to bring criminal charges against alleged purveyors of obscene materials, the feminist ordinance empowered individual women to file civil suits against traffickers in pornography.

The civil rights antipornography ordinance was twice passed by the Minneapolis City Council, only to be vetoed each time by its civil libertarian mayor. A slightly altered version was approved by the Indianapolis City Council and signed into law by that city's mayor. Before a single suit could be brought under the ordinance, it was challenged on overbreadth grounds by the Media Coalition in conjunction with American Booksellers Association and the ACLU. Playboy lent the services of its legal counsel and flooded local legislators with letters denouncing the feminist law.

The ordinance was eventually held to be unconstitutional by a conservative district court judge, a decision affirmed by a conservative circuit court panel. The truth of the matter was that the feminist law flew in the face of both liberal and conservative legal traditions and so was attacked by forces on both ends of the male-dominated political spectrum. Moreover, many conservatives are sexual liberals. Fundamentalist Marabel Morgan's best-selling *The Total Woman*, which attempted to indoctrinate women into sexual submission, pornography-style, was no aberration of conservatism, and two of the three most popular pornography magazines—*Hustler* and *Penthouse*—are published by arch-conservatives and aimed at politically reactionary audiences.

Political reality notwithstanding, sexual liberals floated the rumor that feminists had formed an alliance with conservatives to fight pornography. It didn't matter that the sexual liberals were unable to muster any evidence to support their allegations. This fantasy was reported as fact in the press, and the actual alliance that had long existed between pornographers and civil libertarians was ignored by the media.

The second development that intensified the opposition of the sexual liberals to feminists fighting pornography was not a feminist effort at all but the appointment by Attorney General Edwin Meese of a commission to study the effects of pornography. The commission held a series of hearings around the country, and a broad array of people testified—social scientists, pornographers, pornography performers, feminists, civil libertarians, and ordinary citizens. Although the commission's conclusion—that pornography encourages attitudes and behaviors of sexual aggression—reflected the consensus among leading social scientists and the overwhelming testimony of women seeking refuge and redress from battering, sexual abuse and harassment, and prostitution, it was attacked by sexual liberals as engineered by the conservative Reagan administration. To prevent the report from doing damage to its business interests, the Media Coalition, an alliance of book, magazine, and newspaper publishers and distributors that included publishers and distributors of pornography, hired a major public relations firm, Gray and Company, at a cost of a million dollars. The firm's assignment was to conduct a media blitz that portrayed opponents of pornography, particularly feminists, as book burners. Ironically, and not incidentally, the result of the Media Coalition's so-called anticensorship efforts was the inability of the commission to find a publisher for its controversial report. (The previous commission's report, which had exonerated pornography, had been published by Random House.) Feminists writing about pornography and related issues encountered greater obstacles to publication than ever before, and feminist protests and press conferences that targeted pornography, once heavily covered, were now shrouded in silence.

The onslaught that the sexual liberals waged against feminists divided the women's movement. Liberal feminists, who had long benefited from alliances with sexually liberal men on the issue of abortion, were frightened by the attacks, and many tried to distance themselves from their more radical feminist sisters.[8] Socialist feminists, who have historically remained distant from the feminist campaigns against pros-

---

[8] Sexually liberal men support abortion for women not because they want women to be able to control their bodies but because they know that unrestricted abortions heighten women's availability to men for sex. And the sex sexually liberal men have in mind is not the kind that emerges from women's authentic desire for physical intimacy and pleasure. Instead, it is the male-controlled, male-defined sex of pornography, in which men are subjects and women are objects.

titution, rape, sexual abuse, and pornography, now turned liberal in theory as well. Radical feminists continued their work against pornography and watched financial and political support evaporate.

Then there was the small group of women who went even further: collaboration with antifeminists. Some of these women held prestigious positions with the ACLU. Most were sexual liberals who considered pornography and even sadomasochism to be sexual liberation for women. They banded together in a group they named FACT (Feminist Anti-Censorship Task Force), debated feminists against pornography, and produced their own pornographic publication entitled "Caught Looking." FACT existed for one purpose alone—to defeat the feminist civil rights antipornography ordinance. When the Supreme Court summarily affirmed the circuit court's decision against the law, FACT's raison d'etre disappeared and the group disbanded.

Pornography was not the only issue to mobilize sexual liberals against feminists. Sexual liberals in Canada fought evidentiary rules that prevented defense attorneys from savaging the character of rape victims on the witness stand and fought the feminists who supported the rules. Back in the United States, sexual liberals defended prostitution as an economic and sexual choice for women and advocated its legalization. Feminists in groups like WHISPER (Women Hurt in Systems of Prostitution Engaged in Revolt), many of whom had survived sexual exploitation and abuse as prostitutes, challenged the claims and agenda of the sexual liberals, arguing that they legitimized and perpetuated female sexual slavery. WHISPER pointed to studies showing that instead of entering prostitution voluntarily, as the sexual liberals claimed, most women and girls who became prostitutes had been coerced into that condition by a complex of factors that included sexual abuse in childhood, poverty, and pimps.

Most recently, the sexual liberals have led the prosurrogacy forces. The debate over legalizing surrogate contracts has revived the conflict between civil libertarians and feminists in a battle that mirrors the fight around pornography. The ACLU contested, as unconstitutional, one of the first state laws prohibiting contractual surrogacy in Michigan *after* it had been passed by the state legislature and been signed into law by the governor. To all appearances, the ACLU made a deal with the state's attorney general who agreed to a different interpretation of the bill— one that permits surrogacy as long as the woman does not give up her rights to the child until after birth. Elsewhere, feminists who organized support for Mary Beth Whitehead and other women deceived and exploited by the reproductive pimps and baby brokers, found themselves confronting many of the same characters from the cast that had rallied to the defense of the pornographers, using the same rhetoric of individual freedom, this time phrased as "procreative liberty."

This was the political backdrop of the conference, although battle-ground may be the more accurate term. The feelings of excitement and exhilaration that swept the audience no doubt stemmed from the realization that feminists had weathered the attacks leveled by far more powerful opponents, that they were still fighting sexual exploitation, and that they at long last had an opportunity to tell the truth about who they were and what they were up against, in their own language and on their own terms. The speakers were angry and witty and inspiring. They had survived pimps and Mormon patriarchs, censorship in the name of freedom of speech, and coercion in the guise of freedom of choice. Their characters had been vilified and their words distorted, but they were still there—with more clarity, commitment, and courage than ever before.

Part I

FEMINISM AND LIBERALISM

Liberalism and the Death of Feminism

Catharine A. MacKinnon

Once there was a women's movement. I first heard about it from the liberated issue of *Rat*, which Robin Morgan and a collective of intrepid women put together by taking over an underground newspaper on which they had worked. What I learned from liberated *Rat* was that something that excluded women from equal participation, that denigrated women's voice, that silenced women's contribution, that did not take women seriously, that patronized women, that no matter what else that something did or didn't do, it had to be publicly repudiated at minimum, and at best taken over and transformed. I did not hear at that time that feminists had censored *Rat*, although no doubt some people thought so. To me, it was speech.

Then, there was a women's movement that criticized as socially based— not natural or God-given or even descended from Congress—acts like rape as male violence against women, as a form of sexual terrorism. It criticized war as male ejaculation. It criticized marriage and the family as institutional crucibles of male privilege, and the vaginal orgasm as a mass hysterical survival response. It criticized definitions of merit as implicitly sex biased, class biased, and race biased. It even criticized fairy tales.

When this movement criticized rape, it meant rapists and the point of view that saw rape as sex. When it criticized prostitution, it meant pimps and johns and the point of view that women are born to sell sex. When it criticized incest, it meant those who did it to us, and the point of view that made our vulnerability and enforced silence sexy. When it criticized battery, it meant batterers, and the point of view that violence expressed the intensity of love. Nobody thought that in criticizing these practices, the movement was criticizing their victims.

It also criticized sacred concepts from the standpoint of women's

3

material existence, our reality, concepts like choice. It was a movement that knew when material conditions preclude 99 percent of your options, it is not meaningful to call the remaining 1 percent—what you are doing—your choice. This movement was not taken in by concepts like consent. It knew that when force is a normalized part of sex, when no is taken to mean yes, when fear and despair produce acquiescence and acquiescence is taken to mean consent, consent is not a meaningful concept.

This movement also criticized concepts that we took and made our own, like equality. It knew that the way equality had been defined was premised not only on a meaningless symmetry, an empty equivalence, but also that it was defined according to a male standard. It knew the limits of being told you could either be the same as men or different from men. If you were the same as men, you were equal to their standards; if you were different from men, you were different from their standards. This movement said if that was equality, we didn't want it.

It also criticized the ruling concept of freedom, especially sexual freedom, unpacked and unmasked it as a cover for the freedom to abuse. When people with power defended their oppression of women as freedom, this movement knew it was the thrill of their power they were defending. This was a movement that was critical of the freedom to oppress, not one that thought women would be free when we had more of it.

Some intrepid spirits even criticized love, saying that it was a lust for self-annihilation that bound women to their oppression. And, eventually and at great cost, some criticized sex, including the institution of intercourse as a strategy and practice in subordination.

Implicit in all these criticisms was a criticism of abstraction as a strategy in male hegemony. This was a movement that always wanted to know where the women were, substantively. Where was *women's* "choice"? Where was *women's* "consent"? Where was equality as *women* define it? What did freedom for *women* mean? As we criticized male reality in this movement that was, we always looked for the prick in the piece. We found that abstractions were a coverup for the gendered reality that was really going on. On this basis, this movement produced a systematic, relentless, deeply materially based and empirically rigorous critique of the male-dominated reality of women's lives and the glossy abstractions that made it seem not male-dominated. It uncovered, in this process, deep connections between race, class, and sexual oppression, and pursued them not as an afterthought, not as a footnote, not as a list, but because they were essential. This was a movement that said that every issue was a women's issue and every place was a woman's place.

This was also a movement that demonstrated against the Miss America Pageant and *Snuff* and understood the connection between the two. It understood that sexual objectification as use and sexual objectification as abuse are two facets of the same problem, that the logic of both is making a person into a sexual thing. Miss America is the foreplay, turning a woman into a plaything. *Snuff* is the consummation, turning a woman into a corpse.

This was a movement that defaced objectifying posters. It marched, it petitioned, it organized, it hexed Wall Street and levitated the Pentagon, it sued, it used whatever it could get its hands on. In the words of Monique Wittig, failing that, it invented.

Why did we do all of this? We did it, I think, because we were a movement that valued women. Women mattered. We were not defensive about it. When women were hurt, this movement defended them. Individually and in groups, it organized and started shelters and groups of and for all women: battered women, incest survivors, prostitutes. We did this not because those women were thought "bad" by society or considered outlaws or shunned. We did it because what was done to them was a systematic act of power against each one of us, although they were taking the brunt of it. This was not a sentimental identification. We knew that whatever could be done to them could be, was being, would be done to us. We *were* them, also.

This was a movement that took women's side in everything. Of everything, it asked the question: "Is it good for women?" Each woman was all women in some way. Any woman who was violated was our priority. It was a deeply collectivist movement. In this movement, when we said "women, we," it had content. It didn't mean that we all had to be the same in order to be part of this common condition. That, in fact, was the genius, one of the unique contributions of this movement: it premised unity as much on diversity as on commonality. It did not assume that commonality meant sameness.

This was a movement in which people understood the need to act with courage in everyday life, that feminism was not a better deal or a riskless guarantee but a discipline of a hostile reality. To say that the personal was political meant, among other things, that what we do every day matters. It meant you become what you do not resist. The personal and everyday was understood to be part of the political order we organized to change, part of our political agenda. To see the personal as the political did not mean that what turns you on grounds the policies you promote.

We also felt and understood, I think, a responsibility to all women. We opposed women's invisibility, insisted on women's dignity, questioned everything that advanced itself at women's expense. Most of all, this movement believed in change. It intended to transform language, community, the life of the spirit and the body and the mind, the definition of physicality and intelligence, the meaning of left and right, right and wrong, and the shape and nature of power.

It was not all roses, this movement that we had. But it did mean to change the face of this earth. It knew that this was necessary. Most of all, it knew that we did not yet have what we need and believed that we could get it.

I learned everything I know from this movement.

Then something happened. Or started to happen, or maybe it had been happening all along and some of us had overlooked it. The first time I noticed this something was with the Equal Rights Amendment. We were told that we could and should have this constitutional amendment because sex equality under law was not really going to do very much, would not really change anything, surely nothing basic. What the movement had identified as the pervasive, basic oppression and exploitation of women by men became transformed into an evil called "sex-based classifications by law."[1] That, suddenly, was what sex equality had to change. Under this notion of sex equality, we were given the choice of being the same as men—the left's choice for us— or different from men—the right's choice. We were told that the left's choice was clearly better and the only route to true equality. So so-called gender neutrality—ignoring what is distinctively done to women and ignoring who is doing it—became termed the feminist position. I heard no one challenge the fact that, under this approach to ERA, either way it was the male standard, either way it was not what the movement had in mind by equality. The ERA strategy based on this analysis was, apparently, that sex equality can be made nonthreatening to the hierarchical status quo and still be real. This approach never identified male supremacy as what we had to contend with. It presented the extraordinary spectacle—which I, frankly, found humiliating—of feminists ardently denying that sex equality would make much difference while urgently seeking it.

Then I started to connect that with what was going on with abortion. While the women's movement had criticized the line between public and private and had identified the private as a primary sphere of the subordination of women, *Roe v. Wade*[2] had decriminalized access to

---

[1] An example of this transformation is Brown, Emerson, Freedman, Falk, "The Equal Rights Amendment: A Constitutional Basis for Equal Rights for Women," 80 Yale L.J. (1971).
[2] *Roe v. Wade*, 410 U.S. 113 (1973).

abortion as a privacy right. A movement that knew that the private was a cover for our public condition was suddenly being told—and saying—that the abortion right was our right *to* that same privacy. If you forgot what this movement knew, this seemed like a good thing, just like being the same as men seemed like a good thing. Men, especially straight white ones, live in a gender-neutral universe. It is a lot better than the sex-specific universe women live in. Men have privacy. Maybe if women had some, things would be better. Then *Harris v. McRae*[3] came along and denied public funding for all women who cannot pay for abortions, playing out the logic of the private as we had known it all along. If you can't pay for it, you can't get it — or there are other ways to get it, which are not what rights look like. A coat-hanger is not a right. The logic was that the government, the public, had no duty to fund publicly what the government was supposed to keep out of, the private. It is not that decriminalization wasn't an improvement over jail. It is that getting a right to abortion as a privacy right without addressing the sex inequality of and in the private sphere is to assume that sexual equality already exists.

These suspicions about the male supremacist nature of the privacy right were furthered by another thing some of us noticed. That was that the freedom of the penis to engage in anal penetration in the name of privacy had become a priority issue for women under the banner of "gay and lesbian rights," without connecting a critique of homophobia with a critique of misogyny. Nothing in the sodomy cases criticized gender, far less gender inequality.

If these suspicions are pursued into sex discrimination law, further difficulties emerge, for example, in *Sears v. EEOC*, a garden variety sex discrimination case.[4] There we see a drastic disparity between women and men in some of the better paying jobs at Sears over a long time, a massive statistical disparity, and the Equal Employment Opportunity Commission suing them. A woman—a feminist—testified that this was necessarily evidence of discrimination by Sears because women want the same things from employment that men want, like money.[5] Another woman — a feminist — testified that this is not necessarily evidence of discrimination by Sears because women want different things from employment than men do. The gender difference is consistent

---

[3] *Harris v. McRae*, 448 U.S. 297 (1980).
[4] *EEOC v. Sears, Roebuck & Co.*, 839 F.2d 302 (7th Cir. 1988).
[5] Offer of Proof Concerning the Testimony of Dr. Rosalind Rosenberg and Written Rebuttal Testimony of Dr. Rosalind Rosenberg before the United States District Court for the Northern District of Illinois in *EEOC v. Sears, Roebuck & Co.*, 504 F. Supp. 241 (N.D. Ill. 1988).

with this statistical disparity because women choose jobs which pay less because they are women.[6]

So you have a large pile of men at the top and a large pile of women at the bottom and the question is, which of the two theories best explains that: the theory that says women are the same as men or the theory that says women are different from men? Obviously the latter theory does, especially if you believe that women do what they want to do, and are free to want anything. Even then, the women's movement was fairly clear that Sears' position, even in the mouth of a feminist, justified an oppressive status quo which kept some women on the bottom, and it was perverse to do this in the name of feminism.

Then it became a good day to go back to bed—if bed is a safe place for you—the day we were told by feminist groups that guaranteeing maternity leave to women is a form of sex discrimination, and a statute that does this violates Title VII of the Civil Rights Act. No feminist group that filed a brief in the Supreme Court case on the subject said that it was sex discrimination *not* to give women maternity leave. No one said that if Title VII required maternity leave be *denied* to women, *that* would be sex discrimination under the Constitution. Nobody said squarely that if all the people hurt by this deprivation are women, *that* makes it discrimination on the basis of sex.

Actually, the Supreme Court figured this out all by itself, better than any brief from any women's group did. The Supreme Court said essentially that granting maternity leaves by law is not sex discrimination, it is sex equality. Women getting what they need to work is what sex equality means. The decision, I might add, was written by Justice Thurgood Marshall, a Black man.[7] Once he did it, some feminist groups cheered and took credit for what they had opposed.

Then there was the debate over sadomasochism. If it had escaped you before, it was hard to miss this breakdown in what the women's movement had meant. The part I want to highlight has to do with our ability to say the word "we" in discussions of sexuality, including of sexual abuse, and to have it mean anything. It seems to me that the advocacy of sadomasochism as women's first love, women's final destiny, what we would all do if we really did what we wanted, is based on the absence of a critique of why women *would* experience sexuality in exactly the way in which it has been shoved down our throats since day one: top down. Actually, women have largely rejected the politics

---

[6] Written Testimony of Alice Kessler-Harris before the United States District Court for the Northern District of Illinois in *EEOC v. Sears, Roebuck & Co.*, 504 F.Supp. 241 (N.D. Ill. 1988).

[7] *California Federal Savings & Loan, et al. v. Guerra*, 479 U.S. 272 (1987).

of sadomasochism. But the residue of its defense has been extremely destructive nonetheless. In discussions of sexuality, women don't say "women" any more, but "speaking only for myself, I . . ." The debate over sadomasochism made "women, we" taboo in the sexual area. It began in a moral morass and left us, politically, with an individualistic analysis of sexuality, undermining a collectivity that was never based on conformity, but on resistance.

Everything some of us had started to notice exploded in the discussion on pornography. As many of you may know, Andrea Dworkin and I conceived and designed a law based on the politics of the women's movement that we thought we were part of and fielded it with others who were under the same illusion. It is a sex equality law, a civil-rights law, a law that says that sexual subordination of women through pictures and words, this sexual traffic in women, violates women's civil rights.[8]

This was done in feminist terms: as if women mattered; because we value women; because it wasn't enough only to criticize oppression, and it wasn't enough only to engage in guerilla activities of resistance, although they are crucial. We wanted to change the norm. To change the norm, we looked for a vulnerable place in the system. We looked for something that could be made to work for us, something we could use. We took whatever we could get our hands on, and when it wasn't there, we invented. We invented a sex equality law against pornography on women's terms.

To no one's surprise, especially ours, it was opposed by many people. It was opposed by conservatives who discovered that they disliked sex equality a lot more than they disliked pornography. It was opposed by liberals, who discovered that they liked speech—i.e., sex, i.e., women being used—a great deal more than they liked sex equality. Then came the opposition from a quarter that labeled itself feminist: from FACT, the Feminist Anti-Censorship Task Force. At this point, for me, the women's movement that I had known came to an end.

In an act of extraordinary horizontal hostility, FACT filed a brief against the ordinance in court as part of a media-based legal attack on it.[9] They did what they could to prevent from existing, to keep out of women's hands, this law, written in women's blood, in women's tears, in women's pain, in women's experience, out of women's silence, this

---

[8] *An Ordinance for the City of Minneapolis,* Amending Title 7, Chapter 139 of the Minneapolis Code of Ordinances relating to Civil Rights, section 139.10 et seq., reprinted in Dworkin and MacKinnon, *Pornography & Civil Rights: A New Day for Women's Equality* (Minneapolis: Organizing Against Pornography, 1988).

[9] Brief Amici Curiae of Feminist Anti-Censorship Task Force et al. in *American Booksellers Association v. Hudnut,* 21 J. of L. Reform 69 (1988).

law to make acts against women actionable—acts like coercion, force, assault, trafficking in our flesh. Pornography, they said, *is* sex equality. Women should just have better access to it. Using the debased model of equality-as-sameness that the women's movement we used to know was predicated on criticizing, they argued that pornography must not be actionable by its victims because, among other reasons, "the range of feminist imagination and expression in the realm of sexuality has barely begun to find voice. Women need the freedom and socially recognized space to appropriate for themselves the robustness of what traditionally has been male language."[10] Men have it; FACT women want it. Thus, "even pornography which is problematic for women can be experienced as affirming of women's desires and of women's *equality*"[11] (emphasis added). This is a subquote from Ellen Willis in the brief, "Pornography can be psychic assault,"—get it, that rape only happened in your head—"but for women, as for men, it can also be a source of erotic pleasure. . . . A woman who enjoys pornography, even if that means enjoying a rape fantasy, is, in a sense, a rebel." From what is she rebelling? Their answer: "Insisting on an aspect of her sexuality that has been defined as a male preserve."[12] Now who can't tell the difference between rape and sex? Rape has been a male preserve. But to insist on being defined by what one has been forced to be defined by is, to say the least, a rather limited notion of freedom. And choice. And a women's movement that aspires to inhabit rapist preserves is not a women's movement I want any part of.

Equality in the FACT brief means equal access to pornography by women. That is, equal access by women to the population of women who must be treated in the ways that the ordinance makes actionable, so that pornography of them can be available. The FACT brief further objects that the ordinance "makes socially invisible women who find sexually explicit images of women in positions of display or penetrated by objects to be erotic, liberating, or educational."[13] In other words, an entire population of women must continue to be treated in the ways the ordinance makes actionable so that this other population of women can experience its eroticism, liberation, or education at their expense.

The FACT brief was critical of the politics of the ordinance for implying that in a society of sex inequality—where sex is what women *have* to sell, sex is what we are, sex is what we are valued for, we are born sex, we die sex—that if we don't choose all of that, if we don't

---

[10] Ibid. at 121.
[11] Ibid.
[12] Ibid.
[13] Ibid. at 129.

recognize that that is a choice, then *we* are demeaning prostitutes and oppressing women. It said that when the ordinance told courts that they could not use all the excuses they have always used to disbelieve women when we say we are sexually coerced, that *we* are not respecting women's consent. This was a movement which understood that the choice to be beaten by one man for economic survival was not a real choice, despite the appearance of consent a marriage contract might provide. It was not considered demeaning or oppressive to battered women to do everything possible to help them leave. Yet now we are supposed to believe, in the name of feminism, that the choice to be fucked by hundreds of men for economic survival must be affirmed as a real choice, and if the woman signs a model release there is no coercion there.[14]

You might be wondering what the FACT response to all the knowledge, data, understanding, and experience of women's sexual victimization presented in support of the ordinance was. What their response was to all the women who wanted to use the law, the women who had the courage to speak out so it could exist, who put their lives, their reputations, and, yes, their honor on the line for it. Mostly, FACT did not even mention them. They were beneath notice. Coerced women, assaulted women, subordinated women became "some women." In fact, the FACT brief did what pornography does: it makes harm to women invisible by making it sex. It makes harm to women into ideas about sex, just like the right-wing male judge did who found the ordinance unconstitutional. On the bottom line, the FACT brief was a pure address to the penis. It said, "We like it. We want it. All we want is 'in.' Want to watch?"

And you know, it worked. Women's equality, in the decision that invalidated the ordinance as a prohibition on ideas, became one "point of view" on sex.[15] Doing something about acts of inequality became the regulation of a point of view. FACT does not deserve all the credit for this, because their power comes from fronting for male supremacy. Nor do they deserve all the blame. That belongs with the pornographers, their legitimate media cohorts, and the ACLU. But as an upfront antifeminist vehicle in the name of feminism, FACT made it possible for that right-wing judge to write, as he struck down the ordinance: "Feminists have entered this case as *amici* on both sides."[16] Yes: Linda Marchiano, the woman who was coerced into the pornographic film *Deep Throat,* and Dorothy Stratten, who was in *Playboy* and was mur-

---

[14] Ibid. at 122, 127–28, 130, 131.
[15] *American Booksellers v. Hudnut,* 771 F.2d 323, 327 (7th Cir. 1985).
[16] *Id.* at 324.

dered by her pimp, rape crisis centers, community groups representing working class neighborhoods and communities of color — they filed on one side. FACT, an elite group mostly of academics and lawyers, filed on the other.

The Black movement has Uncle Toms and Oreo cookies. The labor movement has scabs. The women's movement has FACT.

What is the difference between the women's movement we had and the one we have now, if it can be called a movement? I think the difference is liberalism. Where feminism was collective, liberalism is individualistic. We have been reduced to that. Where feminism is socially based and critical, liberalism is naturalistic, attributing the product of women's oppression to women's natural sexuality, making it "ours." Where feminism criticizes the ways in which women have been socially determined in an attempt to change that determination, liberalism is voluntaristic, meaning it acts like we have choices that we do not have. Where feminism is based on material reality, liberalism is based on some ideal realm in the head. And where feminism is relentlessly political, about power and powerlessness, the best that can be mustered by this nouveau movement is a watered-down form of moralism: this is good, this is bad, no analysis of power or powerlessness at all. In other words, members of groups, like women, who have no choice but to live life as members of groups are taken as if they are unique individuals. Their social characteristics are then reduced to natural characteristics. Preclusion of choices becomes expression of free will. Material reality is turned into ideas about reality. And concrete positions of power and powerlessness are transformed into mere relative value judgments about which reasonable people can form different but equally valid preferences. Women's experience of abuse becomes a "point of view."

The way this gets itself up in law is as gender neutrality, consent, privacy, and speech. Gender neutrality means that you cannot take gender into account, you cannot recognize, as we once knew we had to, that neutrality enforces a non-neutral status quo. Consent means that whatever you are forced to do is attributed to your free will. Privacy protects the sphere of women's intimate oppression. Speech protects sexual violence against women and sexual use of women because they are male forms of self-expression. Under the First Amendment, only those who already have speech have protected speech. Women are more likely to *be* men's speech. No one who does not already have these rights guaranteed them socially gets them legally.

What has been achieved for women through these politics of liberalism? The ERA has been lost. Abortion funding has been lost. Nothing very significant has been accomplished with rape law reform. The Supreme Court is fashioning some progressive law on sex discrimination largely on its own. You know, it is an incredible insult when the state does sex equality better than the women's movement does it. We would have *lost* statutory maternity leave if this feminism had its way. And pornography has been saved.

Liberalism makes these results necessary, in part because it cannot look at sexual misogyny. This is because misogyny *is* sexual. To be clear, it is sexual on the left, it is sexual on the right, it is sexual to liberals, and it is sexual to conservatives. As a result, sexuality, as socially organized, is deeply misogynist. To male dominance, of which liberalism is the current ruling ideology, the sexual misogyny that is fundamental to all these problems cannot be seen as a sex equality issue because sexuality is premised on sex *in*equality. Equality law cannot apply to sexuality because equality is not sexy and inequality is. Equality cannot apply to sexuality because sexuality occurs in private and nothing is supposed to interfere in the private, however unequal it is. And equality cannot be more important than speech because sexual expression is sex and unequal sex is something men want to say.

Having said that, here we are in this room—there are more people at this conference than it took Bolsheviks to topple the czar. You make me begin to believe that we may have a women's movement to get back. In your workshops, perhaps you could think about ways—the ordinance is one, we know others, and there are many waiting to be discovered—to mobilize women's sex-based physical and economic insecurity, women's vulnerability and desperation, not to be defeated by women's sex-based personal indignity, women's boredom, and women's despair. Think about how to change women's fear, so that fear is no longer the most rational emotion we feel, how to transform women's invisibility and exhaustion and silence and self-hate. If we loosed all of that, what could stand against it? Also, think about how, against all odds, against history, against all the evidence, we can create—invent—a sex-based hope.

Sexology and Antifeminism

Sheila Jeffreys

I have been involved in Britain in feminist activism against pornography since 1978. In the first few years of that struggle there was a wonderful, burgeoning movement and then, to our astonishment, we discovered that we were getting strong opposition to our efforts from a direction which we had not expected. Perhaps we should have expected it, but we had not. At socialist-feminist conferences — in particular, at leftist conferences — some women who were describing themselves as feminists were doing nothing but trashing the feminists who were fighting against pornography.

This attack from within feminism really surprised us especially as the attack grew and grew. Our activism became more and more difficult. Some feminists were being quoted in all kinds of journals and at all kinds of places, saying how ridiculous the fight against pornography was. For many years we had all agreed, as very good feminists, that it was important not to have horizontal hostility. Indeed, it had been felt that we should not devote our time and energy to countering the campaign that women who were describing themselves as feminists were waging against us. I felt in the end, however, that it was important to challenge this backlash directly.

The attack has not, of course, simply come from those women who describe themselves as feminists. It has also come from sexual liberals on the left — in particular, from men — and from a large part of the gay male movement. That is where the backlash is coming from, but it is being represented within feminism as well. What I have really wanted is to approach head on the arguments these people have been making against us. It's about time, I think, that we stood up for ourselves.

ANTIFEMINISM AND SEX REFORM IN THE EARLY TWENTIETH CENTURY

I want to show that a very similar backlash against feminists has happened before, against the first wave of feminism. This backlash at the beginning of the twentieth century, which carried on into the 1920s, has been called by historians the first sexual revolution of the twentieth century. There are supposed to have been two, one in the 1920s and one in the 1960s. What I suggest is that this so-called sexual revolution was in fact a backlash against feminists, and the values produced by this revolution are the values now being promoted by the sexual liberals in their attack again on feminism.[1]

I don't think I'm saying anything controversial because the sexual liberals themselves are only too pleased to point out their links with the sexologists and sex reformers who took part in that backlash against feminists at the beginning of this century. For instance, Gayle Rubin, a promoter of sadomasochism and a sexual libertarian, sees herself as being in a pro-sex tradition with a pedigree going back to Havelock Ellis, the sex reformer (Gayle Rubin, 1984). The feminists fighting pornography and male sexual violence are in what she calls the antisex tradition, starting in the first wave of feminism. And I am pleased to see myself as being in that tradition, although of course I wouldn't see it as being an antisex tradition exactly.

I take Gayle Rubin seriously. She's certainly in the Havelock Ellis tradition. I want to tell you some things about Havelock Ellis which those of you who have read my book will know. His work needs to be considered because he is said to be so tremendously important by sexual liberals. Whole books are being written about him now saying how good he was for women and for everybody.

Before I look at what he was saying, I'd like to address feminism at the end of the nineteenth century and how it dealt with sexuality (Sheila Jeffreys, 1985; Sheila Jeffreys, 1987). When I started looking at these efforts, although I had received a master's degree in late Victorian and Edwardian social studies which had covered the feminist work on other issues, I had no idea there were struggles of any seriousness around

---

[1] Sexual liberals are those who subscribe to the 1960s' agenda of sexual tolerance, to the idea that sex is necessarily good and positive, and that censorship is a bad thing. Sexual libertarians have a more modern agenda and actively advocate the "outer fringes" of sexuality, such as sadomasochism, with the belief that "sexual minorities" are in the forefront of creating the sexual revolution.

sexuality or violence against women, because those efforts were not mentioned in the textbooks. Documents were not collected in the anthologies telling us what those women were saying. There was no way of having access to their ideas. I don't think it is by accident that these huge efforts which feminists were engaged in have been eliminated from the history of feminism. I think it is very deliberate. It's a big struggle to pull them out of history, to bring them back to consciousness, and make them available to us. I fear very much that the campaigns we are engaged in today can disappear from history in a precisely similar way.

The sexologists and sex reformers attacked feminists in the last wave of feminism as antisex prudes who were acting against the interests of women. This is how historians have represented them up to the present day. This is how we are being represented right now by the sexual liberals. This is the way they are writing our history.

When I started looking at feminist efforts at the end of the nineteenth century, I knew that women had been involved in work against prostitution because there has been some feminist historical work on the Contagious Diseases Acts. What astonished me about these feminists was that the language they were using was so fiercely feminist. They described men's use of women in prostitution as an abuse of women, as dividing what they called the class of women, and putting aside one half of that class simply for men to use for their own purposes. I was surprised by the strength of the language that was used and the way in which these writers were very directly pointing out men's abuse of women in prostitution, and targeting men directly in everything they said.

I went on to discover something I had no knowledge of and about which there was virtually no information in secondary sources: there was a fifty-year campaign by those women against the sexual abuse of children. This started out of the struggle against prostitution, and it centered at first on raising the age of consent for girls so that young girls could not be used in prostitution. There wasn't a law against men using women in prostitution, but age of consent laws would have removed young girls from men's reach. That campaign culminated in the raising of the age of consent for sexual intercourse in Britain to 16 in 1885, and for indecent assault to 16 in 1922. It took fifty years.

Feminists were not simply trying to raise the age of consent. They were fighting incest, pointing out that incest was a crime of the patriarchal family, of men against women, and that sexual abuse of children was a crime carried out by men of all classes. They were fighting for women jurors, magistrates, women police to look after victims, fighting for all kinds of reforms that I thought had been invented by this wave of feminism. They were involved in setting up shelters for women escaping prostitution, something that is happening again in this wave of feminism.

I was enormously impressed by these feminists. In fact, I sat in the Fawcett Library in London getting terribly excited and wanting to tell everybody what I was finding out. Feminist theorists like Elisabeth Wolstenholme Elmy and Frances Swiney were writing at this time about sexuality. We haven't had access to their work because it hasn't been taken seriously. Where they are written about at all in history books, they are simply called prudes and puritans and their ideas are seen as retrogressive. What these women were arguing was that the sexual subordination of women—men's appropriation of women's bodies for their use—lay at the foundation of the oppression of women.

Interestingly, these two women, Swiney and Elmy, made clear their opposition to the practice of sexual intercourse. This practice has become so sacred that it is almost impossible to imagine any serious challenge being made to it. What we have seen in the last hundred years is the total and compulsory enforcement of that sexual practice upon women so that women are allowed absolutely no outlet or escape from it.

But at the end of the nineteenth century there were feminists who were prepared to challenge intercourse. They were prepared to say, for instance, that it was dangerous for women's health; that it led to unwanted pregnancies or forced women to use forms of technology, contraception, that reduced them simply to objects for men's use; that it humiliated women and made them into things. Feminists pointed out that sexual diseases transmitted through sexual intercourse were dangerous to women's lives. They felt sexual intercourse to be a humiliating practice because it showed men's dominance more obviously than anything else. They believed that this practice should take place only for the purposes of reproduction, maybe every three or four years. I know these are ideas which if you voiced them today would make people think that you had taken leave of your senses. But these were ideas that were absolutely mainstream; they were being put forward by respectably married women, one married to a general.

These women were campaigning fundamentally for a woman's right to control her own body and to control access to her own body. The integrity of a woman's own body was the basic plank of their campaign.

The efforts of these women are now said by the sexual liberals to be retrogressive and dangerous. An example of such criticism is the paper by Linda Gordon and Ellen Dubois, two American historians, presented at the Barnard Conference on sexuality (Ellen Carol Dubois and Linda Gordon, 1984). Some of you may be familiar with this conference and with the anthology that came out of it called *Pleasure and Danger*. The title article in that volume, "Pleasure and Danger: Seeking Ecstasy on the Battlefield," was written by Gordon and Dubois about feminist struggles at the end of the nineteenth century. In that article, they suggest that although these feminists may have been well intentioned, they nonetheless allied themselves to conservative forces and were dangerous in the end to feminism, and to woman's sexual pleasure.

So how did these feminists get removed from history? How did their work get interrupted? When I wanted to answer these questions I went to look at the writings of the sex reform movement, and at the "science of sex" founded at the end of the nineteenth century. You probably know that in the nineteenth century male Victorian scientists were setting up classification systems for insects, stones, all kinds of things. They were keen on classification because they wanted everything under their control, and finding the correct pigeonhole made them feel secure. At the end of the nineteenth century they started doing this with sexuality. Doctors, for example, started defining sexual "perversions." The so-called new science of sex was formed to tell people which were the correct ways to act sexually and which were the incorrect ways.

At the beginning of the twentieth century the most famous name in sexology in Britain, and I think probably in the world, was Havelock Ellis. Although Freud is a more familiar name and he was of course a sexologist and in correspondence with Havelock Ellis, if we look at the average marriage advice manual, it is the words and ideas of Havelock Ellis we will find there, not those of Sigmund Freud. Havelock Ellis is your friendly neighborhood sexologist.

Ellis has been seen as the founder and father of sex advice literature, so Jeffrey Weeks, a gay male sexual libertarian historian of the present, describes Ellis's work as "one of the springs from which the stream of sexual liberalism has flowed with apparent ease" (Sheila Rowbotham and Jeffrey Weeks, 1977). Edward Brecher describes him as "the first of the yea-sayers" to sexuality (Edward Brecher, 1970). There is no doubt he was and is a crucially important influence.

He argued first of all that men and women were entirely different biologically and therefore psychologically. Using this idea of difference, he set out to show how male and female sexuality were entirely distinct. Not surprisingly, the map he gave us of male and female sexuality showed that male sexuality was absolutely and inevitably aggressive, taking the form of pursuit and capture, and that it was normal and inevitable for men to take pleasure in inflicting pain on women (Sheila Jeffreys, 1987). Woman's sexuality, he said, was passive. Women were supposed to be captured and took "delight" in experiencing pain at the hands of male lovers.

According to Ellis, female sexuality was based upon evolution, and derived from female animals who were coquettish and led the male animals on. The human female was supposed to be coquettish, too. She was supposed to keep looking over her shoulder, egging on the male animal. At the last moment she was supposed to give in. Female sexuality was passive and masochistic. How did Ellis know this? Well, he said, it was obvious. Women in France enjoyed being beaten up by their pimps; working-class women in the East End of London enjoyed being beaten up by their husbands; and then there was the woman undergoing a clitoridectomy who had an orgasm as the knife passed through her clitoris. Ellis insisted that you could tell from the expression on a woman's face during orgasm that it was pain she was feeling. For women, he concluded, pain and pleasure were inextricably linked.

It is important to remember that throughout this century feminists have criticized these sexologists. They criticized Ellis, too. He responded by saying that, despite what feminists might say, women's delight in pain was so obvious that there was no point in even taking feminists' arguments seriously.

Apart from insisting that sexuality was inevitably based on sado-masochism, Ellis had other contributions to make. Woman's delight in pain and aggression meant that sexual abuse couldn't be taken seriously. Women who complained of rape were simply women who had stayed out later than their parents wanted—they had to say something when they got home. The vast majority of cases of child sexual abuse were invented. There should be separate spheres for men and women. Women should stay at home and shouldn't go out to work. They should put all their energies into pregnancy because "The breeding of men lies largely in the hands of women" (Havelock Ellis, 1917).

Ellis was crucially important in fighting all the feminist ideas developing at the end of the nineteenth century. Why then was he seen as so progressive? One reason is that he didn't just say women should engage in sexual intercourse and that they must enjoy it. He talked about foreplay. According to the concept of foreplay, before men engaged in the act which they wished to pursue, things should happen which would get women ready for it. It was like winding up the clock. And it was necessary because women were slow, slow to realize what they really wanted to do, slow to realize what really gave them pleasure. They needed an inducement to get them ready for the enterprise.

This was called foreplay, and Ellis is regarded as having invented it. It's an amazing concept of sex, but do you know any sex education book not based upon it?

Before we leave Havelock Ellis, I would like to say something about his sexual proclivities. I think it is very important that we understand these male sexologists in depth. I think it's important to us to understand what they were really interested in. Havelock Ellis has taught, through his influence on a hundred years of sex advice books, how sexual intercourse was to be carried out, what men were to do, and what women were to experience during that act. As far as we know, he virtually never, if ever, engaged in that act himself. Now this is not unusual. This is typical for the sexologists of the twentieth century. If you go into their biographies you discover that they never did what they said everybody should do.

Havelock Ellis's favorite sexual practice was urolagnia—watching women urinate. He got women to visit him and he got them to go into a room and urinate into a potty with the door open so that he could hear, if not exactly see, what they were doing. He got some quite well-known women and sex reformers to do this for him. We are fortunate that he left us a record of his feelings about this sexual practice: he wrote poetry about it. Since he is considered a great thinker and the father of sex advice literature, his poetry has got to be worth recording. It goes like this:

> My lady once leapt from the bed,
>> Whereon she naked lay beside my heart.
> And stood with perfect poise, straight legs apart,
>> And then from clustered hair of brownish red,
> A wondrous fountain curve, all shyness fled,
>> Arched like a liquid rainbow in the air,
> She cares not, she, what other women care,
>> But gazed as it fell and faltered and was shed.
> (Eric Trudgill, 1976)

You may have thought that there was something odd about this description, something that did not accord with what you know about women's biology. There are not many women who have fountain curves and rainbows. I think that it would indicate to us that it was not *women* urinating that Ellis was really interested in.

Another so-called sign of Ellis's progressiveness is that he advocated women's right to sexual pleasure. He wrote an article called "Women's Erotic Rights," in which he stated that women both could and should have sexual pleasure (Havelock Ellis, 1913). You can imagine, considering what is supposed to have been the benighted state of sexual practice in the nineteenth century, that quite a lot of people reading this article today would see it as enormously progressive. It is important to look at Ellis's concept of sexual pleasure.

THE CONCEPT OF
SEXUAL PLEASURE

It is generally accepted as truth that sexologists, sex reformers, and sex therapists of the twentieth century have strived to ensure that women enjoy the act of sexual intercourse. For this reason women have sometimes mistakenly seen the industry of sex therapy as being in women's interests. This misperception has prevented some from taking a critical look at the industry.

It is very unfortunate that we do not have a word in our language which would allow us to talk about sexual response, sexual feeling, that is not positive. The only word we have is pleasure. Therefore, there is an assumption running through sexual libertarian literature and through the general understanding of sex that any kind of sexual response or feeling is somehow positive. This linguistic shortcoming leads to considerable confusion. We desperately need and will, I hope, soon acquire a word that will allow us to describe sexual feeling that is not positive, not in our interest. Such a word would need to sum up the feelings of humiliation and betrayal, the totally negative feelings that women often have when we experience this thing called sexual arousal. These negative feelings are associated with sexual arousal arising from literature, pictorials, acts, experiences, and fantasies that are forced on us, that are humiliating to us, that degrade us.

In "Seeking Ecstasy on the Battlefield," Gordon and Dubois provide an example of the problems that arise from having a one-dimensional notion of "sexual pleasure." They state that middle-class women in the late nineteenth century were resisting the patriarchy in a very positive way (Ellen Carol Dubois and Linda Gordon, 1984). How do we know this? Well, it is because a lot of them apparently had orgasms. Forty percent, according to one survey, had orgasms occasionally; 20 percent frequently. This Gordon and Dubois saw as wonderfully revolutionary.

These middle-class women were in relationships which were unregenerately patriarchal, in which men had all the power. These women were probably simply being used as spittoons in the act of sexual intercourse. Was orgasm in such a situation something positive, empowering, something that meant resistance to patriarchal oppression? I would suggest not, unless we see the much-lauded happiness of the Japanese worker in factories as a form of resistance to capitalism. If we do not see happiness at work as a form of resistance, then there is no way we can see the orgasm of the middle-class woman in the nineteenth century as inevitably meaning resistance to patriarchal oppression. Rather, I would see it as accommodation of that oppression. These women had learned to take "pleasure" in their own subordination. Was it actually pleasure?

There are other examples which show that orgasm can not always be seen as positive and pleasurable. For instance, Vietnam veterans had orgasms while killing women in Vietnam; rapists have orgasms while raping women (Deborah Cameron & Elizabeth Frazer, 1987). All of this we know. So for men in particular, surely something called orgasm or sexual response cannot be seen as necessarily positive. Women have had orgasms during sexual abuse in childhood and can have orgasms during rape. This is something which we should make no secret of because this is what happens. How can we see this as pleasure? It's called sexual pleasure because we don't have another word. But we need another word and we need it fast.

We have got to understand that sexual response for women and orgasm for women is not necessarily pleasurable and positive. It can be a very real problem. It can be an accommodation of our oppression. It can be the eroticizing of our subordination. We need to appreciate that the word pleasure is often used for what we experience as humiliation and betrayal. We need to trust those feelings and go with them, instead of being persuaded by the sexual libertarians that our responses are not really humiliation and betrayal, that they are really something good.

Bearing this in mind, we have to look rather differently at the hundred years of sexology and sex reform aimed at ensuring that women take "pleasure" in sexual intercourse. We should bear in mind, also, that these sexologists have been antifeminist from the very beginning.

Sex advice literature produced in the 1920s, the period of the first sexual revolution of the twentieth century, excoriates the spinster and the lesbian. It insists that all women must engage in sexual intercourse, and that they must enjoy it. This period, immediately after World War I, was a time in which many women had considerably more freedom and independence than they had had before. The fact that large numbers of women were not marrying, were choosing to be independent, and were fighting male violence caused considerable alarm. This alarm is apparent in sexological literature.

In response to their alarm, the sexologists invented the concept of women's frigidity. They discovered that an enormous number of women were not enthusiastic about intercourse, as they were supposed to be, but had absolutely no interest in it. Late nineteenth-century feminists, you must remember, had often said they had no wish to do it at all. Moreover, they thought politically that no woman should have to do sexual intercourse. Obviously something had to be done about this problem. The concept of frigidity was invented.

Throughout the twentieth century, women have been the problem for sexology and sex reform. Gradually the frontiers have been pushed back, as the sexual revolutionaries would tell us. More and more practices are becoming perfectly normal. More and more practices are becoming the sorts of things that women should enjoy and be enthusiastic about. Women have been a problem all along because they have never shown the right enthusiasm. In the beginning women simply had to enjoy sexual intercourse. Then along came *Forum* magazine. In the late 1960s and 1970s, women were to enjoy spanking and deep throat. In Alex Comfort's *Joy of Sex*, women were to enjoy sadomasochism and dressing up as a cross between a "snake and a seal" (Alex Comfort, 1979). All of these things women had to enjoy, so you can see why women's lack of enthusiasm has presented a difficulty. It still presents a difficulty.

In the 1920s when the concept of frigidity was invented to explain women's lack of enthusiasm for having to enjoy sexual intercourse in an unregenerately male-dominated relationship, the sexologists tried to work out how many women were frigid. Some said 100 percent, but they weren't sure. Some said 60 percent, and some said 40 percent. What caused it? They suggested lesbianism, masturbation, constipation. So we can tell that what they were calling frigidity was not absence of sexual feeling, because women were clearly experiencing sexual feelings in masturbation and lesbianism. Frigidity meant absence of the right degree of awe and enthusiasm for the act of sexual intercourse.

When I read this literature, I was staggered to find that these sexologists were absolutely upfront about what they considered the nature and purpose of women's sexual pleasure. I read, for instance, Wilhelm Stekel's two-volume work, *Frigidity in Woman in Relation to Her Lovelife*. In this work Stekel, an analyst, is crystal clear. He believed that women must enjoy sexual intercourse because their enjoyment would subordinate them to the man in that act, and subordinate them in every aspect of their lives. Stekel summed up this message in a brief remark: "To be roused by a man means acknowledging oneself as conquered" (Wilhelm Stekel, 1936). Stekel saw women's frigidity as a weapon in the war of the sexes. It was a threat to civilization that so many women refused to accept sexual intercourse. Civilization of course meant male dominance. So women had to engage in sexual intercourse if male dominance was to survive.

Van de Velde's *Ideal Marriage*, which was selling well right into the 1960s and early 1970s, was one of the main works of sex advice literature in this century. Van de Velde defined frigidity as "hostility of the wife towards her husband" (Thomas Van de Velde, 1931). Frigid women had to be sent to gynecologists or psychoanalysts, to somebody who would resolve their problem, which was, as Van de Velde made clear, that they were resisting male power.

So then, in the 1920s, women's pleasure in sexual intercourse became a way of subordinating women in that sexual act and subordinating them to men in every aspect of their relationships and in the whole of their lives. This theme predominates in sexological works throughout the twentieth century.

The late 1940s and early 1950s was a very interesting period. It was another post-war period when something had to be done about the independence of women and the fact that a lot of women again were not showing the right enthusiasm. There was a panic about frigidity during this time too. To solve the problem there were books telling women the pleasure they were to take from sex, with titles like *The Sexually Adequate Female*. This book, by Frank Caprio, is an absolute classic (Frank Caprio, 1953). After saying how important the orgasm was and how many women were frigid, and what a great tragedy this was, Caprio has a section called "Serious Bedroom Mistakes." These were mistakes made by women during the act of sexual intercourse. They were serious because the act of sexual intercourse was sacred, and women were supposed to approach it with what Eustace Chesser, famous British sexologist of the period, called "joyous anticipation" (Eustace Chesser, 1946). "Joyous anticipation" was an almost religious attitude. Women were supposed to feel it before they went into the room for the act of sexual intercourse. Then they would have the right kind of pleasure. It was all in the mind, so women had to psych themselves into the right state.

In the "bedroom mistakes" chapter, we have the cases of two women who didn't show enough enthusiasm and hadn't bothered with "joyous anticipation." One of them continued reading a book while her husband engaged in sexual intercourse. The other continued to apply her nail polish (Eustace Chesser, 1946). These were serious bedroom mistakes, you've got to admit!

The sexologists in the late 1940s and 1950s were just as determined as those of the 1920s that women's sexual pleasure would and should subordinate them. Eustace Chesser said that a lot of women in sexual intercourse would only "submit." Submission, he said, was not enough. They had to "surrender themselves" and "surrender themselves entirely" in the sexual act. This is a Chesser quote about a girl who was in love but was having difficulty achieving the proper state of mind:

> She may find it impossible to surrender herself completely in the sex act and complete surrender is the only way in which she can bring the highest pleasure to both herself and her husband. Submission is not the same thing as surrender. Many a wife submits but retains deep within herself an area which is not conquered. And which indeed is in fierce opposition to submission. (Eustace Chesser, 1946)

Woman's pleasure in the act of sexual intercourse would eradicate that little area of resistance to male power.

The literature of the so-called sexual revolution of the 1960s continued these themes, but now what women were expected to do was more complicated. Now they had to join in and be energetic. This was a big change. After World War II there was a great worry that if women showed too much enthusiasm in the act of sexual intercourse, as British sexologist Kenneth Walker put it, the penis might drop out (Kenneth Walker, 1949). So women had to be careful: they couldn't move around too much. In the 1960s all this changed. Women were expected to hang from lampshades, swallow erect penises, and perform numerous other feats to prove to men how much they liked it.

During the 1980s the sexual libertarians have followed the traditions of sexology and sex reform. The sexual libertarians of the present, such as the organizers of the Barnard Conference, Jeffrey Weeks, and other gay male historians and theorists, see themselves in the tradition of sex reform and regard Havelock Ellis as their founding father (Carol Vance, 1984; Simon Watney, 1987; Jeffrey Weeks, 1985). Like Ellis, they are involved in eroticizing dominance and submission. The libertarians have an agenda on sexuality that is in fundamental opposition to that of feminists. Where feminists seek to transform sexuality in the interests of keeping women and children safe and ending women's inequality, the libertarians seek to promote and legitimize the traditional sexuality of dominance and submission. They eroticize practices that rely on power imbalance, such as sadomasochism, butch and femme, and so-called erotica that display women's humiliation and degradation. They see themselves as being in the so-called pro-sex tradition. Pro-sex turns out to mean pro-sexual dominance and submission.

Unfortunately, the sexual libertarians have had quite an influence on the women's movement. I have a quote from an article in a 1985 health issue of *Ms.* Magazine to show how acceptable their ideas have become. I assumed that, since it was a health issue, if there was anything about sex, it would of course cover the health problems women have as a result of male sexual violence and the use of pornography against them. Nothing like that appeared in this issue. The article on sexuality was a piece on "The Big 'O' " (orgasm), and how women were to have more of them (Sarah Crichton, 1986).

The article explained that women would have to psych themselves up for three or four days before an act of sexual intercourse in order to get enough orgasms, because one was no longer enough and they should have many. How were they going to psych themselves up? Well, they should engage in fantasies of sadomasochism, bondage, and so on. In other words, they should humiliate themselves within their own heads in order to be in the right mood by the time they got to the act of sexual intercourse so that they could have the correct number of orgasms.

The authors realized that because they were writing in a magazine that is supposed to be feminist, it might be a problem to advocate that women surrender themselves in a sexual act with a man. They got around this. They said that women in sexual intercourse weren't surrending themselves to men at all; women were surrendering to "Nature" or to themselves. They said:

> But—and this is a very important concept for a woman to understand—when a woman lets go, gives up, she is surrendering herself not to her partner, but to Nature. She's giving herself to herself. (Sarah Crichton, 1986)

You will not, of course, find sexual advice to men telling them to surrender themselves to themselves or indeed to nature in sexual intercourse. If they did so, sex as we know it would probably disappear. I think it would be a good idea if men started surrendering themselves to themselves every so often.

What this demonstrates is that the message of the sexual libertarians has gotten into feminist culture. Even within the feminist movement, women are encouraged to be complicit in their own oppression by becoming consumers of pornography, by engaging in sadomasochistic practices, by eroticizing their own oppression.

A hundred years of sexology has told us that when women learn to take pleasure in submission in sex, we will be subordinating ourselves in our lives as a whole. In this respect, the sexologists knew their business. And their business was to ensure that women were undermined, unable to fight their oppression. Today the sexual liberals who are fighting feminist activists, who see themselves as being in the progressive pro-sex and anticensorship lobbies, are continuing the sexologists' work. Through eroticizing our subordination in the name of "sexual liberation," they shore up the foundations of male supremacy.

REFERENCES

Brecher, Edward. (1970). *The sex researchers.* London: Andre Deutsch.

Cameron, Deborah, and Frazer, Elizabeth. (1987). *The lust to kill.* Cambridge: Polity.

Caprio, Frank S. (1953). *The sexually adequate female.* (Reprint 1963). New York: Citadel Press.

Chesser, Eustace. *Love and marriage.* (Reprint 1957) London: Pan.

Comfort, Alex. (Ed.). (1979). *The joy of sex.* London: Quartet.

Crichton, Sarah. (1986, May). Going for the big "O." *Ms.*

Dubois, Ellen Carol, and Gordon, Linda. (1984). Seeking ecstasy on the battlefield: Danger and pleasure in nineteenth-century feminist sexual thought. In Carol Vance (Ed.) *Pleasure and danger: Exploring female sexuality.* Boston: Routledge and Kegan Paul.

Ellis, Havelock. (1913). *The task of social hygiene.* London: Constable.

Ellis, Havelock. (1917). *The erotic rights of women.* London: British Society for the Study of Sex Psychology.

Jeffreys, Sheila. (1985). *The spinster and her enemies: Feminism and sexuality 1880–1930.* London: Pandora.

Jeffreys, Sheila, (Ed.). (1987). *The sexuality debates.* London: Routledge and Kegan Paul.

Rowbotham, Sheila, and Weeks, Jeffrey. (1977). *Socialism and the new life.* London: Pluto Press.

Rubin, Gayle. (1984). Thinking sex. In Carol Vance (Ed.). *Pleasure and danger: Exploring female sexuality,* Boston: Routledge and Kegan Paul.

Stekel, Wilhelm. (1936). *Frigidity in woman in relation to her love life,* vol. 2. 1926. (Reprint). New York: Livewright.

Trudgill, Eric. (1976). *Madonnas and magdalens: The origins and development of Victorian sexual attitudes.* London: Heinemann.

Van de Velde, Thomas. (1931). *Sex hostility in marriage.* London: Heinemann.

Vance, Carol, (Ed.). (1984). *Pleasure and danger: Exploring female sexuality.* Boston: Routledge and Kegan Paul.

Walker, Kenneth. (1949). The art of love. In Sybil Neville-Rolfe, (Ed.). *Sex in social life.* London: George Allen and Unwin.

Watney, Simon. (1987). *Policing desire: Pornography, AIDS and the media.* Minneapolis: University of Minnesota Press.

Weeks, Jeffrey. (1985). *Sexuality and its discontents.* London: Routledge and Kegan Paul.

Woman-Hating Right and Left

Andrea Dworkin

It's been a long time since we've come together to say what we mean by feminism and why the struggle for women's freedom matters to us enough that we devote our lives to it: not three hours on Saturday afternoon; not an occasional letter here and there; not an outraged "Oh, my God, you don't mean that!" We actually don't think our lives are trivial. Imagine. And we don't think the crimes committed against us are minor and insignificant. And that means we have made phenomenal progress in understanding that we are human beings who have rights on this earth; that nobody can take those rights away from us; and that we have been injured by the systematic subordination of women, by the systematic sexual abuse we have been exposed to. And we are politically organized to fight back and to change the society in which we live from the ground up.

I think as feminists we have a way of looking at problems that other people appear not to understand. To name names, the right and the left appear not to understand what it is that feminists are trying to do. Feminists are trying to destroy a sex hierarchy, a race hierarchy, an economic hierarchy, in which women are hurt, are disempowered, and in which society celebrates cruelty over us and refuses us the integrity of our own bodies and the dignity of our own lives.

Now, that's not a problem that the left has decided must be solved. You may have noticed. And that is not a problem that the right thinks is any problem. The right hasn't gotten to the point of saying the problem is not important yet—as the left has, because the left is always avant-garde. Since the left is avant-garde, it can be out there in front saying, "Well, yes, we understand the problem. It just isn't particularly important." The right, being the dinosaurs, just say there is no problem. And we're supposed to pick between them.

So feminists look at the society we live in and try to understand how we are going to fight male power. And in order to try to figure out how we're going to fight it, we have to figure out how it's organized, how it works. How does it survive? How does it work itself out? How does it maintain itself as a system of power?

In the course of looking at male power, at all the institutions of male power, trying to understand how they work—you know, it's like putting sand in their gas tanks; we've got to stop them from working. So we try to figure out how we can do that.

We have to look at the role of the right in upholding male power over women and we have to look at the role of the left in upholding male power over women: not at what they say but at what they do. And so we have to go beyond the reality they present to us when they say, as they often do, one way or another: "Little girls, we know what's good for you. We are acting in your best interests." The right wing will promise you a husband whom—yes, it's true, you have to obey him, but then he has to love you for doing it, for obeying him. Now, there are circumstances—like the ones we live under—in which for a lot of women that's not a bad offer. Because you cut down the number of men you have to listen to by several million.

And the left says—and they think this is a good deal—they say also: "Little girls"—unless they are being particularly politically progressive at the moment, in which case they can sometimes say "big cunts," because that's their idea of freedom—they address us in whichever tone of voice they are using at the moment, and they say to us—"Well, what we'll do is that we will allow you to have an abortion right as long as you remain sexually accessible to us. And if you withdraw that accessibility and start talking this crap about an autonomous women's movement, we will collapse any support that we have ever given you: monetary, political, social, anything we have ever given you for the right to abortion. Because if your abortion right is not going to mean sexual accessibility for us, girls, you can't have it." And that's what they've been doing to us for the last fifteen years.

So feminists come along, and we say: Well, we are going to understand how it is that these people do what they do. We are going to approach the problem politically. That means that we are going to try to isolate and describe systems of exploitation as they work on us, from our point of view as the people who are being hurt by them. It means that even though we're on the bottom and they're on the top, we are examining them for points of vulnerability. And as we find those points of vulnerability—and you might locate them anatomically, as well as any other way—we are going to move whatever muscles we have, from whatever positions we are in, and we are going to get that bastard in his collective manifestation off of us.

And that means we are politically organizing a resistance to male supremacy. We used to talk about having a revolution. We all smiled and laughed and were giddy. And we thought it was going to be easy. We didn't understand, for some reason, that the people who had power weren't going to enjoy the revolution as much as we were. They started not to have a good time when we started to organize. Well, they got more and more unhappy as they began to see that they were vulnerable, that male supremacy wasn't just this giant, monolithic thing that had, in fact, been given to them by God or nature. God is the right; nature is the left.

And it began to appear that while the overnight revolution wasn't going to be possible, a consistent, serious, organized resistance to male power and to the institutions of male power that hurt women *would be possible*. We began to see it, and they began to see it.

Then the hard days for the women's movement began. The people we were trying to take power from weren't just going to continue to assault us in the ways that they had been privileged to do in all the many hundreds and thousands of years before. They were also going to organize politically to stop us. And that is what they have done.

Now, when I talk about a resistance, I am talking about an organized political resistance. I'm not just talking about something that comes and something that goes. I'm not talking about a feeling. I'm not talking about having in your heart the way things should be and going through a regular day having good, decent, wonderful ideas in your heart. I'm talking about when you put your body and your mind on the line and you commit yourself to years of struggle in order to change the society in which you live. This does not mean just changing the men whom you know so that their manners will get better—although that wouldn't be bad either. It has been fifteen years. Their manners haven't gotten appreciably better, even. But that's not what a political resistance is. A political resistance goes on day and night, under cover and over ground, where people can see it and where people can't. It is passed from generation to generation. It is taught. It is encouraged. It is celebrated. It is smart. It is savvy. It is committed. And someday it will win. It will win.

We all embody, as well, a personal resistance to male dominance. We do it the best way we can do it. And part of the problem in the last years has been to suggest that one or the other—the political or the personal resistance—will be sufficient because feminism is some kind of a lifestyle choice. You're a young, modern woman. Of course you're a feminist. That's not what being a feminist is. Feminism is a political practice of fighting male supremacy in behalf of women as a class, including all the women you don't like, including all the women you don't want to be around, including all the women who used to be your best friends whom you don't want anything to do with any more. It doesn't matter who the individual women are. They all have the same vulnerability to rape, to battery, as children to incest. Poorer women have more vulnerability to prostitution, which is basically a form of sexual exploitation that is intolerable in an egalitarian society, which is the society we are fighting for.

Part of what we have to do in this resistance I'm talking about is to refuse to collaborate with male power. Refuse to be used by it. Refuse to be its chicks up front. Refuse to collaborate with it to make our lives a little bit easier. Refuse to collaborate with it even though that's really how you get a platform to speak in this society. A ventriloquist could be moving your mouth if you're a woman who is fronting for male power. You are not working in behalf of your sisters. You're working for the boys. And you're making it easier for them to hurt other women. It's very hard not to collaborate with male power because male power is ubiquitous. It is everywhere.

Part of having a feminist resistance to male power includes expanding the base of that resistance to other women, to women you have less in common with, to women you have nothing in common with. It means active, proselytizing dialogue with women of many different political viewpoints because their lives are worth what your life is worth. That's why.

We have to go past the conventional political barriers, the lines that the men have drawn for us. "*Our* girls are over there; we'll call them Democrats, we'll call them socialists, we'll call them whatever we want to call them. *Those* girls are over there; that's *their* girls. The girls on our side aren't allowed to talk to the girls on their side." Well, if the girls on either side talked to the girls on the other side, they just might find out that they're being screwed the same way by the same kinds of men.

And so when we look at women's real experience—which is what feminists do that neither the right nor the left does—what do we find? We find that women all over the political spectrum, whatever their ideologies, are raped and that women experience battery, in marriage and out of marriage. We find that a huge number of adult women have been incest victims even as the current rate of incest is growing in this country. Right now, experts believe there are 16,000 new cases of father/daughter incest—which is only one kind of incest—every year.

Women's real experience includes prostitution, and women's real experience includes pornography. And when we look at women's real experience — and when we don't accept the pabulum that we're being fed by the boys from both sides who are telling us what to think and what our lives really are — what we find, for instance, when we look at the pornography, is that we can trace its use in sexual abuse back generations. We can take generations of women: girl, young woman, mother, grandmother. The pornography did not have to be all over the streets to be a functioning part of the sexual abuse of women in this society. I'm only reminding you of what you already know, which is that most sexual abuse of women takes place in private. It takes place, really, where we can't see it. And the astonishing achievement of the women's movement was to say: "We no longer respect your privacy, rapist."

Women are isolated in their homes. This is not to say that women can't go out; women can go out. But the things that happen to women mostly happen in the home. The home is the most dangerous place for women in this society. More women are killed in their homes than anywhere else. A woman is battered in this country—a woman married or cohabiting—every eighteen seconds. The home is a dangerous place for women.

And before the women's movement, the women who were raped, the women who were beaten, didn't know that anybody else was. It only happened to her alone in all the world. Why? Because of something she did; because of something she was; because of something she did wrong; because she was bad in some way. The problem—the violence—was effectively hidden by male supremacy. The fact was that you could go down a block in a city and find massive numbers of women who had had precisely the same experiences of violence by men against them for precisely the same reason. And the reason—there is really only one reason—is that they're women. That's it. They're women. The society is organized not just to punish women but to protect the men who punish women. And that's what we are trying to change.

Now, in terms of dealing with the right and the left and woman hating, I want to talk to you especially about pornography and some of the strategies around pornography where the right and the left coalesce to keep the pornography safe, to keep women subordinated through the pornography, and to keep the sexual abuse that pornography does cause—*cause*—protected and safe as well.

Pornography existed in the home and was used in sexual abuse. Pornography was available to men in men-only groups. Many of us growing up—if we're forty or fifty—we didn't see pornography. It didn't saturate the environment the way it does now. As a result, there was always a missing piece when later as feminists we tried to understand sexual abuse. There was never any way of understanding how all these rapist values and ways of abusing women got communicated —or how all the rationales for the abuse got communicated. How did men learn them? They didn't just fall out of the sky; we don't think they did. I guess some people think they did. Down with the Ten Commandments they came. This is the way you hit her. This is the way you tie her up.

But we don't think it's like that. So: we have women as private property, owned by men, in houses, isolated. And then to deal with what is called the pornography problem we have something called obscenity laws. And what obscenity laws do when they work in a society is that they hide the pornography from women and children. They keep us from seeing it. They don't keep it from being used on us by men in sexual abuse. The men can get it and use it. But we don't get to see it, to talk about it, to organize around it, to learn everything that we can learn about how male supremacy works from it. We don't get to do that.

One of the ways the social structure has protected male supremacy has been the right-wing strategy of using obscenity laws to keep pornography a secret from women but to keep it available to men, to men as individuals, to all-male groups.

We have this strange notion that surfaces in the women's movement now and then—it's a great trivialization of our lives; it's also wrong— that there is a division of women in the world that is phenomenologically real into good women and bad women. And we have some very proud leftist women who want to be recognized as, perceived as, and considered bad. Baaad. Now, the reality is that you can do everything in the world to be a good woman in this society but when you are in the private house with the private husband whom you've attracted through your conformity to being what is on the surface a good woman, when that man starts hitting you, he hits you because you're bad. And the underlying premise of this society is that all women are bad, that we have a nature that's bad and we deserve to be punished. And you can be the baaadest woman on the left—which means being a good woman from the point of view of the left—and when the leftie starts hitting you, he hits you because you're a woman, because you're bad the way a woman is bad, not the way a leftist is bad; you're bad because you're a woman and you deserve to be punished.

You can look at the way that is manifested in institutions. I ask you to consider it in relation to pornography, because in pornography there is nothing that can be done to a woman that can punish her enough for being a woman. And the very nature of her being is that she gets sexual pleasure out of being punished. You don't have to ask to be a bad girl. You live under male supremacy; you are one. You are a woman; what is hateful in you—*in you*, defining you—is the reason that men have for hurting you. It's the reason that they don't say: "I'm hitting a human being, and I'm hurting that human being." They say: "I'm punishing a bitch. I'm punishing a whore." They say what the pornography says: "You really like it, don't you. There's something in you that really . . . it really satisfies."

And then when you go for help, thinking you're an individual person who does not like to be hurt, the psychologist says, "There's something in you that really liked it, isn't there?" You say: "Gosh, no. I don't think so." And he tells you: "Well, you're not being honest and you certainly don't know yourself very well." And you go to your yogi, and he's liable to tell you the same thing. It's a little discouraging, isn't it? Even the vegetable people believe that if you're a woman, you're bad.

We're supposed to have this nature that craves abuse. Pornography is about punishing us to the point of annihilation for being women and both the right and the left have a role to play in protecting pornography. They act in concert to make sure we get punished. This public fight they're always having, from our point of view and for our purposes, is a diversion. They each do their part to keep us down. And the important thing is to understand what their part is.

What happens around obscenity laws is that the right-wing judges —these authoritarian people who supposedly hate pornography more than they hate anything in the world (believe that and I have swampland I want to sell you)—have established the legal formula that protects pornography. In defining obscenity, they have established the formula the pornographers use to protect legally the material they publish. The Supreme Court says: "Do it this way, this way, and this way. As long as you have this, and this, and this, we won't touch you." That's what all those obscenity decisions say.

And then we have our wonderful, left-wing, avant-garde writers who join in and say: "Fine—and I'll provide the socially redeeming material so that you can meet the standards of the formula that the right-wing men have given you." And occasionally a right-wing writer does it too. William Buckley or somebody like that. He doesn't turn down the money. Feminists turn down the money. People who don't turn down the money aren't feminists.

So you have this extraordinary social agreement between the right and the left—who act as if they're fighting all the time—that in fact they can put any amount of woman-hating exploitation, torture, viciousness, or savagery in their magazines, just so they wrap it in a piece of writing that will meet the standard the Supreme Court set. That's all they have to do. They barely have to be literate to meet that standard. And they do this together. And if you let them distract you by the public cockfight they're always having, you miss the fact that when it comes to producing the social product called pornography, they agree.

The woman hating in the pornography doesn't bother either side. The woman hating does not "offend"—to use a current word—the right or the left, and that's whether the woman hating is women as bunnies and pets and pussy and beaver, or women being tortured. They're fine with any of it. Both sides.

The way the pornographers actually run their business has to do with their relationship to municipal governments throughout the country. We have so-called good governments in cities all over the country —Democrats and Republicans on city councils—who are making incredible decisions about our lives every day. Most of us are too highfalutin' to pay any attention to them. We've got ideology we have to consider. We have more important political fish to fry. Meanwhile they're giving the pornographers pieces of our cities, those little city councils that don't mean anything to any of us.

So you have the local politicians standing up, as they do, right and left, denouncing pornography. The liberals are appalled. I mean—they're just appalled—but they must defend it. They must. Why must you? They change the subject. Zoning is legal permission to exploit and traffic in women. That's what it is. It doesn't stop pornography. It puts it into a certain neighborhood. The way the pornographers get vast municipal power is that they *do* go to the zoning board meetings. They do, and their lawyers do. They find out what parts of what cities are slated for city development, whether it's a city center, a housing project, or a shopping mall. And they go and buy the land. And then they hold that land hostage until the laws of that city become friendly to them. And they get to sell their product—which is woman hating—in officially sanctioned parts of the city. And where are the parts of the city that they're given? The places are mostly where people of color live, and some poor white people.

For instance, Minneapolis is a city in which the population is 96 percent white and 4 percent people of color, mostly black and Native American people. How did 100 percent of the pornography land in their neighborhoods? I mean, if you were dropping it down from the sky you couldn't do that.

This is what happens. Those parts of cities become economically devastated. Legitimate businesses move out. Men from all parts of the city come in at night to buy pornography and hunt women. Crimes of violence against women and children in those neighborhoods go up. No one will come into those neighborhoods from other neighborhoods unless they want pornography. So we have a new form of segregation in our cities created by the social effects of pornography. We have an increase of violence against the women and children.

Now, here is the collusion of the right and the left. We have the Republicans and the conservatives, who are sometimes Democrats, talking about property values. They're going to save property values. And whose property values are they going to save? The property values of rich and white people. That's why they put the pornography where they put it. Does the left rise up in fury and say, "How dare you do this? We want economic equality. We don't want economic devastation here." The left doesn't do anything, because while the right is talking property values, the left is talking speech.

And so we have—in vast areas of municipalities in this country—a new form of segregation created by pornography. We have new areas of economic blight created by pornography. And we have a new despair of the people who have to be there.

What is the role of the state in all this? People like to talk about the role of the state. It's blessedly abstract. It's like reading an inkblot test; you can sort of say whatever you want. Nobody ever knows if you're right or if you're wrong. So, what I would like to say is that we actually have a particular state that we could look at, and that's the state we live under. We could actually pay some attention to what it is and how it works and how it came into being.

One thing that appears to be clear is that neither the right nor the left thinks that the role of the state is to create economic or sexual justice. That seems to be clear. Equality is no longer a left-wing goal if it has to include women. The left has disavowed equality as a goal. And equality never was a right-wing goal.

Here's the reality of it, and I beg you to think about this when you hear all the shit that you hear about the First Amendment. I beg you to think about this Constitution that was *crafted* to protect the institution of slavery; *crafted* not to interfere with it, with the buying and selling of human beings. It is not a surprise that this state, regulated by this Constitution, is deeply insensitive to crimes against people that involve buying and selling them.

And I will remind you that the Founding Fathers were—many of them—slave owners. But especially—especially—that James Madison, who crafted the First Amendment, not only owned slaves but bragged that he could spend $12 or $13 a year on their upkeep and make from each slave $257 a year.

The First Amendment doesn't have anything to do with protecting the rights of the people who historically have been chattel in this country. And it is not a surprise that right now the First Amendment is protecting people who buy and sell people: the First Amendment is protecting pornographers. And we're told that their rights of speech make our rights of speech stronger. You see, they take one of us, or ten of us, or thirty of us, put gags in our mouths, hang us from something, and our speech rights are stronger. It defies comprehension but they keep saying it's true. I keep saying it's not true.

Please understand that we now live in a country where the courts are actively protecting pornography and the pornography business. When the civil-rights ordinance was passed in Indianapolis, the city was sued an hour after the ordinance was passed for passing it. For *passing* it. It was never even used. For *passing* it.

The first judge, in federal district court, was a Reagan-appointed judge, a woman, a right-wing woman. She said in her decision that sex discrimination never outweighs First Amendment rights in importance. That's the right-wing position. The First Amendment is more important than any harm that's being done to women. This First-Amendment-first decision was then appealed. Another Reagan-appointed judge, Frank Easterbrook, wrote the appeals court decision striking down the ordinance. He said that pornography did everything that we said it did. He said it promoted rape and injury. He said it led to lower pay for women, to affronts to women, to insult, to injury. And then he said that that proved its power as speech. Its ability to hurt women proved its power as speech and was the reason it had to be protected. A right-wing, Reagan-appointed libertarian.

So if your theory says that the right is against pornography and will use any means in its hands to stop pornography from existing, it seems to me that reality forces you to change your theory because your theory is wrong. Both the right and the left agree that a woman being hung from something is somebody's speech. Somebody's speech. And this means there is a new legal way in which women are legally chattel. Do you understand that once we're made into speech, we are owned as speech by men in the age of technology? Once we're technologized, once the abuse of us is technologized, we are legally their chattel.

The left is supposed to not value the free market too much. I mean, the free market is not a left-wing idea, is it? I mean, the free market means that you sell what you can sell, and you sell a lot of it, and you get your prices up high, and you make as big a profit as you can. And the market tells you what's popular and what's not popular and what you can do and can't do. And if a whole lot of people die because they're not worth very much, that's the breaks, because the highest value is on the competition of the free market.

Now, you may have heard a lot of left-wing people talking about something they call "the free market of ideas." You see, you're not just supposed to sell pigs and cattle and onions and apples and cars in the free market. There's a free market of ideas. And in this free market of ideas, ideas compete. And the good ideas win and the bad ideas lose.

You might think—as I did—that an idea is ineffable and is not a commodity. I mean, you sort of can't pull it out of the air and put it on the market to sell it and say, "It weighs so much, and I'm selling it for so much per pound." It turns out that if you trace the ideas that the left is talking about, they mean women. They mean women being objectified in pornography, being used in pornography, being exploited in pornography. That's "the free market of ideas." And the ideas look strangely like us. We're the ideas, and they've got a free market in us, folks. And they *do* have a free market in us.

The truth is that oppression is a political reality. It is a state of power arrangements in which some people are on the bottom, and they are exploited and used by people who are on the top, or who are on top of them. In this country, where everything has to be psychologized, and also used by sociologists, we don't talk about oppression as a political reality. Instead, we talk about people being victims. We say so-and-so was victimized. So-and-so was a victim of rape. And it's an all right word. It's a true word. If you were raped, you were victimized. You damned well were. You were a victim. It doesn't mean that you are a victim in the metaphysical sense, in your state of being, as an intrinsic part of your essence and existence. It means somebody hurt you. They injured you.

And if it happens to you systematically because you are born a woman, it means that you live in a political system that uses pain and humiliation to control and to hurt you. Now, one of the things that has happened to us is that a whole bunch of people have said not that we are victims but that we *feel* victimized. We feel it. It's a state of mind. It's a state of emotional overreaction. We feel it. It's not that something happened to us; instead, we have a state of mind that's bad. And feminists are responsible for this state of mind, because we make women feel victimized.

When we point out that there is a rape every three minutes, that a woman is beaten every eighteen seconds in this country, that's very bad for women because it makes them feel victimized. And we're not supposed to be bad and make women feel bad. This is the ultimate mind fuck. It takes away all the ground that we can stand on to say: "We have a political problem. We are going to find a political solution. And we are going to have to change the society that we live in to find it."

If you take a bunch of people and suddenly you find out that one is being beaten every eighteen seconds, that one is being raped every three minutes, that ten billion dollars a year now is being spent on watching them being raped for fun, watching them being exploited and objectified and violated for fun, and you don't feel a little bit put upon, I mean a little bit frazzled around the edges by that, it seems to me that one would be not only a victim but half dead, totally numb, and a true fool.

Exploitation is real and identifiable, and fighting it makes you strong, not weak. Sexual violation is real, and it is intolerable, and fighting it makes you strong, not weak. Woman hating is real, and it's systematized in pornography and in acts of sexual violence against women, and fighting it makes you strong, not weak. And the right and the left both—whether it's Phyllis Schlafly lecturing on how if you had been virtuous you wouldn't have been sexually harassed or the left explaining to you that you should celebrate your sexuality and forget about rape, forget about it, don't have a bad attitude, don't feel like a victim—they both want women to accept the status quo, to live in the status quo, and not to organize the political resistance that I talked about earlier. Because the first step in resisting exploitation is recognizing it, seeing it, and knowing it, and not lying about where it is sitting on you.

And the second step is caring enough about other women that if today you are fine, and yesterday you were fine, but your sister hanging from the tree is not fine, that you will go the distance to cut her down.

Feminism is opposition to woman hating in order to achieve a truly egalitarian society. And there can't be any women's movement that is rooted in political defenses of woman hating. Those who think that woman hating is all right—they're not feminists. They're not. Those who think that it's all right sometimes, here and there, where they like it, where they enjoy it, where they get off on it—especially sexually—they're not feminists either. And the people who think that woman hating is very bad some places, but it's all right in pornography because pornography causes orgasm, are not feminists. Pornography does cause orgasm in people who hate women — it sure does. And people who hate women so much that they believe that the exploitation of women is speech or is an idea are not feminists. People who believe that women are not quite human beings like they are — or that women in pornography are not quite human beings like they are — are not feminists. Anybody who fronts for those who hate women, who produce woman hating, who produce pornography, who celebrate woman-hating sex, those people are not feminists.

I would like to see in this movement a return to what I call primitive feminism. It's very simple. It means that when something hurts women, feminists are against it. The hatred of women hurts women. Pornography is the hatred of women. Pornography hurts women. Feminists are against it, not for it.

Part II

FAMILY STRUCTURES: THE PATRIARCH AND THE PIMP

Making an Issue of Incest

Louise Armstrong

When we first spoke out, ten years ago, on the subject of incest, of our abuse, as children, by fathers and stepfathers, of our childhood rape by older brothers, stepbrothers, funny uncles, grandfathers—there was, for all the pain, sometimes humor.

And there was, even through the anguish, a terrific mood of ebullience, of fantastic hope. Not only was it thrilling to pull insight and clarity from turmoil. But then—in the late 1970s—there was that sense of empowerment, of possibility for real change.

In these ten years things have become unimaginably worse—for child victims, now, and for the women, their mothers, who try to protect those children. And for survivors, who now find the very stuff of their trauma, their degradation, their violation as children, the common currency of talk show guest "experts" and "professionals"; find their courageous speaking-out transformed into no more than a new plot option for ongoing dramatic series.

People say to me, "Well, but at least we're talking about it now."

Yes. But it was not our intention merely to start a long conversation.

In breaking the silence, we hoped to raise hell. Instead, we have raised for the issue a certain normalcy. We hoped to raise a passion for change. Instead, what we raised was discourse—and a sizable problem-management industry. Apart from incest educators, we have incest researchers, incest experts, incest therapists, incest awareness programs, incest prevention programs.

And, of course, we have that immense backlash from fathers' rights groups, which now threatens to re-entomb children and women in silence—in fear for their very safety once again.

This society has now devised systematic torments for children who tell of abuse. We label these torments "help." We now tell children in schools to tell. And when they do tell, we either disbelieve them, or we encourage the empowered intervention system to yank them from their mothers into foster care. We call this "help."

After we have yanked the child into state care, we now turn to the mother and we explain: "We have done this because you 'failed to protect' the child. We have done this because, even though you didn't happen to know of the abuse, even though you just found out, you 'should have known'." We call this the "best interest of the child."

When a mother now attempts to protect her child by divorcing the abuser, or when she discovers the abuse after divorce, on visitation, there is a near certainty that she will be disbelieved: perceived as a "vengeful" woman in an "acrimonious" divorce dispute. She is a sitting duck for abuse by the system; for vilification by the courts; for charges of vindictiveness, instability, "delusional psychoses" by the mental health professionals; and for charges of outright lying by the father and his lawyers. As well, she faces serious disbelief by a public already brainwashed to believe in that pillar of the new incest mythology: the "incest mother"; that weak, needy, domineering, cowardly, passive, manipulative, frigid, and sexually rapacious creature who (a) always tells her child to shut up and never say that again, and (b) always chooses her husband over the child.

In a nutshell, a child's disclosure of rape by the father will be believed by those in power, and by the public, so long as the mother disbelieves the child. And she will be punished for that. A child's disclosure of rape by the father will not be believed by those in power and by the public, so long as the mother believes the child and acts to protect her. And she will be punished for that.

And so even as 800-numbers continue to blare out from radio and TV sets across the nation—protect kids, report abuse, help is available —women are doing jail time for refusing to send the child who's disclosed abuse for her weekly "visitation." And the clear message deriving from experiential reality, rather than propaganda, is reaching an increasing number of women: take the kid and run.

The media is abuzz and atwitter with reports that *women* have formed an Underground Railroad. That *women* are helping other women escape! That they are offering sanctuary to those many, many mothers whose children have disclosed sexual abuse by their fathers—and who are being vilified, pilloried, jailed by the courts, for trying to protect those children; who are, in fact, apt to lose not only custody, but all visitation with those children.

Underground Railroad. It certainly has resonance (although the news accounts and TV presentations seem oblivious to the full implications of the phrase). It sure puts the slavery piece in place. It tells us just how uppity it was of us to speak out about paternal child-rape; just how deeply our defiance of a longstanding presumed male prerogative cuts.

Underground Railroad. Alas, for all its splendor as simile, it is inaccurate in one crucial way: for these women and children, *there is no North*. There is no state, no place, where safety can be relied on; no area in the country that promises protection. Indeed, ironically, I am told that women from Canada are seeking haven here—even as U.S. mothers and children look toward Canada with hope.

Yet the sad fact is that many, many feminists have so far failed to identify what is being done to these children and women as a "feminist" issue. Nor have I noticed many incest survivors impassioned by this backlash which has all the genuine menace of a full-scale declaration of war. They seem not yet to understand. Our speaking out, as adult survivors, about our childhood incestual assault, did not threaten the status quo. It challenged nothing in the present; cost those in power nothing in the present—economically or politically. In fact, our coming forward opened a new frontier for therapeutic specialization.

It is the women now acting to protect child-victims who are radically defying the patriarchy—challenging it in the arena where all women are most vulnerable: the courts. And they are being hounded and punished—even unto death.

Such was the fate of Dorrie Lynn Singley—dead, at 27. Her story— the stuff of legend and ballad—may help illuminate what we are speaking of here.

A young Southern woman, of ordinary rural background, who loved to cook, sew, clean, and mind her kids, Dorrie was divorced from her husband, Tim Foxworth, in February, 1984. According to newspaper reports, she later swore in an affidavit that she left Foxworth because she found him requiring her daughter, Chrissy, to fondle his genitals.

Dorrie took the child and went to Texas, evading visitation. In July, 1986, when she returned to Marion County, Mississippi, she was jailed for ten days for denial of visitation, for contempt.

On November 26, an Assistant District Attorney, Margaret Alfonso, interviewed Chrissy. A year later, Alfonso would write to psychologist Franklin Jones, "I had no doubt this child is being abused."

Meanwhile, in December, 1986, Foxworth filed for custody of Chrissy.

And meanwhile, as well, another woman in Mississippi was in a similar circumstance. Karen Newsom, described in the press as articulate, intelligent, a teacher, had medical and psychological testimony that her young children, Katy and Adam, were being sexually molested by her former husband.

Both women shared an attorney, Garnett Harrison, a longstanding feminist activist: founder of the Jackson, Mississippi rape crisis center, author of the Mississippi Protection from Domestic Abuse Act passed by the legislature in 1984.

And they shared a judge, Judge Sebe Dale, described as a "stern rural judge." "Witchhunt!" Judge Dale opined about Newsom's allegations. "Shades of Salem!" he cried as he reversed custody, and sentenced Newsom to indefinite time in jail when she refused to comply and secreted her children away.

Forty-three days Karen Newsom would hold out in that jail before crying uncle and revealing her children's whereabouts. Forty-three days in a Mississippi jail is a long, long time.

Dorrie's ten days in jail had given her real feeling for what that was like. She swore she would never go back (and then swore she would if she had to).

On August 4, 1987, Judge Dale awarded custody of Chrissy to the father. Dale produced, as support for his decision, the fact that Dorrie's eight-year-old son and her six-month-old son were "born out of wedlock." He spoke of her "nebulous" plans about marrying the baby's father.

Judge Dale called Dorrie a liar. And he said, in conclusion, that "the environment for Chrissy while in Tim's custody was a stable one, and wholesome and well-suited to Chrissy's needs and best interests."

In defiance of the court, Dorrie did not turn Chrissy over to Foxworth. In defiance of the court, she had Chrissy examined at the New Orleans Children's Hospital by sexual abuse expert, Dr. Rebecca Russell. Russell found "marked hypervascularity (an increase in the number and size of the blood vessels) of the hymen and perihymenal tissue." She found gaps and scarring of the hymen. In short, there were, in Dr. Russell's opinion, genital findings which "could only be caused by molestation, and not from vaginal infections or self-stimulation by the child."

"2 Women Refuse to Let Children Return to Alleged Sexual Abuse" headlines a story in the *Mobile (Alabama) Press Register*, August 16, 1987.

> Two women say they'll go to jail before they turn over their children to fathers they accuse of sexually abusing the youngsters.
> "I don't intend to turn them over," said Newson, 30, of Gulfport. . . .
> "I'm sure I'll be found in contempt, which I am in contempt. I'll stay in jail," said Newsom. . . .
> "And I'll follow in right behind her," said Singley.

Both Karen and Dorrie had supporters. With the turn of events, a group of women were galvanized to action as Mothers Against Raping Children (MARC). Karen Newsom's two children were hidden away. And Dorrie and Chrissy went into hiding as well. Sometimes together, for more time separately, they became fugitives. The women were labeled kidnappers and hostage-takers—and said to be using tactics that were terrorist.

Here is what Dorrie, our young kidnapper-terrorist, wrote in her journal on August 27, a week after Karen had been jailed.

> Lord, how much longer can this mess continue? The whole system is crazy. What more can they do to these children? First, these sick men have sexually used them, Dale gives them to the perverts, Karen & I protect them by hiding them. . . . The State refuses to hear these children's cries. . . . I can't even begin to express what I feel right now. Anger, fright, loneliness and even hatred. I don't want to hate. It's not in me.

On August 28, at Dorrie's contempt of court hearing, Garnett Harrison tried to get Judge Dale to look at Dr. Russell's medical report. The judge refused. Then he held Dorrie in contempt.

Dorrie, however, did not attend the hearing. Instead, she took cover.

And, later that day, after learning the outcome, she wrote in her journal:

> I'm glad I didn't go. I think they intended to lynch me. . . .
> It's a shame when so many are so blinded. Even worse is when it's a whole town. And to protect a *RAPIST*, instead of a 5½-year-old child. Who has repeatedly said her FATHER DID IT.

On September 2, Dorrie developed what she believed to be a severe migraine headache.

On September 3, she was brought to the New Orleans home of Judy Watts, a children's advocate. Watts says that Dorrie "was sick off and on throughout the time she was with me. When she wasn't in pain, though, she kept busy around the house. She cleaned, washed dishes, did laundry. She sewed and cooked. She'd have dinner waiting for me when I got home. She read magazines and books."

Dorrie's journal, though, testifies to chronic torment, acute isolation, and to the abysmal dislocation experienced by someone who has suddenly stepped outside the world as she has always known and believed it to be.

On September 14, she wrote:

> I guess they picketed yesterday at jail. I hope so. I know this is getting to Karen. It's been 26 days. She must be feeling totally helpless.
> I know I feel that way. Somehow trapped and unable to help yourself or speak up for yourself. And (especially) when you have finally gotten to where you could speak out.

And, virtually without relief, there were the terrible headaches.

> I still have the migraine. I sure could use a hug. Even a sticky hug &
> kisses.
> My head is worse today. I can't tell you how alone I feel. . . . Oh and
> Karen still in jail.

On September 15, Dorrie's ability to speak was impaired.

She had insisted vehemently from the time she came to this house
that she would not go to a hospital. They'd learn who she was and
she'd be sent back to jail and she'd probably stay there the rest of her
life because she would never, ever tell where Chrissy was.

However, the severity of the attack left no real choice. She was examined at Charity Hospital and told her physical condition was good
and she was suffering from nerves. Well, that certainly sounded credible.

What seems—if not incredible, then at least uncanny—is that Dorrie suffered this temporary loss of speech on the very day when Karen
Newsom's spirit broke and she decided to speak. After more than forty
days in jail, she told the whereabouts of her children. She was then
held a few more days until she disclosed the whereabouts of her children's "protectors."

In the event, about thirty women courageously stepped forward to
"confess" their participation in the protection of Karen's children.

However, the screws were tightening.

Now Foxworth's attorney started threatening the members of MARC
with kidnapping charges. Garnett Harrison's phone records were sub-
poenaed, and she was threatened with prosecution. The FBI was on
the case. A federal grand jury was convened.

Dorrie missed most of this.

On October 13, she was stricken severely with the brain aneurysm
which would rupture and kill her. She was taken to the hospital, where
she died the next day.

Her last journal entry was made on September 21:

> I decided to add this to my journal today. It may never be read. But
> writing it helps.
> Judge Dale, Honorable, isn't that what they call you? Honorable, isn't
> that what you're supposed to be? I find this hard to believe.
> An honorable man would protect the innocent rather than the ac-
> cused. At least that's what I always believed. I thought justice was what
> protected a victim. How wrong I've been for 27 years.
> Over the past months, I've seen how honorable you are. I've seen
> how you chose to protect the innocent. For now, my children as well as
> I, am a victim of your justice.
> It sickens my soul to think you have such power. The power to de-
> stroy a human being's life. To turn that person inside out, without even
> blinking. To turn your head on a criminal who could destroy another
> life. Literally destroy this time.

I've managed to keep the life that was set out to be destroyed pro-tected. I chose to protect that life through your so-called courtroom, and now I have to do it alone without your so-called courtroom of justice.

That life being a five-year-old child. A child whose life has barely be-gun. She's a victim of today's society. A victim of a courtroom that does not serve with justice. A victim of a so-called father who takes his sexual pleasures from his daughter. How sickening? How horrifying to a five-year-old child.

The saddest day in my life was telling my 8-year-old goodbye and my 9-month-old son. And then came my 5-year-old daughter, who I've tried and will continue to protect, goodbye. They know I love them. I hope God helps each one through this horrid time we're going through.

My other hope is for justice to work for the innocent. No child de-serves to be raped. And no child should be forced to live with her rapist. And no mother should be punished for loving what God gave her to love and protect.

This entry is signed, "A Loving Mom, Dorrie Singley."

In early December, Chrissy surfaced in San Francisco and was turned over to the juvenile authorities there. For a moment, there was hope that they would protect her and not return her. However, that did not happen, although the Mississippi authorities made some promises about a correct investigation toward the child's protection. To begin with, she was placed in the home of the district attorney. Next, she was given into the custody of Foxworth's parents. And on New Year's Eve she was returned to the custody of Foxworth.

How did we get here? How did we get from the starting point of a "dread taboo" to the point where another mother worn out, beaten down, defeated, said, "The court just gave my baby to a rapist." How did we get from the so-newly-reached vantage point of believing chil-dren—to the backlash which renders any particular child suspect, in any particular instance, where she identifies any particular of-fender?

In retrospect, it was frighteningly easy. Our understanding of incest as a longstanding male prerogative, a routine behavior traditionally permitted to men, was based on history, based on theory, and, of course, utterly corroborated by women's testimony. For centuries, men have molested their children because it has been their privilege to do so. Whether incest was overtly permitted—as it once was—or tacitly per-mitted—as it once was—or whether continuance of the permission was ensured by denial, as when Freud held sway, a certain proportion of the male population sexually exploited their own children for a simple reason: they chose to, and they could.

And our simple, homespun analysis of the situation as one of ordi-nary, everyday patriarchal prerogative was completely congruent with the understanding of the molesters themselves. One father, on national TV, said, "You have to understand. At the time I thought I was doing her a favor." Another said, "I'm a good man. I don't run around. I provide for my family. And I've never slept with anyone except my wife and my daughters."

We correctly identified the permission for men to molest their own children as a method by which girl children learned, at a very tender age, their sexual vulnerability, their status as sexual objects for male gratification; and by which boy children, molested by fathers and step-fathers at a very early age, learned what their future possibilities and prerogatives could be with their own children.

We identified incest as effectively *legal*, and we called for the repeal of the license. We challenged the system to make it a crime—as it is to molest the neighbors' kids.

However, what we saw, and what the offenders saw, as a license to exploit, the powers-that-be saw as a potential threat to the status quo. And the mental health professionals saw as a business.

We called it traditional, they called it deviant. We called it criminal, they called it sick. And the offenders—the perpetrators—when they finally caught their breath—they called it a big lie. Our political under-standing was all but completely obliterated.

"Sick" became so thoroughly ingrained as the correct way to "un-derstand" that even the appearance, in 1980, of a group of perfectly respectable doctors and professors under the banner of the "pro-incest lobby" could not shake the public's need to disbelieve the obvious. These men were passionately promoting the healing powers of "posi-tive incest": they sought an open permission for sex with their chil-dren. They said incest was sometimes beneficial (take two children every four hours and call me in the morning). And the media and the pop-ulace looked at these perfectly normal men and as one voice they cried, "Sick! That's sick!"

What we failed to apprehend, in our exuberance, was the sheer pas-sion and intensity that lay behind the endorsement and behind the permission: the power of the backlash that would press its thumbs to the eyeballs of anyone who tried to withdraw that permission.

We failed to apprehend, too, what would happen when the state took one look at the size of the problem and had an epiphany: If they treated paternal child molestation as a crime, there was the prospect that one-tenth of the otherwise law-abiding, productive, economically useful and prosperous male citizens would be diverted to making li-cense plates in jail.

And so to label these crimes against children a disease was itself, in fact, a child of necessity. The problem was that they could not identify the offender, singly, as the sick one. For one thing, in the public mind, to be so sick as to orally rape a two-year-old is to be very sick indeed. In fact, it made the fathers' protestations that they didn't see they were doing anything wrong seem like an insanity defense.

For another thing, to identify the offenders singly as the sick ones would raise the idea of an offense, and have everyone wondering why you were trying to keep the bastard in the home. There was nothing for it, really, but to see it as a "family disease," a "symptom of family dysfunction."

Enter, the "incest mother"—that dreadful, "collusive" woman, who "always knew on some level"; who positively shoved her daughter in as a sexual surrogate; who invariably chose her man over her child; who was at once sexually rapacious and frigid; who denied and who lied. The "incest mother."

Never in history has the rotten mother been of such service to her country.

It was this "incest mother" who provided the very foundation on which the experts built their "disease model," their treatment intervention schemes, their decriminalization defense. It was she around whom intervention was structured, toward whom counseling was aimed. She, who was the justification for the proliferation of treatment programs designed to "keep the family intact." The fact was she seldom existed. But by now facts didn't have much power to bother anybody. The state had its new mythology. The "experts" had their problem-management industry. The paternal child molesters of America were once again safe.

The children and their mothers, however, were not—and are not. In placing themselves outside the "profile" of the typical "incest mother," in trying to protect the children, in choosing the children and not the offenders, women were placing themselves dangerously outside the convenience of public policy, and outside the available remedies in law.

Nor did these women have any real credibility with a public already thoroughly brainwashed about what a woman who chanced to find herself the mother of a child-victim should be like.

The offenders picked up on this readily. It gave them heart. It gave them hope. And it gave them a voice of such raucous outrage at the sheer injustice of things as to make our voices, when we spoke out, seem the very model of dignified, ladylike reason.

One of the backlash group's flyers tells me that "there is new hope" for those accused of sexual abuse. "We have," they say, "developed a specialized team capable of assisting on cases anywhere in this nation. . . . The team is made up of the best experts available in the United States. . . . We call it the 'annihilation team,' because our aim is to destroy false allegations. You can call it the 'A-team' for short. We mean business." The flyer is signed "The Avenger."

I have no opinion about the impact of television on small children. However, it clearly has an impact on the fantasies of some adult men.

These backlash groups, also, are being very well served by the "incest mother."

Dr. Lee Coleman, a psychiatrist based in Berkeley, California, and founder and director of the Center for the Study of Psychiatric Testimony, said before a meeting of Victims of Child Abuse Laws (VOCAL) that an allegation of child sexual abuse *might* be true under these conditions: Where you found a mother saying to the child, "How could you think such a terrible thing?"; or where you found the mother saying, "Don't let me ever hear you say anything like that again!" Paternal child molestation *might* exist, that is, wherever you had an intact family, and you had your good old prototypical "incest mother."

Coleman said,

> Now, in a classic situation where the male figure is the alleged perpetrator, that is the kind of statement you might hear from a mother who is still married to the father, or who is still living with, and wants to continue to live with, the live-in boyfriend. Yes indeed, that is the kind of thing you might hear. That is the classic, intact family situation.
>
> That makes sense when a mother who hears that her husband has molested a daughter may, in fact, have more loyalty to her husband than to her daughter, for emotional reasons, for financial reasons, and there may be a lot of other reasons. . . . And that most certainly is an abuse that anybody who becomes aware of should try to protect the child. . . . So far so good.
>
> Now, we have a situation where the mother and the father have divorced each other. They hate each other. And they are fighting over custody of the child. Do you think you are going to hear that mother say to the child, "How could you ever think of such a terrible thing?" "Don't let me ever hear you say that again?"

"Well," he says, addressing this group with a membership of those claiming to have been falsely accused, "I don't need to tell *this* audience how totally ludicrous that is."

And so it is the nominally liberal ideology—of illness and cure, rather than crime and accountability—turned to by the state in its own interest, and enthusiastically embraced by professionals, which is providing a new shield of protection of offenders. The mental health "understanding" has generously given them a new framework for denial, a new justification for retaliation and vengeance toward child-victims and women who break the silence.

The backlash literature expresses a kind of petulant concern over what they see as "man-hating radical feminists" (which appears to include anyone who perceives child-rape as a gender, rather than gender-neutral, issue). But it is not a very serious concern that they are expressing. And, alas, at least until now, we have given no cause why it should be. Incest in the present has not been a priority political issue for feminists.

It was not long after we first spoke out that it began to become clear that many feminists had also succumbed to the medical model. Survivors in significant numbers fell prey to the litany of shame and guilt. They fell victim to the litany of childhood sexual abuse as an individual emotional problem, and they—with the help of many of the new therapeutic "experts"—lost sight of the political/power issue at hand. That is not to say, of course, that there is no place for individual counseling, individual help, individual support. It's just to say that when you are looking at a systematic, system-endorsed power abuse, individualized solutions—exclusively individualized solutions—are antithetical to change.

It was depressing, as well, to watch formerly feminist therapists seduced into paying the price of the ticket of access. To be fair, however, there was no other way into the incest club than to check your political persuasions permanently at the door; to agree with the "illness model"; and to speak of dynamics, etiology, of dyads, triads; and to tinker around with ever-more-fantastical methods of "behavior modification" for an "illness" in perfectly normal men.

With the re-introduction of *Kiss Daddy Goodnight* as *Kiss Daddy Goodnight: Ten Years Later* (Louise Armstrong, 1987), I had occasion to get back in touch with some of my friends who first joined me in speaking out. How did they feel about what had happened in these ten years? Here is what one woman, Maggie, wrote:

> Dear Louise,
> Ten years! My god! I remember how brave I felt saying the words, getting my story out there. All those valiant thoughts of how it would change the world, help thousands, get it out of the closet, shake foundations. In many ways the outcome has been somewhat surprising. It's sort of like, "She labored and labored and brought forth a mouse!" *Nothing's really changed.*
> We've been sold a bill of goods, particularly by the mental health people and the courts. The whole message is that those kids will just have to grow up fast and learn to understand daddy and give him another chance and that daddy just somehow got off to a bad start and if we will all sit down rationally and discuss it, that:
> 1. Daddy will see the error of his ways and be good.
> 2. Mommy will realize that if only she'd been more understanding and available to daddy and more intimate, she would have stopped it from happening.
> 3. We would get over our shame and realize we were not to blame. And we'd all live happily ever after.
> Bullshit.

Recently, I went to yet *another* seminar on incest and child abuse which you must understand is good business for the "helping" professions, and they expounded all day on early recognition, immediate involvement and intervention, etc., etc. We spent the whole day learning what we as clinicians could do to *save the kids*.

Then the bureaucrats from the state got up to speak and the first thing they said was that unless you had proof positive—i.e., caught everyone red-handed—there wasn't really much that could be done. Talk about intellectual masturbation.

All this funding, all these incest programs are a total abuse of power. If the kids are taken away, what good does that do the kids? And where are they putting those kids? We keep hearing that they're sometimes re-molested in foster care. Do you think those kids are going to come forward and speak about it again? And go through it all *again?*

The mother can't win. She's wrong no matter what happens. If she leaves, she didn't support her husband and work it through to keep the family intact. If she stays, somehow she's condoning it. Usually, she's so burned by her first experience, trying to leave or trying to get help to protect the child, she doesn't ever want to confront it again. She's burned out.

Ten years. I'm married to a wonderful man. He's my best friend. My heart still skips a beat when I see him. I still think he's beautiful. We're great together. Our lives work. We travel. We went to Africa to see the gorillas, rode elephants in Thailand. We love spending time together. And I still, deep down, don't trust him.

I'm successful, well liked, have substance, humor, joy, and on some level I still hate myself.

It still goes back to the damage of childhood, and it pisses me off. I'm bored to death with "my story," and furious that it can still get in my way at times. All those neurotic fears have *nothing* to do with me, with my husband, with us, with the reality of us. I've swollen up like a blimp since we married for fear of the kind of wonderful intimacy we have. I'm losing weight again. It's tiring, boring, and redundant. But when I look around me—I'm more alive than most people. I have more joy in my life, more variety, more pizzazz, and part of me loves who I am. I just think it would have been one hell of a lot easier if my folks had been Ozzie and Harriet. (Maybe just Harriet?) All that *wasted* energy and all those moments of self-hatred. . . .

There are incest counselors, incest programs, incest awareness groups, incest survivor groups, incest education for mothers and kids. . . . And it's still happening. And it's still legal. They're still getting away with it. There's a whole business around it, a structure to protect it.

And we're getting used to it. "Hey, did you hear about so-and-so? She was molested by daddy." "No kidding. I assume she's getting some counseling. Where shall we go for lunch?"

God, when I think back to the hope we had, the ideas we had, the significance we attached to what we were doing, the belief we had that we could change things for kids now—and then when I look at how things really are for kids now. . . .

I hate to say we made things worse. I guess *we* didn't, but I think things *are* worse, and maybe somebody has to say so out loud before anything can ever change.

I'd like to see survivors wake up to the power abuse, and the abuse by professionals, talking about them as depersonalized victims, objects of study to be quantified and described in terms of some prefabricated set of personality specifications.

Ten years later. Damn. I am pissed off. I think it's time for a survivor revolt. No more "poor little things," or "how hard it must be for you." Let's just get some action to stop it.

Yes. I agree. It is time, ten years later, to begin action for change. If there is to be change.

How long are we going to watch the protective women we wished our mothers had been, relentlessly hounded, legally crucified—and do nothing? How long are we going to watch as the "Chrissies" of today become—if they are lucky, if it is a very good day—the survivors, the "Maggies," of tomorrow?

REFERENCES

Armstrong, Louise. (1987). *Kiss daddy goodnight: Ten years later*. New York: Pocket Books.

Eberle, Paul, and Eberle, Shirley. (1986). *The politics of child abuse*. New Jersey: Lyle Stuart.

2 women refuse to let children return to alleged sexual abuse. (1987, August 16). *Mobile (Alabama) Press Register*.

Taking Our Eyes Off
the Guys

Sonia Johnson

All of us—all women in patriarchy—are seasoned to be slaves, are seasoned to be prostitutes. All of us, in some sense, are, or have been, prostitutes and slaves, and most of us will continue to be for the rest of our lives. And it is the essence, the very nature of seasoning, to blind us—to our condition as well as to the mechanics of our enslavement.

Those of us, however, who grew up in and were seasoned in traditional, fundamentalist Judeo-Christian environments, got a closer look at the mechanics of that seasoning process than some others. And although we're sometimes matronized in the movement—the assumption being that if we could ever have believed that preposterous, dangerous nonsense, we can never again be trusted to be clear—the truth is that we can probably be trusted *more* to have kept the vision of feminism clear once we had seen it than those of you who grew up as Unitarians or Quakers or even Methodists and Presbyterians because, you see, we saw patriarchy naked before us all the time, all around us all day long, every day.

And what we knew, what we realized as soon as we were able to *see* what we were seeing and to reject it—wrench it out of our souls and throw it all away—what we were left with was the understanding of the patriarchal family as the model for all oppression: the patriarchal family with the man on top as god and the women and children as worm under him—and far too often very literally under him.

We understood then that that paradigm—that power-over paradigm, that sadomasochistic paradigm which is patriarchy—extends to everything, that it is the model for all social institutions, for all economic structures, for international politics. It's white on top in male position as god, people of color underneath in woman position as worm.

It's the rich as male on top, the poor as female on the bottom. It's humans on top, all other living things on the bottom. It's large on top, small on the bottom—large countries as male, small countries as female—and so on.

Now where we learn that this is "natural" and "normal" is in the family. All of us had one of those, and some of them, as I say, were more blatantly patriarchal than others. Some of us got a really thorough-going education, and as was said in my introduction, I got one of the best there ever was! I'm grateful to the Mormon elders for a truly matchless education in patriarchal ontology. I can't be fooled again, and neither can you graduated Catholics or any others of you who were true believers in any religion.

When I say that all women have been seasoned as slaves and prostitutes, I'm talking about seasoning that began at home. All other societal institutions avidly participated in it, of course. But no matter how we're seasoned—as prostitute or as wife, which is the same thing—we're seasoned in the patriarchal family almost exclusively to serve sexual functions.

No matter what form seasoning takes, it always has the same goal —to make us feel worthless and dependent. Obviously, incest is a seasoning tool par excellence; one incident of incest is really all that is necessary to teach us our role in patriarchy. It is such a profound betrayal of trust, primarily of our trust in ourselves. It is designed to make us feel powerless, to shatter our inner core of confidence, and therefore to make us feel utterly dependent on men. It functions to make us believe passionately that we need a savior, that men must save us, that we have to go through them to be saved. That somehow we've got to get them to *change their minds* about us. We've got to make them agree that their behavior is terrible and get them to stop it. Our seasoning teaches us nonsense: that we've got to get the slaveholders to free the slaves.

That's the goal of seasoning: to make us believe that we must always go through someone else to be free. Of course, the reason we're taught this is because freedom never happens that way. Tyrants never free the slaves. It's an historical truth that the oppressed must always rise and free themselves, and in freeing themselves, free everyone. The truth is that radical change, change at the root, must be made by *us*.

There are many reasons for our being in the only position, historically speaking, to change things. One of these is the basic paradox of tyranny, that the oppressors are always less free than the oppressed. Another is that, as women, we are truly outside men's system. Virginia Woolf said that, you know. She said in *Three Guineas* that women are the Society of the Outsiders, that that's where we have our power.

We have power—meaning the ability to act, to effect change—outside the system because that's where we truly live, politically, psychically; it is therefore the only place where we are authentic, and we can only have power where we are authentic. We also have power there because being outside and being slaves means being flexible; slaves have to be almost preternaturally flexible in order to survive. And one of the most important laws of cybernetics is that the most flexible element in any system is the controlling element. Privileges are chains. Men are bound by their privilege, have no flexibility, cannot change their system even if they wished—and they don't wish. Being the most flexible elements in this system, women are now in control of the planet. Our behavior, not the men's, will determine the course of human events.

But conditioned, seasoned as we are, this is the most difficult possible conception for us, and most of us continue to believe that we must make *men* change their ways, that we are dependent upon legislators to pass laws, for instance. Good grief! When have those in control ever given up a significant amount of it to those they control? Can you think of a single time in history?

Well, it has never happened and it's not going to happen. We should have learned that with the Equal Rights Amendment. If we didn't learn it then, what is it going to take to teach it to us? Our not learning it is part of our seasoning, our profound conditioning. We're deeply dependent, deeply servile in ways that our surface militance camouflages.

That is the main goal of seasoning: to make us believe the men must change the world for us and that we're powerless to change reality unless the men change first. But the truth is that they're not *going* to change—*can't* change—so we don't have to waste our time trying to get them to any more. *We* are the ones who must change, because we *can*. And when *we* change, everything outside us will have to change to accommodate our new way of being in the world—including men, but that's beside the point.

The principle underlying all seasoning—how you get this effect, how you reach this goal of getting women to believe that our salvation depends on someone else's behavior — is that you get someone to do everything *in relation* to someone else who they perceive as more powerful; you get them always to consult an image of someone else in their minds, to say to themselves—to say to ourselves as women, for instance—"Now, how will the *men* respond to that?" every time we make a decision, or "If we do this, what will *they* do?" Always to be relational, to consult the masters in our psyches every time—this is bondage.

When women make our internal states, our well-being, contingent upon men's behavior, behavior we can neither control nor change, we give up all chance for independence and freedom. Our freedom must depend exclusively on us; we are the only ones we can change and control.

We must understand and internalize the fact that men are totally irrelevant now as far as change is concerned. So we can take our eyes off them and look at ourselves to make a shining new reality right here, right now in the midst of the old putrescent, collapsing world of the fathers.

As long as we're focused on the men, we're never going to see that the door to our jail cell is open, that it's open *not* into patriarchy but into our own power. As long as we're concentrating on the men, doing everything with our pimps in mind, we're never going to break free. Our pimps are the men around us. They're the legislators, professors, ministers—none of you still *has* ministers or priests, I trust? Our pimps are our fathers, our husbands, our sons. To be everything in relation to them is slavery.

I learned this as a prostitute-in-training in Mormondom, in a Mormon home as well as the church. And in the Democratic Party. And in liberal and progressive and leftist groups. And in the National Organization for Women, which is modeled, also, on the patriarchal family. I learned these things in the same place *you* learned them. We have all learned them the hard way.

When I escaped from Mormonism, I looked out and saw that all churches were the Mormon church. I looked out further and saw that the whole world was the Mormon church. Over the years as I kept looking, I saw that Congress and the legislatures and the political parties and *Mother Jones* and National Public Radio were also all the Mormon church—you know, "Nothing New Considered," "The Same Old Stuff Considered." I saw that they were all the Old Boys' Club.

I decided I wasn't going to escape from one brothel just to get myself trapped in another; that something was basically wrong with thinking that any of these institutions was the New World. So it seemed to me that it was time for me to take my eyes off the guys, to get rid of the superstitious belief that if I didn't monitor every single thing they did, if I didn't clutch at them and beg them and plead with them and lobby them and kick and scream and stamp my foot and demand, they would go berserk and kill us all.

But this is nonsense, of course, because all evidence shows that men have gone berserk *anyway*. With our eyes fastened unblinkingly on their faces day and night for thousands of years, they have grown increasingly mad. With our attention *riveted* upon them they are killing us and the world around us daily. The evidence is that with our reactive, fearful, dependent behavior we have been facilitating patriarchy in all its manifestations throughout its history. We have been seasoned to do this, to keep our eyes on our patriarchs, our pimps, so we won't look at ourselves and see the stunning alternatives.

I saw that since it hadn't gotten us anywhere, it was time to stop doing that. We don't have a thousand years to get enough women in our legislatures and our Congress. And even if we did, they would all be female impersonators by the time they got there, anyway.

We don't have time. We've only got, maybe, ten years. That means we've got to learn from history that resistance to and cooperation with the oppressor don't work. All the ways we've tried to change things didn't work. They didn't work! Hierarchical structures don't work. They are all copies of the patriarchal family, a paradigm that has failed us utterly.

So I've decided it's time for me to refuse that seasoning. It's time to deprogram myself and to stop concentrating at all times upon the masters, upon the pimps of the world, stop doing all I do in relation to them, in reference to them, in reaction to them; stop making my feelings of well-being contingent on their behavior; stop thinking about them—they are so *boring,* so numbingly boring! We can predict everything they will do, every savage, gruesome, gross, crass thing they're going to do. We know it all by heart. We don't need to watch it anymore, do we? Do you? I certainly don't. I've seen plenty of it, and I know it inside out.

It seems to me that what I have to do is what my deep conditioning tells me *not* to do, to do the thing that scares me most of all, to do what I've been taught *never* to do or I would die—and that is to take my eyes off the guys and to take *myself* seriously. To stop enabling men's system, patriarchy. To stop believing that they are going to change the world, that I ever have to try to get them to do anything redemptive again. They will not, *could* not if they would. And to come to grips with the truth that if I want the world another way, I must make it that way *myself.*

The most important message my wise old woman within has ever given me is that the transformation of this world is up to me—and you. What a relief! Thank goodness it's up to the women because now it will get done!

Family Matters

Ann Jones

When we consider the structure of the family and what goes on within it, the sexual liberals seem beside the point. When we consider the family, we have to talk about child sexual abuse, incest, and the area of family violence that I've focused on: wife abuse, marital rape, and battering—often culminating, in the cases I've looked into, in homicide. I've written particularly about cases in which a woman fought back and attacked or killed a man who abused her. But we know that far more often the outcome is the other way around, that it is the woman who dies. Exploring our sexuality requires freedom, and for women the family structure is still a prison.

The family is grounded in the same kind of repression that brings us capitalism and what Freud and others have been pleased to call "civilization." These days the American family is touted as a last bastion of red, white, and blue American life. The family is also said to be the first line of defense (or the last) against sexual license, drug addiction, homosexuality, widespread depravity, and crime. We are charged to defend the family at all costs. The military terminology is no accident.

We have come to expect this kind of language from people on the right, and in fact the right waves the bright banner of the American family to justify almost any of its schemes—no matter how vicious—from book banning to bombing abortion clinics. But it's a little disconcerting when feminists, whom we have more or less learned to trust, talk about the family in this way—when feminists find nothing fundamentally wrong with the family as an institution but seek only "equality" within it.

What that implied in the early days of the current feminist movement was some sort of contract about the housework. If you could just get him to *make* the bed you had to lie in, perhaps things would work out after all.

Many feminists in those embattled early days refused altogether to fill the conventional woman's role within the family; instead they went out into the world and there struggled to be independent women in a system designed to make that as difficult as possible—and suddenly unsurprisingly, they wanted to get back in. We watched a rather embarrassing procession of women marching in quick step to the altar and the maternity ward, and telling us how wonderful it all was, as though they had just invented it. (This parade still continues, though the joyous song is once again drowned out by the lament of the overburdened supermom, an old dirge meant to inspire a rising generation of women to just stay home in the first place.)

It's useful to study history. We learn from it how institutions and laws, social and economic forces, traditions and habits of mind converge to keep women in marriage and in a subordinate position within the family. We can name a long list of factors: inadequate job training for women, lack of access to jobs, lower wages paid to women, absence of child care, discriminatory promotion policies, discrimination in housing, sexual harrassment, rape, and so on.

These considerations led women in the movement to work for equality outside the family, in economic, political, and social life. We didn't speak much about sexual equality, for history also teaches us that whenever feminists turn from the body politic to the body they somehow wind up in the master bedroom. Yet surely there are connections to be made, for self-defined sexuality is one more thing—like autonomy, self-determination, safety, and the minimum wage—that is denied women in the family.

Family "stability" in a patriarchal system depends upon sexual repression of women. The same repression of woman-defined sexuality is also essential to pornography, and in both cases it is based on the separability of love from lust. This is no mere coincidence. In the traditional scheme of things, women love while men lust. The whole "desire" of a woman—ladies don't feel "lust"—is supposed to be encompassed in her love for her husband. In the perfect woman, desire, and marital duty perfectly coincide. Male sexuality, on the other hand, is based on a lust so powerful and apparently uncontrollable that grown men find themselves raping their own "seductive" children. Pornography, like prostitution, has always been a permissible outlet for male sexuality—which, to hear men tell it, is as glorious as it is boundless. Indeed, in this scheme, pornography and prostitution are not only necessary but good, for they safeguard the family structure by draining off excess male lust. Thus do these "social evils" sanitize and maintain "civilization."

The problem is not simply that this traditional view of sexuality maintains the family at the expense of female sexual pleasure, but that it makes violence against women inevitable.

It is in the interests of pornography, prostitution, and family mythology to stress as much as possible the difference between male and female sexuality. That difference lowers our expectation of passionate companionship between women and men. Young college women I've met recently, for example, expect that they will marry men they passionately love. But they also expect that passion will soon pale—they call this "being realistic" —to be replaced by the "other advantages" of marriage and the family structure. They expect to remain in the family for the sake of those other "advantages," though what those benefits may be is not quite clear.

Traditionally, the main "benefit" for a woman in marriage was that the man made the living, or at least in certain classes he was supposed to. We all know what women traded for that. But wars, tough economic times, and periods of active feminism have brought more and more women into the work force, and the old arrangement has broken down. And when a woman gains neither love nor support, when she finds no advantage to being in the family, then a man has only muscle and terror to keep her.

We still cite economic dependence as one of the main reasons why battered women remain in the family as long as they do. But I meet more and more battered women—severely battered women and women who have struck back—who were not being supported by the men who were their abusers. Rather the economic arrangement is often the other way around: the man lives off the woman, off her wages or her welfare check or the proceeds of her prostitution. He dominates and exploits her economically, just as he does physically and sexually. The parties may be husband and wife or a cohabiting couple, but the arrangement is the classic one of pimp and prostitute. The man maintains the arrangement by terror and violence, for when traditional bargains break down, what other sources of power do men have?

We know that men beat women because they can. No one stops them because to do so would be to interfere with the family. It would be un-American. But men beat women also because they think they must. Like the American generals in Viet Nam who destroyed cities in order to "save" them, men batter women in order to hang on to them. We know that batterers inflict the greatest violence and the greatest damage not when women "take it," but when women try to get away.

Men rape and batter women not for what women have done but for what they are about to do: escape.

Violence has always been an important tool for maintaining the family to serve the purposes of patriarchy. We can see that women who act against that violence—women who denounce those arrangements, women who try to leave, women who work on behalf of women—are the very ones accused of breaking up the family. It is the women who expose violence, not the men who commit violence, who are said to be "dangerous." And indeed they are, for the family depends upon violence and its concealment.

Women who successfully escape pay all sorts of real costs for having done so. Middle-class and upper-class women who leave lose their class status and the "privileges" their children might have enjoyed—better health care, better education—if they had remained with highly paid men. Poor women may slide deeper into poverty. Any woman may lose her children. And women who fight back against batterers are punished most severely of all. Most of those who kill their assailants serve long, long terms in prison.

What part does a positive sexuality play in all this? Very little. In violent marriages, in violent families, sex is a weapon. Whether it is used in rape or incest, whether it is directed against a woman or a child, sex is used in the same way that terrorists use, say, genital torture or mutilation—to humiliate, to shame, to destroy a sense of autonomy and authority, to erase identity. Rapists and batterers within the family are, in fact, domestic terrorists and they use exactly the same methods that international political terrorists use for exactly the same purposes: domination and control. The purpose of all domestic terrorism is to control the lives of women. To my way of thinking, that has everything to do with gender, but little if anything to do with a positive sexuality.

The abuse of children in the family perpetuates this system to the next generation through the process of socialization. It doesn't seem to matter much whether the children are girls or boys, or even whether they suffer abuse themselves or merely witness it. They are taught the same lesson: that violence is "normal" behavior, that men are powerful abusers, women and children powerless abused.

Susan B. Anthony knew all of this, and she wrote about it in *The Revolution*. And then somehow the knowledge got lost. It took us a long time to resurrect it. And now we are in danger of forgetting it again. Susan Brownmiller's book, *Against Our Will*, is a milestone in the women's movement because it demythologized—desexualized— rape. We learned—and not for the first time in history—that sexual and physical violence against women is not "sexual" at all but simply violent. Men use it to dominate women. Are we now to erase this knowledge again, to make violence and dominance glamorous and "erotic" once more?

Bernadette Powell, a black woman from Ithaca, New York, is now serving a 15-year-to-life sentence in New York's maximum security prison for women because in 1978 she shot and killed her ex-husband. She was a battered woman. At her trial she and several other witnesses testified about her battering and about torture with cigarettes, scalding water, ropes. Much of the testimony sounded like your standard home video porn flick scenario. Bernadette Powell had been subjected to all of it.

Although she said she acted in self-defense, she was convicted of murder, and she appealed. In response, the Tompkins County prosecutor—a man whose wife had just divorced him, charging that he also was a batterer—argued in his legal brief that Bernadette Powell had no reason to fear bodily harm from her ex-husband because although the man admittedly had committed many violent acts against her— there were hospital emergency room records and eye-witnesses to prove it — his motivation was "sexual." In other words, a woman's broken bones and broken spirit don't count if the man who broke them had sex on his mind. On the basis of this argument and several others, the New York State Appellate Court upheld the conviction of Bernadette Powell.

"Experts" debate the impact of pornography, but you have only to talk to battered women to know that it is used as a recipe book for violent scenes in the home. Many battered women report that their husbands keep pornographic magazines beside the bed and consult them as they proceed step by step to "have sex." But pornographic attitudes also may bend the minds of officials in the criminal justice system who in turn determine the future of women who fight back. Our prisons today are filled with women like Bernadette Powell, women who have been victims of a pornographic family structure at home and victims of a pornographic mythology in the courtroom. I'd like to see a mass appeal for clemency on behalf of these women imprisoned for fighting back, for with these attitudes fogging the court, none of the women was fairly tried.

The sexual liberals, as I understand them, want feminists to talk less about women as victims and more about women as autonomous people: women who choose freely and who act. We are all familiar with real limitations on women's freedom and women's choices, but if ever there were women who acted freely and willingly and with unbeatable spirit to tell us how they feel about the family in America, it is battered women who have left their husbands by the thousands, by the millions, over the years—women who faced extreme difficulties and danger and yet freed themselves from violent homes to make new lives. These women not only managed to save themselves and their children but they also organized to save other women from violent men. Now after more than a decade of intensive work on the issue of violence against women within the family, we must still cite woman abuse as the only major crime for which the only significant relief comes from organizations of survivors acting on behalf of victims. This movement, I think, is one of the most remarkable chapters in the history of women. And it's not finished.

Yet many of those battered women go back—not to the man who battered them, but to another man, another marriage, another nuclear family. Some of them are battered again, but most of them are not. They think they are smarter, and they probably are. They think they know the danger signs, and they probably do. Similarly, women who have not been battered believe that they are both wise and in control, that it can't happen to them, that if it did they wouldn't stand for it. What all these women still believe, you see, is that violence erupts spontaneously from the individual man.

We should know better than that. Susan Brownmiller showed us that rapists serve all men by enforcing male supremacy. Batterers do on the home front what rapists do both there and in the streets—they are the home guard of male supremacy. So as we continue to work against what is euphemistically called "domestic violence," as we continue to work for those women and children who are the immediate victims of male violence, we should be clear that our quarrel is not only with certain abusive men but with male supremacy. Our goal should be not merely to redefine our sexuality but to redefine the world and our place in it. Our fight should be not just "against domestic violence" but against that peculiar "domesticity" which couldn't carry on without it.

REFERENCES

Brownmiller, Susan. (1986). *Against our will.* New York: Bantam.

Confronting the Liberal Lies About Prostitution

Evelina Giobbe

WHISPER[1] is a national organization of women who have survived the sex industry. Our purpose is to expose the conditions that make women and children vulnerable to commercial sexual exploitation and trap them in systems of prostitution, to expose and invalidate cultural myths about women used in prostitution and pornography, and to end trafficking in women and children. We define systems of prostitution as any industry in which women's or children's bodies are bought, sold, or traded for sexual use and abuse. These systems include pornography, live sex shows, peep shows, international sexual slavery, and prostitution as it is commonly defined.[2] All these industries are merely different commercial vehicles through which men traffic in women and children.

We chose the acronym WHISPER because women in systems of prostitution whisper among themselves about the coercion, degradation, sexual abuse and battery upon which the sex industry is founded, while myths about prostitution are shouted out in pornography and the mainstream media, and by self-appointed "experts." This mythology, which hides the abusive nature of prostitution, is illustrated by the ideology of the sexual liberals which erroneously claims that prostitution is a career choice; that prostitution epitomizes women's sexual liberation; that prostitutes set the sexual and economic conditions of their interactions with customers; that pimp/prostitute relationships are mutually beneficial social or business arrangements that women enter into freely; and that being a prostitute or a pimp is an acceptable, traditional occupation in communities of color.

---

[1] Women Hurt In Systems of Prostitution Engaged in Revolt, Lake Street Station, Box 8719, Minneapolis, Minnesota 55408.
[2] Streetwalkers, "Call Girl" or "Escort" Services, brothels, saunas, massage parlors, etc.

The sexual liberals have developed three major arguments which attempt to explain away the central role of pimps in the recruitment of women and girls into so-called voluntary prostitution: "pimp as business manager"; "pimp as stigmatized minority"; and "pimp as lover or boyfriend." All three models have been embraced and promoted by Priscilla Alexander[3] of NTFP (The National Task Force on Prostitution) and COYOTE (Cast Off Your Old Tired Ethics) and Arlene Carmen and Howard Moody, speaking from the pulpit of the Judson Memorial Church and in their book, *Working Women: The Subterranean World of Street Prostitution* (1985). Since their collective views are representative of the sexual liberals' promotion of, and apology for, the commercial sexual exploitation of women through pornography and prostitution, this article will address their work.

In order to understand how pimps and panderers came to be redefined as "business managers," one needs to examine the myth that prostitution is a job just like any other job. According to the sexual liberals, "Prostitution is a traditional female occupation, a daily occurrence where biological desire and economic needs meet." They continue—in double-speak—to advise us that it is at once "an act that is primarily personal and intimate" and at the same time "one of the last bastions of small, free-enterprise, laissez-faire capitalism" (Arlene Carmen and Howard Moody, 1985). The fact that prostitution requires the commodification of women's bodies to be sold in the marketplace removes the act from the personal realm. Furthermore, survivors have described the act of prostitution as "disgusting," "abusive," and "like rape," and explained that they learned to cope with it by disassociating themselves from their bodies or by using drugs and alcohol to numb physical and emotional pain (WHISPER, 1988). Thus it would be more accurate to describe the act of prostitution as intrusive, unwanted, and often overtly violent sex that women endure rather than as a "personal and intimate act."

The central flaw in the sexual liberals' analysis is that it ignores survivors of prostitution who have testified repeatedly that they did not experience prostitution as a career (WHISPER, 1988). Further, the analysis doesn't consider the social function of prostitution: to extend to all men the right of unconditional sexual access to women and girls in addition

---

[3] Alexander, who has never been in prostitution, is the director and chief spokesperson of both NTFP and COYOTE. Neither organization has a visible membership or board of directors. Neither organization has produced any original research to substantiate its claims. Both organizations share the same address and phone number, I will assume that they are, in fact, one and the same and as such reflect primarily Alexander's philosophy.

to those privileges enjoyed by husbands and fathers within the institution of marriage. These dynamics are clearly understood by women used in systems of prostitution, as illustrated by the remarks of a survivor who made the connections between the physical and emotional abuse to which she was subjected in her family and her marriages, and her subsequent recruitment into prostitution by a pimp: "I basically just thought that women were put on this earth for men's sexual pleasure in exchange for a roof over your head and food in your stomach" (WHISPER, 1988).

Some sexual liberals justify prostitution as the altruistic creation of women of color. "Prostitution is no alien thing to Black women," write Carmen and Moody. "In every southern city in the 1920's and '30s the red light district was on the other side of the tracks in the Black ghetto [where] young white boys 'discovered their manhood' with the help of a 'two-dollar whore' . . . Prostitutes . . . were integrating blacks and whites long before there was a civil rights movement" (1985: pp. 184–185). Astonishingly, Carmen and Moody consider the buying and selling of women of color by white men and their sons to be the vanguard of desegregation.

White-male supremacy intensifies oppressive conditions that make women of color particularly vulnerable to recruitment or coercion into prostitution. By limiting educational and career opportunities and fostering dependence on an inadequate and punitive welfare system, racism creates economic vulnerability. This is illustrated by the testimony of a woman of color who survived prostitution:

> As a Black coming up in Indiana in the steel mill industry up there, they hired men. All the men got jobs in the mills there; very few women. You really had to be very cute or know someone, and so there wasn't jobs in the field, there wasn't jobs in offices for you, unless you knew someone or something; but there were lots of jobs for you in strip joints, dancing, or even down at some of the restaurants and bars outside of the steel mills for when the guys came in. (WHISPER, 1988)

Racist stereotypes of women of color in pornography and racist policies that zone pornographic bookstores, peep shows, topless bars, and prostitution into poor black and ethnic neighborhoods, create an environment in which women of color are particularly vulnerable.

> Young girls get their role models from somebody. In my family and in my neighborhood and around me was that kind of lifestyle, the fast lifestyle and that's where I got mine . . . pimps taught me, society taught me, my neighborhood taught me how, men in general, taught me that the way to get over is to use my good looks and my body. (WHISPER, 1988)

By not providing effective intervention programs to women of color who are trapped in abusive relationships—including prostitution—in their own communities, racist policies send out a message to these women that they are not deserving of help:

> I feel that social service agencies ignore the needs of Black women . . .
> In my community, coming up as a Black girl and even now, there weren't
> any agencies dealing with battering or prostitution or rape . . . For me,
> being abused sexually by men and not being able to talk about it, not
> having anyone to talk to about it, by being swept under the rug as this
> being a way of life . . . caused me to go out there and be abused again
> because no one was telling me that this was not okay so I felt I had to
> conform to this. (WHISPER, 1988)

Racist law enforcement policies disproportionately target women of color for harassment, arrest, imprisonment and fines (Bernard Cohen, cited in Nancy Erbe, 1984). Such actions create a revolving door through which women are shunted from the streets to the courts to the jails and back onto the streets again to raise money to pay these penalties. Selective application of laws prohibiting prostitution creates a kind of de facto regulation in which a tax is levied primarily against women of color by white men who design, maintain, control and benefit from the system of abuse in which the women are trapped.

Lastly, institutional racism puts women of color in a double bind by forcing them to go to white-dominated agencies to seek relief and redress for their injuries. If they speak out about the abuses they sustained in their own communities, they risk isolation, the possibility that their complaint will be used to fuel racist stereotypes and the probability that they will not receive effective advocacy. If they remain silent, they are left with limited resources with which to find an effective solution. Thus, racism holds women of color hostage to familial loyalties and community ties. This dilemma is well articulated by another woman of color who survived prostitution:

> I was taught what goes on in here you keep in here. That's not only in
> the house but you don't talk about other people's business in the com-
> munity, in the neighborhood, so it becomes a closed thing that extends
> from my house to the neighbor's house to the church . . . By not being
> able to go to white agencies and ask for help I was kept in the commu-
> nity in sexual violence—that is, prostitution and battering—because I
> didn't have information, I wasn't able to get the information. The only
> people I was allowed to talk to are people right there in my house, in
> my neighborhood, my environment that have said this is okay, that have
> agreed to this or adjusted to this. (WHISPER, 1988)

The role of racism in the recruitment of women into systems of prostitution and as an impediment to their escape is complex and multifaceted. This is a problem that survivors have begun to investigate with women of color in the larger feminist community. This discourse must begin with an understanding of the social realities under which women of color are forced to live in a white-male supremacist culture and the acknowledgment that any strategies for change must come from women of color, particularly those who have survived commercial sexual exploitation. Without this kind of leadership, racist and misogynist analyses of prostitution in communities of color — like those put forth by Carmen and Moody — will continue to facilitate and maintain the traffic in women and children of color.

"Prostitution involves an equation of sex with power," asserts COYOTE. But instead of recognizing the power that pimps and johns wield over women used in prostitution, COYOTE sees an antithetical arrangement: "For the woman/prostitute, this power consists of her ability to set the terms of her sexuality, and to demand substantial payment for her time and skills" (Priscilla Alexander, 1987: p. 189). Grossly distorting feminism, Carmen and Moody contend: "In a society where women are at the threshold of equality with men, beginning not only to enjoy sex but also to decide when and with whom to have it, the prostitute becomes the embodiment of that freedom which until now has only been a fantasy" (Arlene Carmen and Howard Moody, 1985: p. 80). They expose their support of the male sexual imperative as the measure of women's sexual freedom, however, when they describe the prostitute's primary function as ". . . indulging for pay the sexual fantasies of our brothers, fathers, and sons . . ." Caught with their pants down, so to speak, they rush back to the rhetoric of sexual liberalism and in doing so confuse sexual exploitation with sexual choice by championing "a woman's right to exercise her sexual autonomy [including] mercantile promiscuity" (Arlene Carmen and Howard Moody, 1985: p. 191).

COYOTE's Priscilla Alexander picks up this thread and informs us, "Whatever you or I think of prostitution, women have the right to make up their own minds about whether or not to work as prostitutes [including] the right to work with an employer, a third party, who can take care of the administration and management problems" (Priscilla Alexander, 1987: p. 211). Indeed, exploitation by pimps is redefined by Alexander as "an employer-employee relationship in which several prostitutes turn over some or all of their earnings to a third party (Priscilla Alexander, 1983: p. 13). "Pimping and pandering," COYOTE explains, "are inflammatory words used to refer to third-party management of prostitution [and as such] should be recognized as legitimate businesses and regulated only by business and labor law, not criminal law" (COYOTE/NTFP, 1984–86: p. 3).

In an attempt to turn straw into gold, the sexual liberals spin an argument in support of prostitution based on false assumptions and outright lies. They claim that prostitution is a manifestation of both women's sexual freedom and gender equality. They claim that women freely choose prostitution as a career alternative. They claim that women control both sexual and financial interactions between themselves and their customers. They claim pimps are small-business managers who can and should be made accountable to their employees through labor negotiations.

There are approximately one million adult prostitutes in the United States (Charles Winich and Paul Kinsie, 1971: p. 14). Many are women of color (Pasqua Scibelli, 1987: p. 120). Many have dependent children. The average age of entry into prostitution is fourteen (D. Kelly Weisberg, 1985: p. 94). Others were "traditional wives" who escaped from or were abandoned by abusive husbands and forced into prostitution in order to support themselves and their children. Additionally, there are approximately one million children used in the sex industry in this country (D. Boyer, 1984). Although estimates vary due to the covert nature of child prostitution, we know that without effective intervention most of these children will grow up to be adult prostitutes.

Women in prostitution have few resources. Most have not completed high school.[4] Few have had any job experience outside of the sex industry.[5] Most have been victims of childhood sexual abuse, incest, rape, and/or battery prior to their entry into prostitution. WHISPER has pointed out that the function of the institution of prostitution is to allow males unconditional sexual access to women and children limited solely by their ability to pay for this privilege. A preliminary analysis of data collected by the WHISPER Oral History Project has isolated culturally supported tactics of power and control which facilitate the recruitment or coercion of women and children into prostitution and effectively impede their escape. These tactics include child sexual abuse, rape, battery, educational deprivation, job discrimination, poverty, racism, classism, sexism, heterosexism, and unequal enforcement of the law. These same tactics are used by individual men to keep women trapped in abusive relationships outside of prostitution.[6]

---

[4] Mary Magdalene Project, Reseda, California (1985); Operation De Novo, Minneapolis; WHISPER Oral History Project (1988).

[5] Council for Prostitution Alternatives, Portland, Oregon; Genesis House, Chicago; WHISPER, Minneapolis; PRIDE, Minneapolis.

[6] The WHISPER Oral History Project is an ongoing research project designed to document common experiences of women used in prostitution. Respondents participated in a single 2–3 hour oral interview which was subsequently transcribed for data analysis. Preliminary findings are based on 19 interviews with women ranging from ages 19–37.

Ninety percent of the women who participated in the WHISPER Oral History Project reported having been subjected to an inordinate amount of physical and sexual abuse during childhood: ninety percent had been battered in their families; seventy-four percent had been sexually abused between the ages of 3 and 14.[7] Of this group, fifty-seven percent had been repeatedly abused over a period of one to five years; forty-three percent had been victimized by two or three perpetrators; ninety-three percent had been abused by a family member.[8] Additionally, fifty percent of this group had also been molested by a non-family member (see, for example, Mimi Silbert, 1982).

Once in prostitution, these women and girls were further victimized by both pimps and customers. Seventy-nine percent of the women interviewed had been beaten by their pimps. Seventy-four percent reported assaults by customers; of these, seventy-nine percent reported beatings by a customer, and fifty percent reported rapes. Seventy-one percent of these women were victims of multiple customer assaults. (These findings are consistent with Mimi Silbert, 1982; Diana Gray, 1973.) The conditions these women were subjected to in prostitution replicated the abuse they had sustained at the hands of their fathers and husbands.

Carmen and Moody attempt to exonerate pimps by presenting a pseudo-psychological profile of these men. What's really important, they write, "is the self-image of the man, the way he perceives himself in the relationship with the prostitute. . . . He doesn't see himself as an enslaver of women; he rather thinks of himself as a business entrepreneur. . . . He is running a small business." And as we read on, we learn that, in his business, "he usually chooses to pay the women in goods and services rather than cash" (Arlene Carmen and Howard Moody, 1985: pp. 107–108). This is the equivalent of attempting to construct an analysis of sexual assault by asking a convicted sex offender the way in which he perceives himself in relation to his victim: he doesn't see himself as a rapist; he rather thinks of himself as a lover.

In explaining how the pimp is viewed by society, Carmen and Moody write, "The pimp as a category of human being suffers from the same fate as other members of deviant or minority subcultures" (Arlene Carmen and Howard Moody, 1985: p. 100). They claim that ninety-nine percent of pimps are Black and then bolster this misconception by presenting a racist/misogynist interpretation of history. "In times of slavery," they state, "white masters raped Black women with impunity." However, they add, "some Black women cooperated with the white

---

[7] Of these, 36 percent were rape victims.
[8] 50 percent were abused by a natural, step-, or foster father.

masters to gain a more secure place." Dismissing the gender-specific horrors to which enslaved women were subjected, including forced breeding, and the labeling of some as collaborators with their oppressors, Carmen and Moody quickly move on to what they perceive to be the real degradation of slavery: "White masters socially castrated Black men by not allowing them to be heads of their own households, and denied them access to white women." To Carmen and Moody, the contemporary pimping of women by Black men rights this historical wrong. "The Black pimp has reversed history," they explain. "He dominates over black and white women [and has] also humiliated the white man by making him pay for what his women lavishly give the Black man" (Arlene Carmen and Howard Moody, 1985: pp. 106–107).

This racist paradigm defining pimps as Black men fueled by historical sexual revenge, ostensibly because they've been deprived of unconditional sexual access to both Black and white women, diverts attention from the organized traffic in women owned and controlled by white businessmen in America — brothel owners in Nevada;[9] owners of massage parlors and escort services throughout the United States; owners and managers of bars, nightclubs and "dance studios" where prostitution is promoted;[10] owners of "mail-order bride" businesses;[11] organized crime rings that operate in collusion with American GI's to fraudulently induce Asian women into this country and imprison them in massage parlors (Crime syndicate, 1985: p. A1, A2); pornographers and owners of "peep shows" and "live sex shows";[12] and the leftist self-

---

[9] For example, Joe Comforte, owner of the Mustang Ranch, Nevada; Russ Reade and Kenneth Green, owners of the Chicken Ranch, Nevada; and Jim Fondren, owner of the Sagebrush Ranch, Nevada.

[10] For example, Earl Montpetit, owner of the OZ nightclub in St. Paul, Minnesota, convicted of promoting prostitution and awaiting trial on charges of engaging in prostitution with a minor in 1988; Walter Montpetit, former owner of the Belmont Club in St. Paul, Minnesota, convicted of promoting prostitution in 1988 (*Minneapolis Star and Tribune*, April 1988); David Fan, current owner of the Belmont Club, lost liquor license this year for employing a 13-year-old girl as a nude dancer and evidence of prostitution-related activities (*Minneapolis Star and Tribune*, September 1989); Patrick Carlone, proprietor of Hollywood Stars Dance Studios in St. Paul, Minnesota, convicted of two counts of promoting prostitution of his employees in 1988 (*Minneapolis Star and Tribune*, January 1988).

[11] There are over 150 "mail-order bride" companies operating in the United States. *The News and Observer*. (Raleigh, 21, November 1986: p. 20A).

[12] Martin Hodas, owner of "Paradise Alley" in New York City; Clemente D'Alessio and Scott Hyman, convicted child pornographers and former managers of adult bookstores subsidiaries of "Show World" in New York City (Ritter, 1987: pp. 166–69); Feris Alexander, owner of a number of "adult bookstores and peep shows" in Minneapolis, Minnesota.

proclaimed revolutionaries who "turned out" their women comrades during the 1960s and 1970s. By feigning concern for the subordinate socioeconomic status of Black men in America, sexual liberals point a finger at the individual visible pimp and absolve themselves of culpability. Yet their portrait of the typical American pimp is false. Conveniently omitted from their picture are the husbands who pimp their wives and the fathers who pimp their daughters. One survivor of prostitution described how her stepfather forced her into prostitution at age eleven:

> He would sell me to his bar buddies . . . we would drive to a bar and then he'd go into the bar while I was left in the car and he would bring his bar buddies out to the car. (WHISPER, 1987)

Such scenarios of pimping, commonly intra-racial, are ignored in both the popular and academic literature. Thus the family, under the control of the father, is held blameless for the sexual enslavement of women and girls publicly and privately. This is not coincidental, for it is the family that serves as a training ground for prostitution. It is in the interest of the sexual liberals, most of whom are husbands and/or fathers, to keep that institution intact. They protect it through the enforcement of privacy laws, which prevent any interference with men's absolute authority in the home just as these laws protect their right to traffic in women through pornography in public.

Attempting to absolve men of any responsibility for trafficking in women, Carmen and Moody argue that it is "[myth] that the pimp is the primary reason for a women being in the life" (Arlene Carmen and Howard Moody, 1985: p. 101). Claiming to speak for prostitutes, they assert: ". . . the woman more often than not chooses the man she wants to be with and give her money to . . . women leave one pimp for another. Or a woman with no man decides to work for the pimp she wants" (1985: p. 104). Alexander goes as far as claiming that, "young girls (runaways) deliberately go to the big cities to find pimps to turn them out" (1985: p. 10).

Both of these victim-blaming theories ignore the seasoning techniques employed by pimps to recruit women and girls into prostitution, for example, targeting emotionally and/or economically vulnerable women, fostering trust and dependency by feigning love and friendship, and using overt acts of physical and sexual abuse (Kathleen Barry, 1981: pp. 121–122). They do not consider the fact that prostitutes who do not have pimps are considered "outlaws." Because an "outlaw" is not the property of one pimp, she is fair game for all pimps. Also ignored is the fact that pimps trade women among themselves and "steal" them from each other. In a preliminary investigation, the WHISPER Oral History Project found that all the women interviewed thus far had been harassed, assaulted, raped, kidnaped, and/or forced to turn tricks by a pimp or a gang of pimps. That some of the women had pimps at the time of the assault did not dissuade other pimps from preying on them.

In spite of this reality, Carmen and Moody portray pimps as benign. "The pimp," they write, "enacts a multifaceted role in relating to his . . . women: . . . [as] a father correcting his wayward daughter . . . [as] brother . . . [as] lover. Perhaps the most important role is assumed when . . . he plays the role of husband." They claim, "He is desirable because she believes that he will be a good provider who will give her the things she needs . . . and the things she desires . . . and that he will give her the ultimate gift—he will let her bear his child." Blaming the woman, they state "[I]n the subculture of prostitution the man is still king of the hill while the woman is a submissive servant, albeit for the most part a willing one" (Arlene Carmen and Harold Moody, 1985: p. 126).

What Carmen and Moody have just described is the traditional patriarchal family, and by doing so, they have unwittingly exposed the truth about prostitution. Prostitution is taught in the home, socially validated by a sexual libertarian ideology, and enforced by both church and state. That is to say the male hierarchies of both the conservative right and the liberal left collude to teach and keep women in prostitution: the right by demanding that women be socially and sexually subordinate to one man in marriage, and the left by demanding that women be socially and sexually subordinate to all men in prostitution and pornography. Their common goal is to maintain their power to own and control women in both the private and public spheres.

Prostitution isn't like anything else. Rather, everything else is like prostitution because it is the model for women's condition. The line between wife and prostitute—madonna and whore—has become increasingly blurred, beginning in the 1960s when women's attempts to free themselves of the double standard was frustrated by the liberal left's adoption and promotion of the "Playboy Philosophy." This resulted in the replacement of the double standard by a single male standard in which sexual liberation became synonymous with male sexual objectification of and unconditional sexual access to women. With the invasion of the home by pornographic cable programs and video cassettes, the "good wife" has become equated with the "good whore," as more and more women are pressured into emulating the scenarios of pornography. In this context, the wife is pressured, seduced, and/

or forced into the role of the prostitute while her husband adopts the role of the "john." Contests promoted by pornographers, like *Hustler's* "Beaver Hunt"[13] and pornographic computer bulletin boards like *High Society's* "Sex-Tex,"[14] have resulted in a proliferation of homemade pornography. In this situation the wife is compelled to assume the role of "porn queen" when her husband adopts the role of the pornographer. The growth of "swingers' magazines" and "wife-swapping clubs" have allowed men to assume simultaneously the role of john and pimp, paying for the use of another man's partner by making his wife available in exchange. The last barrier separating the roles of wife and prostitute is smashed when men engineer sexual encounters with prostitutes which include their wives. One prostitution survivor describes the dynamics of such an experience:

> A lot of men enjoyed bringing me in as a third party with their wives. Usually what would end up happening is we'd watch some pornographic film, say, and then he'd say, "All right, I want you to do that to my wife." Now, in these instances, I felt the wife was the victim, and that I was there to hurt the wife. I felt there was a real power play there, where the man was obviously saying to the wife, "If you don't do this, I'm going to leave you." I mean there were great overtones of manipulation and coercion. (WHISPER, 1988)

In each of these ways the prostitute symbolizes the value of women in society. She is paradigmatic of women's social, sexual, and economic subordination in that her status is the basic unit by which all women's value is measured and to which all women can be reduced. The treatment that a man pays to inflict on the most despised women—prostitutes—sets the standard by which he may treat the women under his control—his wife and his daughters.

The role of prostitute is imposed on women in the home when the courts uphold the marital rape exemption in penal codes. These laws codify the traditional moral imperatives of the church which demand that women be unconditionally sexually available to their husbands. Through this legally sanctioned victimization, the state supports a man's right to use a woman's body for his own sexual gratification, regardless of the emotional and physical impact on her, based on a social contract (marriage) which assumes blanket consent on the part of the wife. This

---

[13] *Hustler* offers payment to readers who submit the best "beaver shots" (pornographic photographs) of wives or girlfriends.

[14] "Sex-Tex" is a computer service of *High Society* Magazine which provides an unregulated market through which pornographic material can be distributed.

same logic has been used against prostitutes who have attempted to bring charges against customers who have sexually assaulted them. A California court recently ruled in favor of a john charged with raping a prostitute, on the grounds that the courts were "not in the business of adjudicating breaches of illegal contracts" (*LA Times*, 1986: pp. 1, 7).

The role of prostitute is taught to girls in the home through paternal sexual abuse. The fact that an estimated seventy-five percent of women in the sex industry were sexually abused as children suggests that the ramifications of incest and sexual assault in childhood contribute to the recruitment of women and children into prostitution.[15] One survivor asserts,

> I believe that I became a prostitute because of the physical abuse that I experienced in my childhood. It made me very intimidated and afraid of men, and I was very easily pushed around by men. I also believe that another factor that played a large part in my getting involved in prostitution was the sexual abuse that I encountered at a very young age, 12 . . . and it was like three encounters that happened—boom, boom boom— to let me know it was not just an isolated incident. (WHISPER, 1988)

The role of prostitute is taught to women individually and as a class through the social sanctioning of commercial sexual exploitation of women by pornographers, which maintains our second-class status yet is touted by sexual liberals as women's sexual liberation. Preliminary data collected by the WHISPER Oral History Project refute the sexual liberals' argument that pornography is harmless fantasy or sexually liberating entertainment, suggesting instead that pornography is an important factor in the seasoning of women and girls into prostitution. Fifty-two percent of the women interviewed revealed that pornography played a significant role in teaching them what was expected of them as prostitutes. Thirty percent reported that their pimps regularly exposed them to pornographic material in order to indoctrinate them into an acceptance of the practices depicted. One survivor explained:

> He used pornography to give me role models to follow, you know, women to try and portray. He'd say, "This is what I want you to look like." (WHISPER, 1987)

This situation is compounded by the use of pornography by johns. Eighty percent of survivors reported that their customers showed them pornography to illustrate the kinds of sexual activities in which they

---

[15]The Mary Magdalene Project in Reseda, California, reports 80 percent of the women they've worked with were sexually abused as children; Genesis House in Chicago reports 94 percent were abused as children (in The First National Workshop For Those Working With Female Prostitutes, Wayzata, Minnesota, October 16–18, 1985).

wanted to engage, including sadomasochism, bondage, anal intercourse, urination and defecation, and the shaving of pubic hair to give
an illusion of prepubescence. This information is consistent with testimony given by survivors of prostitution at public hearings and before
fact-finding commissions:

> Porn was our text book. We learned the tricks of the trade by men ex-
> posing us to porn and us trying to mimic what we saw. I could not stress
> enough what a huge influence we feel this was.[16]

Fifty-three percent of the interviewees reported that their customers
took pornographic photographs of them in addition to engaging in sexual activities.[17] Further investigation is required to assess whether the
use of pornographic material is a common factor in the seasoning of
women into prostitution; whether johns routinely demand that prostitutes engage in sexual practices promoted in pornography; whether
pornography has a modeling effect on prostitutes compelled by customers to act out scenarios depicted in pornographic material; and
whether pornography shapes the sense of self of women compelled to
pose for pornographic photographs and films as a function of prostitution. It is evident, however, that pornography does not have a liberating effect on prostitutes' lives, nor does it enhance their sexual autonomy, as sexual liberals contend.

We, the women of WHISPER, escaped the brutality of the patriarchal family only to find ourselves at the mercy of pimps, panderers,
and procurers, who have built a multibillion dollar industry selling what
our fathers and husbands stole from us originally. We are here to expose the lie that prostitution is the answer to women's social, sexual,
and economic subordination.

Prostitution is *not* a "career choice":

> I look at my life and when I came into this world, you know as a child,
> I expected to be fed, clothed, sheltered and to be treated with respect
> and kindness as any human being would so desire . . . . I don't think I

---

[16]Public Hearings before the Minneapolis City Council; Session II, December 1983, p. 70.
[17]None of the women used in pornography received additional compensation, signed a
contract affirming consent and none maintained possession or control of the material.
Furthermore one woman disclosed that a customer threatened her with a knife when
she refused to pose for pornographic pictures. He subsequently tied her with ropes,
photographed her in bondage, withheld payment, and left her tied up in a motel. Mimi
Silbert also recognized the role played by pornography in legitimizing victimization in
her study on the sexual assault of prostitutes (1982, p. 21).

came into this world with the desire to be a prostitute. I think that that was something that was put on me by the dynamics of society. Something that was taught me. (WHISPER, 1988)

Prostitution is *not* a "victimless crime":

Prostitution is violence against women . . . it's the worst form of violence against women because you get abused by the johns, you get abused by the pimps, you get abused by the police. Society in general turns their back on you. (WHISPER, 1988)

Prostitution is a crime committed against women by men in its most traditional form. It is nothing less than the commercialization of the sexual abuse and inequality that women suffer in the traditional family and can be nothing more.

The laws are made by men and men desire to keep women in prostitution because they desire to control them, so the thing that would change prostitution is not legalizing it, but by putting an end to it and stopping it, and I don't believe that men want to do that. I think women are going to have to do that. (WHISPER, 1988)

Dismantling the institution of prostitution is the most formidable task facing contemporary feminism.

REFERENCES

Alexander, Priscilla. (1983, July). Working on prostitution, California: NOW, Inc., Economic Justice Committee.

Alexander, Priscilla. (1987). Prostitution: A difficult issue for feminism. In Delacoste and Alexander (Eds). *Sex work*. Cleis Press.

Barry, Kathleen, (1981). The underground economic system of pimping. *Journal of International Affairs*.

Boyer, D. (1984, January). A cultural construction of a negative sex role: The female prostitutes.

Carmen, Arlene and Moody, Howard. (1985). *Working women: The subterranean world of street prostitution*. New York: Harper and Row.

COYOTE/NTFP (National Task Force on Prostitution) Policy Statement. 1984–1986.

Erbe, Nancy. (1984). Prostitution: Victims of men's exploitation and abuse. *Law and Inequality*, 2:609.

Genesis. (1986). Unpublished Report.

Crime syndicate's web snares Oriental women. (1985, March 8). *Kansas City Times*, pp. A1, A2.

Gray, Diana. (1973). Turning-out: A study of teenage prostitutes. *Urban Life and Culture*.

Hunter, Susan. (1986, June 30). Report to the Council for Prostitution Alternatives. Portland, Oregon.

"I'm blunt," says judge to outraged feminists. (1986, May 11). *Los Angeles Times*, Part IX, pp. 1, 7.

St. Paul Star Tribune. (1989, September 7). St. Paul, Minnesota.

Star Tribune. (1988, January 22). Minneapolis, Minnesota. p. 1B.

Star Tribune. (1988, April 19). Minneapolis, Minnesota. p. 1A.

Silbert, Mimi. (1982, November). *Sexual assault of prostitutes*. Phase I, Final Report. San Francisco: National Center for the Prevention and Control of Rape, National Institute for Mental Health.

WHISPER. (1987). WHISPER Oral History Project. Transcript of interview. Portland, Oregon.

WHISPER. (1988). *Prostitution: A matter of violence against women*. Video. Minneapolis: WHISPER.

Part III

THE NEW
REPRODUCTIVE
LIBERALISM

The New Reproductive Technologies

Gena Corea

The new reproductive technologies represent an escalation of violence against women, a violence camouflaged behind medical terms.

Violence against women has been a part of obstetrics and gynecology ever since it was formed as a specialty in the United States. To give a hint of that violence, let me tell you about the "father of gynecology," J. Marion Sims.

In 1845, Sims hit upon a method of opening the vagina to view, thereby making it possible to repair a heretofore incurable female condition, vaginal-vesico fistula. This condition, acquired during childbirth, was a tear in the vaginal wall resulting in constant seepage of urine from the bladder through the vagina. The condition was sometimes caused by unusually hard labor but was often associated with aggressive use of instruments like forceps in delivery.

After Sims got his idea for the operation, he wrote in his autobiography, he "ransacked the country" for cases of vaginal-vesico fistula among black slave women. He made a deal with the owners of these women that allowed him to experiment on them. The owners were to clothe the women and pay taxes on them but Sims was to feed and house them. He kept the women in a building behind his home—a building he called a "hospital."

He acquired several women in this way and kept them in his "hospital" for four years, during which time he performed up to thirty operations on each, entirely without anesthesia. Anesthesia, though just beginning to be used by Dr. James Simpson in Scotland, was unknown to U.S. doctors (Seale Harris, 1950).

The operations he performed on his experimental subjects, Sims wrote, were "so tedious, and at the same time so painful, that none but a woman could have borne them."

After several years filled with unsuccessful attempts to devise an operation to repair the vaginal tears, Sims found himself in an embarrassing situation. His biographer Dr. Seale Harris explains: "Socially, the whole business was becoming a marked liability, for all kinds of whispers were beginning to circulate around town—dark rumors that it was a terrible thing for Sims to be allowed to keep on using human beings as experimental animals for his unproven surgical theories."

Dr. Harris argues that the slave women were willing experimental subjects, that they clamored for the operations, that the suffering caused them by their condition was so great they would go through any torture if it held promise of a cure.

"They love it. They beg for it. When we cut them and torture them, we're giving them what they want." This rationale sounds sickeningly familiar to feminists who fight pornography and rape.

After Sims did succeed in perfecting his operation, he was ready to perform it on paying, white, middle-class women. But at that time, anesthesia was still not available. The white women, who had to endure the already perfected operation only one time—not thirty—often cried out to Sims to stop in the middle of the operation. Even though they were women, they could not endure the pain. Yet they too suffered from the ailment just as the black slave women had. Why weren't they, like the slave women, prepared to go through any torture in order to be relieved of their condition?

The discrepancy in responses of the white and black women to the operation can be explained by this hypothesis: Someone was lying. Those black women, forcibly separated from the babies they had just delivered and imprisoned in a "hospital" for four years, never entreated the man who imprisoned them to experiment on their bodies, never begged to be tortured.

There is a bust of Sims on Fifth Avenue and 103rd Street in Manhattan near the New York Academy of Medicine. In 1978, the Medical University of South Carolina established a chair in honor of Sims. Dr. Sims, who practiced surgical violence against women—and here, I've described only his opening gambit—remains a respected figure in U.S. medicine.

Since the days of Father Sims we have had operations to remove ovaries in order to cure "ovariomania," a disease—essentially female sexuality—we don't hear too much about these days (Gena Corea, 1986a). We have unnecessary hysterectomies, a continuing scandal. We have prophylactic mastectomies that entail cutting off healthy breasts on the grounds that some day they might become unhealthy. (There are no prophylactic removals of testicles.) We have unnecessary cesarean sections—again, a scandal. We have experimentation on us with brutal contraceptives like Depo-Provera and drugs like diethylstilbestrol (DES). A few of the many books that provide documentation are Diana Scully, 1980; Janice Raymond, 1979; Michelle Harrison, 1982; Boston Women's Health Book Collective, 1984; Gena Corea, 1977; 1980; Barbara Seaman and Gideon Seaman, 1977.

This kind of violence against women is escalating with the new reproductive technologies (Gena Corea, 1986b). Under these technologies, I include in vitro fertilization (IVF), the test-tube baby procedure. That entails pumping a woman full of hormones so she will release more than the usual number of eggs from the ovary; placing her under general anesthesia, usually, and sucking her eggs out; fertilizing the eggs in a dish and, when she's kneeling on a gynecological table, her head down by her hands and her rear end pointed upward, inserting the embryo through her vagina and into her uterus. It sounds simple. In fact, it is a complicated procedure that rarely works.

Embryo flushing is another of the new reproductive technologies. You artificially inseminate the woman, flush the embryo out of her, and then insert the embryo into another woman. That's done in cows. A couple of brothers who worked on cows for seven years figured it was time to move on to women. So they started a company to do that (Gena Corea, 1987). Their procedure is highly experimental. Only two births have resulted from it.

Sex predetermination—that is, predetermining the sex of a child—is also one of the new reproductive technologies.

Surrogate motherhood could be used with the embryo flushing technique or with in vitro fertilization or with sex predetermination. Many combinations of the different technologies are possible.

Before discussing the violence of the new reproductive technologies, let me point out briefly that these technologies were not developed out of compassion for infertile women nor are they just for the infertile. They will eventually affect the vast majority of women.

A pattern has emerged in the spread of a new reproductive technology. When it is introduced, it is presented as something for a small proportion of women in certain groups. But then, quickly, physicians expand the indications for the technology so that it is used on a large proportion—or even the majority—of women. For example, in obstetrics, electronic fetal monitoring was introduced for use on women judged to be at high risk of obstetrical complications. But now in many industrialized countries, it is used on most birthing women. The same pattern is evident with ultrasound, amniocentesis, cesarean section, and genetic testing and counseling.

It is likely that this pattern will emerge with newer technologies such as IVF, egg donation, sex predetermination, and embryo evaluation.

IVF, for example, was originally proposed for use on a small group of women—those whose infertility was caused by blocked or absent fallopian tubes. But physicians quickly extended the indications for IVF so that now even fertile women are among IVF candidates. These are women married to men with low sperm counts. Instead of physicians saying, "Maybe there's a terrific hormone we could inject into men to see if we could raise the sperm count," they operate on women's bodies.

Very early on, technodocs began saying that once they found a way to use donor eggs with in vitro fertilization, many more women—for example, women with bad eggs—would become candidates for this procedure. I asked one reproductive technologist, "How do women get 'bad eggs'?" He said that women who work in places where there are toxic chemicals may have their eggs damaged by those chemicals. These women could simply use another person's egg, he said, and they won't mind because the process of birth is much more important to women than the genetic content of the child. (I guess he'd say that the average woman is very unlike Bill Stern, the man who hired Mary Beth Whitehead as a so-called surrogate and for whom the genetic content of the child—*his* genetic content—was so overwhelmingly important it justified impairing the lives of scores of people around him, most notably Mary Beth Whitehead's.) The technodoc said this was a large group of women and would grow larger as we learn more and more about the effects of toxic chemicals on eggs.

In Melbourne, Australia, a couple of years ago, we learned from Carl Wood, a physician heading an IVF program, that some women in his program were asking him to use donor eggs rather than their own in the in vitro fertilization attempt. The allegedly said they didn't want to reproduce themselves because they were dissatisifed with some of their own qualities, like their appearance and intelligence. They wanted to use donor eggs, the eggs of women who, unlike themselves, were adequate human beings (Karen Milliner, 1984; John Schauble, 1984; and Fiona Whitlock, 1984.)

Now, I don't know how women suddenly, without prompting, come to the conclusion that they don't want to use their own eggs. I suspect that Wood's announcement was a trial balloon floated to see if there would be much objection to this selective breeding practice. He was just announcing a fact and was quite helpless before it. He was being subjected to these consumer demands and really, what could the poor man do?

His plight opens up the vision of a whole new clientele for IVF with donor eggs: women who feel inadequate. It is a large clientele.

There's another way in which I think the use of the new reproductive technologies will expand. I talked with one of the developers of the embryo flushing procedure, one of the men who worked with cows for seven years. He said that embryo flushing may become a routine part of prenatal care. In other words, every single pregnant woman would go to the doctor and have the embryo flushed out of her. It would be checked to see if it comes up to snuff. If it does, it would be transferred back to her at some little risk (this, he didn't mention) of a potential ectopic pregnancy. If the embryo did not pass the tests, the woman would try for another, more acceptable, pregnancy. So that's another way in which use of the technologies could expand widely.

In the literature on reproductive technology, the suggestion appears again and again that female sterilization could be combined with the various technologies. This practice would always be carried out in order to benefit women. Women would just be sterilized and then they wouldn't have to worry about all these dangerous hormonal contraceptives. (This is one of those rare times there is an admission that these contraceptives are dangerous.) The women would have their eggs frozen. Then, when they want to have a child, they simply get out a frozen egg or, if they're married, frozen embryo, and have in vitro fertilization. This is tremendously convenient. Various technodocs have indeed pointed out that embryo freezing would offer a terrific new form of family planning.

In 1976, which was two years before the birth of Louise Brown, the first test-tube baby, two physicians wrote in the *Western Journal of Medicine* that in the future, in vitro fertilization may become the standard way to reproduce (Laurence Karp and Roger Donahue, 1976). The rationale for this was that it may be possible to develop embryo evaluation methods and people would want to have their embryos evaluated before implantation so they could be sure the child is free of defects.

Those are the reasons I think these technologies will not be confined to the infertile.

The use of these technologies on women's bodies is an experiment, not a treatment. You may think the technologies are treatments because language is routinely used here to obscure what is really going on. For example, in its section on surrogate motherhood, the American Fertility Society's ethics report uses medical terms to describe the sale of women (Ethics Committee, 1986). A man's desire to have a genetically related child becomes a "medical indication" for buying a woman's body. Such terms sanitize the sale of women and remove the reader emotionally from what is actually going on.

In vitro fertilization and other new procedures are called "treatments" and "therapy." In fact, the success rate for these technologies is extremely low. We don't have accurate figures on success now be-

cause over the years that technodocs have been developing the technologies, they have displayed no interest (for very good reason) in
gathering the information necessary to determine the actual success.

Medical writer, Susan Ince and I did a survey of all the in vitro
fertilization clinics in the United States for the *Medical Tribune* in the
spring of 1985 and for the first time exposed routine deception in the
reporting of IVF success (Gena Corea and Susan Ince, 1985; 1987). Briefly,
we found that half the clinics in the country had never produced even
one test-tube baby. Despite that, they were claiming high success rates,
some as high as 25 percent. They could do that because they were in
total control of the definition of success. No uniform definition exists.
Any clinic can define success in any way it wants. Clinics don't define
it in terms of live births, which is the way many women entering the
clinic would think. "Twenty percent success rate? That means I have a
20 percent chance of coming away with a baby." It doesn't mean that
at all.

One of the definitions of success was "percentage of pregnancies
per laparoscopy," the operation performed in order to suck eggs out
of the ovary. But the fact that there's a pregnancy doesn't mean that
there will be a birth. When it is a chemical pregnancy, as many are,
that simply means that there is a slight elevation in the level of hormones present during pregnancy. There will be no baby. Some technodocs count that as "success" knowing that there will be no baby.

There are many, many tricks with the statistics to make it look as
though a clinic is successful. IVF clinic directors explained the tricks to
us when we interviewed them. They were telling on each other. That's
how we learned what they were doing.

I want to describe briefly some of what the women go through because women's experience of in vitro fertilization has been rendered
invisible. It lies in the shadows, quiet and dark.

Women who go through IVF have already been through an incredible amount of medical probing and prodding, much of which is painful
and humiliating. Many have had biopsies of the endometrium, the
uterine lining; tubal insufflation—the filling up of the oviducts with
pressurized carbon dioxide to see if the tubes are open; injection of dye
into the uterus and oviducts; drug treatments; and blowing out of the
tubes to maintain an opening.

But once in an in vitro fertilization program, the manipulations of a
woman's body and emotions begin in earnest. Drugs are administered;
blood samples are taken, and the hormones within measured; ultrasound exams are done to estimate when the women will ovulate; ster-
ile normal saline is put into a woman's bladder through a catheter for
the ultrasound right before the laparoscopy; the laparoscopy for egg

capture (they actually call it that) is performed, often repeatedly. In an Australian in vitro program, when the woman is sick, drowsy, and sore from the operation she's just had, she is sometimes asked to arouse her husband sexually so that he can masturbate for the sperm sample. (For information on women's experiences in IVF programs, see Renate Klein, 1989; Christine Crowe, 1987; Barbara Burton, 1985.)

Remember that the vast majority of women who go through all this do not come away with a baby. In a study of women's experience of in vitro fertilization in Australia, one woman told a researcher: "It [the in vitro procedure] is embarrassing. You leave your pride at the hospital door when you walk in and you pick it up when you leave. You feel like a piece of meat in a meatworks but if you want a baby badly enough, you'll do it" (Barbara Burton, 1985).

Isabel Bainbridge had seven failed in vitro attempts in Australia before giving up. She now says of in vitro fertilization: "It's a very brutal way of coming to terms with your infertility. I think there could have been kinder ways."

Let me tell you about an unkind incident.

Several years ago technodoc Milton Nakamura arranged for scientists from Monash University in Melbourne, Australia, to give a practical course on in vitro fertilization in his country, Brazil. The Globo television network paid for the travel and other expenses of the visiting Australian doctors, in return for which it received the first—but not the exclusive—shot at the news coverage.

The fourth and tenth floors of the maternity hospital where the course was given and where the operating rooms were located were partly taken over by security guards who were principally employed by the television network. The presence of the press with photographers and television cameras led the president of the Brazilian Society for the Advancement of Science to criticize the project and describe it as "an obstetrics carnival."

Twelve infertile women were used in this course on in vitro fertilization. Following the laparoscopy, one of the women, Zenaide Maria Bernardo, died. Dr. Nakamura's only consolation, the press reported, was that Zenaide may have lost consciousness under the sweet illusion that she was going to have a baby. He wanted to name his test-tube baby center after Zenaide "in honor of the woman who symbolized the iron determination to be a mother."

The Brazilian publication *Veja* reported that Dr. Nakamura considered the accident a "lamentable and rare misfortune," and "water under the bridge." From a scientific point of view, the publication *Manchete* reported, the IVF program had been a success (Ana Regina Gomez Dos Reis, 1987).

When it is asserted in Germany that in vitro fertilization and similar technologies are all about helping infertile women, German feminists impatiently brush that claim aside. They are irritated at any suggestion that they ought to take such a claim seriously. It is, they say, a "Deckmantel," which means "cloak," "disguise." In conversations with them, one hears occasional references to the political naivete of Americans who accept such a "Deckmantel" at face value.

German feminists have known all along that the stakes in this issue are high. They are particularly sensitive to the ways in which these technologies can and are beginning to be used to manufacture human beings to specifications and, in the process, to reduce women to breeders or, less elegantly, to raw material for a new manufacturing process.

Unlike U.S. feminists, they organized as a movement on the issue and began spreading their critique beyond the feminist movement.

That the stakes are indeed high became dramatically evident in December 1987.

The German equivalent of the FBI (the "Bundeskriminalamt") staged thirty-three simultaneous raids, many of them against feminists, throughout the Federal Republic of Germany, December 18 at 4:30 p.m. A total of 430 heavily armed police burst into the workplaces of activists. Fifteen to thirty in a group, the police swept into homes in Cologne, Dortmund, and Düsseldorf. In Essen, Duisburg, Bochum, and Hamburg, the raids were directed overwhelmingly against feminist critics of genetic and reproductive technology, according to Prozessgruppe Hamburg, a watchdog group.

The targeted critics have written and spoken on such issues as in vitro fertilization, amniocentesis, sex predetermination, and genetic engineering. They have actively opposed surrogate motherhood. Many worked together in a massive coalition to stop Noel Keane's attempt to open a branch of his U.S. surrogate business, United Family International, in Frankfurt. (Keane's New York firm arranged the Mary Beth Whitehead surrogate contract.) Their campaign to stop the sale of U.S. women to European men for breeding purposes ended successfully January 6, 1988 when a West German court ordered Keane's business closed, three months after it had opened.

Grounds for the police raids? In many cases, the women were not given any. But the next day, newspapers reported that the police conducted the searches to ascertain whether any of the individuals were members of a terrorist organization. They were specifically looking for a group called Revolutionaren Zellen and its feminist wing, Rota Zora.

The police were operating under Paragraph 129a of the terrorist act, "Support or Membership in a Terrorist Organization."

The women raided were forced to undress. All "non-changeable marks" on their bodies—scars, moles, etc.—were noted down in police records. The women were fingerprinted.

Two well-known and widely respected women were arrested: Ulla Penselin, active in two groups in Hamburg, Women Against Genetic Engineering and another group critiquing population control policies; and Ingrid Strobl, a journalist for eight years with the national feminist magazine, *Emma*. Strobl is accused of buying a clock used in a bombing attack against Lufthansa offices in Cologne to protest the exploitation of Third World women in the sex-tourism industry. Both women were charged under the terrorist act, Paragraph 129a. Strobl remains in prison while Penselin has since been released.

In the nationwide raids, police confiscated materials from an archive on genetic and reproductive technology established by women in Essen and from private homes and apartments. They seized drafts of the women's speeches, material prepared for seminars, names and addresses of those attending seminars, published work, videos, tapes of radio programs, scientific articles, postcards, brochures and private address books.

The police raids appear to be an attempt to stop the widespread antigenetic technology movement in Germany by linking legal organizations with more militant ones, Maria Mies, author of *Patriarchy and Accumulation on a World Scale* and professor of sociology at the Fachhochschule in Cologne, told me in a telephone interview from her home.

"No concrete accusation or crime was being investigated," she pointed out. "This means that women doing 'Aufklarungsarbeit,' that is, researching reproductive or genetic engineering or talking about it or giving seminars, are already doing enough to provide a pretext for the attorney general to launch such a police action."

Mies, an organizer of the world's first massive feminist conference against reproductive and genetic technology in Bonn in 1985, said of the police action: "We think it is an effort to criminalize and intimidate the whole protest movement of women against reproductive and genetic engineering and frighten others away from participating in order to prevent the movement from spreading even more widely."

Mies added: "We are planning another conference against reproductive and genetic engineering just to demonstrate that we are continuing our work."

REFERENCES

Boston Women's Health Book Collective. (1984). *The new our bodies, our selves*. New York: Simon and Schuster.

Burton, Barbara A. (1985, March). Contentious issues of infertility therapy: A consumer view paper presented at the Australia Family Planning Conference.

Corea, Gena. (1980, July). The cesarian epidemic. *Mother Jones.*

Corea, Gena. (1977). *The hidden malpractice: How American medicine mistreats women.* New York: Harper & Row.

Corea, Gena. (1986). *The mother machine: Reproductive technologies from artificial insemination to artificial wombs.* New York: Harper & Row.

Corea, Gena. (1987). Paper presented at the Forum International Sur les Nouvelles Technologies de la Reproduction Humaine organise par le Conseil du Statut de la Femme, Université Concordia, Montreal, Canada, October 29–31.

Corea, Gena, and Ince, Susan. (1985, July 3). IVF: A game for losers at half of U.S. clinics. *The Medical Tribune.*

Corea, Gena, and Ince, Susan. (1987). Report of a survey of IVF clinics in the USA. In Patricia Spallone and Deborah Lynn Steinberg (Eds). *Made to Order: The Myth of Reproductive and Genetic Progress.* The Athene Series. Oxford: Pergamon Press.

Crowe, Christine. (1987). 'Women want it': In vitro fertilization and women's motivations for participation. In Patricia Spallone and Deborah Lynn Steinberg (Eds). *Made to Order: The Myth of Reproductive and Genetic Progress.* The Athene Series. Oxford: Pergamon Press.

Dos Reis, Ana Regina Gomez. (1987). IVF in Brazil: The story told by the newspapers. In Patricia Spallone and Deborah Lynn Steinberg (Eds). *Made to Order. The Myth of Reproductive and Genetic Progress,* The Athene Series. Oxford: Pergamon Press.

Ethics Committee of the American Fertility Society. (1986, September). *Ethical Considerations of the New Reproductive Technologies.* Birmingham, Alabama: American Fertility Society. Available from the American Fertility Society, 2131 Magnolia Avenue, Suite 201, Birmingham, AL 35256.

Harris, Seale. (1950). *Woman's surgeon.* New York: Macmillan.

Harrison, Michelle. (1982). *A woman in residence.* New York: Random House.

Karp, Laurence E., and Donahue, Roger P. (1976). Preimplantation ectogenesis. *The Western Journal of Medicine* 124, no. 4.

Klein, Renate. (1987). When medicalisation equals experimentation and creates illness: The impact of the new reproductive technologies on women. Paper presented at the Forum International Sur les Nouvelles Technologies de la Reproduction Humaine organisé par le Conseil du Statut de la Femme, Université Concordia, Montreal, Canada, October 29–31.

Klein, Renate. (1989). *Infertility.* London: Pandora Press.

Milliner, Karen. (1984, May 17). In vitro babies better adjusted: Team leader. *Canberra Times.*

Raymond, Janice G. (1979). *The transsexual empire.* Boston: Beacon Press.

Schauble, John. (1984, May 17). "Babies: They're better from glass." *Sydney Morning Herald.*

Scully, Diana. (1980). *Men who control women's health.* Boston: Houghton-Mifflin.

Seaman, Barbara and Seaman, Gideon. (1977). *Women and the crisis in sex hormones.* New York: Rawson Associates.

Whitlock, Fiona. (1984, May 17). Test-tube babies are smarter and stronger. *The Australian.*

Mothers On Trial: Custody and the "Baby M" Case

Phyllis Chesler

When *Mothers on Trial: The Battle for Children and Custody* was published, the truth was out: I was not a nice, male-identified, gender-neutral liberal feminist. I was a nice woman-identified radical. I did not believe that men and women had to be the same in order to be treated equally. I mistrusted gender-neutral legislation especially in those areas where women are most obviously different from men: in the areas of reproductive biology, heterosexual relations, pregnancy, childbirth, lactation, mother-infant bonding and the bottom-line responsibility for primary child care. After all, freedom of choice involves the right to have an abortion and the right to have and keep a baby if women so choose.

For saying all this, some feminists accused me of romanticizing the biological chains that bind us; and of biological determinism. I presumably wanted all women to be married, pregnant, and poor. I was against gender-neutral feminism and against women's right to buy or kidnap another woman's child or to rent another woman as a "surrogate uterus"—in the name of feminism.

In *Mothers on Trial* and elsewhere I note that mothers are *women* and therefore have few maternal rights and many maternal obligations; and that feminists fighting for father's rights or for the primacy of sperm are, to me, a pretty shabby spectacle. Were feminists in favor of joint custody because it would empower mothers (who are women) or because it would empower fathers and men, many of whom have no intention of assuming any primary child care responsibility after they win joint custody? Unfortunately relatively few men are trying to assume *some* child care responsibility. Such men do not do as many things, or the same things that women do in terms of housework or children. Nor are such men perceived in the same way as women when they perform a "female" task. However, liberal feminists did not want to sacrifice joint custody as an *ideal;* many were more willing to sacrifice *real* mothers on the altar of abstract notions—real mothers who were suffering under the weight of child care responsibilities, poverty, custodial seige, and the threatened or actual loss of their children.

Once I started organizing around the Baby M Case, I called many feminist leaders. For example, Betty Friedan said she was "up in arms" about what the media and the courts were doing to Mary Beth Whitehead. She said: "I am outraged by this case! Where are the feminists? Where are the feminists?"

I replied, "Well, we're a small, raggedy-assed band out there every week outside the courthouse in Hackensack. Please come and join us. But you're quite right: National NOW, New Jersey NOW, the NOW Legal Defense and Education Fund has, as yet, not gotten involved." I had this conversation with at least thirty other feminist leaders. Many were sympathetic; no one came to help. After a while, it became clear that the "issues" (of surrogacy, adoption, custody) were "complicated" for feminists. And why? Well, there were infertile feminists and single adoptive mother feminists and feminists who had husbands whose ex-wives really didn't deserve custody or child support. There were lesbian feminists who were suffering custodially far more than Mary Beth Whitehead and decent middle class feminist couples (two career families!) who couldn't adopt a child without first being humiliated. And anyway, abortion under seige was the real priority.

All true. But does this mean that women should have the right to exploit other women just like men do? Or the right to call such an arrangement "feminist"?

The refusal of many feminists to get involved in the Baby M Case or to agree with my view of custody did not stop them from asking me for help when one of our "own"—a custodially challenged career woman or lesbian needed a strategy or an expert witness. But feminists still didn't see the connection between supporting Mary Beth Whitehead as a way of organizing for the reproductive and custodial rights of all women.

Custody is not a new issue for feminists. In the nineteenth century, suffragists fought in the abolitionist movement against slavery; some fought for custody for mothers. For example, there was a woman named Mrs. Phelps, the wife and the sister of United States and Massachusetts state senators. When her husband was flagrantly unfaithful, beat her, threw her down the stairs, and when she dared to complain about this—he locked her up in a mental asylum. Eventually, with her brother's help, Mrs. Phelps (whose first name I do not have) was released from this imprisonment. She ran away that very day with one of her children. Why did she have to flee with her child to retain custody? Because in the nineteenth century, and for all the previous centuries of patriarchal history, men have always owned wives and children, as legal chattel property. All during the eighteenth and nineteenth centuries, if a man divorced his wife, she was not legally entitled to ever again see her children. Like surrogate-contract mother Mary Beth Whitehead, legal wives had no legal rights.

Susan B. Anthony came to the aid of Mrs. Phelps, took her in, helped find her sanctuary. She did so without shame. Some of Anthony's abolitionist friends chastised her for doing so. They told her she was endangering the women's rights movement and the anti-slavery cause. Anthony disagreed. She said:

> Don't you break the law every time you help a slave to Canada? Well, the law that gives the father the sole ownership of the children is just as wicked, and I'll break it just as quickly. You would die before you would deliver a slave to his master, and I will die before I will give up the child to its father.

How many liberal, gender-neutral feminists are there today who would utter these words, who would take this risk, who would act on such a belief?

By the end of the nineteenth century, nine states and the District of Columbia finally permitted a judge—a white, middle- or upper-class male judge—to decide if a mother was wealthy enough or morally fit enough to be allowed to continue her obligation to her child. With no child support. And this was progress!

A lot has been said about how much the maternal presumption, a legal doctrine, favors mothers. Let me tell you: the maternal presumption never meant anything in a court of law when the father said, "Well, your honor, this mother has no money. She's been a go-go dancer. I think she's mentally unstable. She's narcissistic. She dyes her hair." For reasons like these, mothers have been denied not just custody but even visitation. These were some of the "deep" psychological problems that William Stern and the court used to deny Mary Beth Whitehead her parental rights. (Parental usually means paternal, not maternal.)

Contrary to myth, when custody is *contested*, fathers win easily and routinely. It is a very different situation when the issue is child support. When a father walks out, there is very little the wife can do to make him stay, make him pay decently (above the level of state welfare), or to make him see his own children. This is the common plight of most custodial mothers. Most fathers don't fight for custody. Most mothers are stuck with it, whether they want it or not. Most mothers rise to this occasion heroically, with no help from anyone. But when fathers fight for custody, fathers win custody anywhere from 60 to 82% of the time, even when they're grossly unfit, as fathers or as husbands, and even when they've never been their child's primary caretaker.

In my study, in the United States, between 1961 and 1981, 82 percent of those fathers who *contested* custody won custody within two years. Eighty-seven percent had done no primary child care. One third were wife batterers. More than one third kidnapped their children and took them on "sprees." Nearly two thirds of these fathers tried to seriously brainwash children against their mothers. Two thirds refused to pay child support for the very children they claimed to love. It is not always the good guys who fight for and get custody. It is — at least two thirds of the time—the bad guys who fight for custody.

Just when feminists began to organize for the right to abortion, and for equal pay for equal work, at that precise moment in history, men in every state legislature and in the judiciary, men running Hollywood studios and T.V. stations and newspapers, men who were economic losers and/or whose patriarchal kingdoms had begun to tremble as wives moved for divorce, men everywhere started to say, "Oh, you want equality? You want men's jobs? You want to leave us? Okay, bitch! We'll take your children. They were only on loan to you. It's our sperm and our dollars that matter. They were only on loan to you."

In the landmark case of Dr. Lee Salk against his wife, Kirsten, Dr. Salk was granted custody—not because Kirsten was unfit and not because he was an involved father, but because the judge found him to be more intellectually stimulating and richer than his legal wife who was, after all, only his womb-man or "surrogate uterus." Many people applauded this decision as a progressive and liberal decision—which indeed it was.

Then there's Mary Beth Whitehead's case. Mary Beth was a New Jersey housewife and mother, who, for reasons unknown to me and, indeed, of no real business of mine, signed a contract to be a surrogate mother. She was psychiatrically interviewed and, once a month for nine months, inseminated by Noel Kean's Infertility Center of New York.

Mary Beth was impregnated with the semen of William Stern. Dr. Stern forced her to undergo, against her will, but by contract, an amniocentesis test. Not only did he want a baby to whom he was genetically related; he wanted one who was genetically perfect.

Whitehead was contractually on notice that, if the baby was genetically defective, she must have an abortion. If she didn't have an abortion, then Dr. Stern would no longer be responsible for the child, legally or economically.

Mary Beth had the amniocentesis test. It made her so angry that she didn't tell the Sterns the sex of her child. And when it was time to deliver, she chose to have her legal husband, Richard, in the delivery room with her.

A woman faces all kinds of medical consequences and physical risks, including death, during pregnancy. Although the initial non-medically facilitated contributions of the future mother and father are comparable —she contributes the egg, he contributes the sperm—the similarities stop there. She is pregnant for nine months. She carries the baby, feels it moving inside her. She goes through labor. She delivers. She begins to lactate. She breastfeeds the baby. Mary Beth did all these things. Additionally, throughout her life she was being socialized into motherhood. Motherhood is not what men are socialized into. William Stern's position was in no way identical to or even comparable with Mary Beth Whitehead's.[1]

On March 27, 1986, when she gave birth, Mary Beth saw that her new daughter looked like herself and like her other daughter, Tuesday. At that point, Mary Beth felt that she had made a terrible mistake. She could not honor that surrogacy contract. It was too inhumane. It was beyond her capacity to do so.

She called Noel Keane, the lawyer who in many ways functions like pimps and profiteers do in terms of women's sexual and reproductive capacities, and said, "I can't go through with this." And he allegedly replied, "Well, Mary Beth, okay. Take your baby home. We will find another surrogate mother for the Sterns. The worst that could happen is that they might want some visitation." And she allegedly said, "I'll give them all the visitation they want. I feel so bad. I feel so guilty."

Mary Beth went home and continued to breastfeed her daughter. On March 30, 1986, three days later, she let the anguished and arrogant Sterns have the baby. Within twenty-four hours, Mary Beth arrived at their door, distraught, weeping, having had no sleep. She pleaded, "I need to have the baby back. It's my baby. I can't give her up." The Sterns gave the baby back. (If they really thought she was crazy or an unfit mother, why would they have done so?) By April 12, 1986, Mary Beth allegedly informed the Sterns that she could not surrender her daughter. Mary Beth Whitehead continued to breastfeed and care for her for four and a half months.

The Sterns went to a lawyer, Gary Skoloff. And he, in turn, went to his colleague, Judge Harvey Sorkow. Now at this point in time, there had been no paternity test. The existing birth certificate said "Sara Eliz-

---

[1]Had Mary Beth wanted to donate the eggs and had their "harvesting" been painful, dangerous or expensive, then in that case, egg donation would not have been the same as sperm donation.

abeth Whitehead." The baptismal certificate said "Sara Elizabeth Whitehead." But Judge Sorkow ignored these facts. All that William Stern had to say to the judge was that he was the genetic father of the child (that it was his sperm) and that he was ready to economically support the consequences of his sperm—and, or yes, that the "surrogate" mother was mentally unstable.

The judge didn't say, "Well, let me interview this woman." He didn't say, "Let me interview this woman's lawyer." He didn't even say, "Well, let's at least have a psychiatric kangaroo court in my chambers." On the basis of hearsay alone, he issued a custody order, and then he ordered it enforced. So one day, five policemen, with guns drawn, came to Mary Beth Whitehead's home, handcuffed her, and threw her into the back seat of a police car. Only then did they actually read the birth certificate in her possession. The child's name was Sara Elizabeth Whitehead. But their order was for a "Melissa Stern." Scratching their heads, the police returned to the courthouse. And Mary Beth fled, with her baby daughter in her arms, to Florida.

William Stern responded by putting a lien on the Whitehead house. He effectively halted all the Whiteheads' cash flow. Remember, the Whiteheads were a struggling, working-class family while the Sterns were comfortably upper-middle-class.

Hiding in Florida, without any financial resources, Mary Beth had that famous conversation with Dr. Stern, a conversation he taped secretly, the one in which she threatened to kill herself and her child.

She said, "Bill, why have you done this to me and my family? Please take the lien off." And he replied, "It's my baby." She said, "It's *our* baby." And then she said, "Okay. What do you want me to do, kill myself? Is that what you want? Do you want me to kill the baby? Is that what you're asking for?" Frankly, if I had been in Mary Beth's place, I might have sounded crazier than she did. Any normal mother under those conditions would.

Detectives hunted Mary Beth down. The police and private detectives hired by the Sterns came time and again, and they finally took "Baby M" away. They did this after Mary Beth had been breastfeeding the child for four-and-a-half months.

After that, Mary Beth was allowed to see her baby only two hours at a time, twice a week, in an orphanage with an armed sheriff standing guard over her. She had to travel four to six hours roundtrip for each of those two-hour visits.

Mary Beth Whitehead was put on trial by the legal system. But she was also put on trial by the media and by society. Watching coverage of her ordeal was, to me, like watching a version of the New Bedford, Massachusetts gang rape on the pool table, over and over again, day after day, where the men in the bar cheered the rapists on. You do something like that to a woman and you kill her. The victim of the New Bedford rape was driven out of town. She allegedly began to drink and take drugs. (I would too—wouldn't you?) And died in a car accident in Florida. They said it was an accident. It was the inevitable consequence of what the rapists and our woman-hating society did to her.

In Mary Beth Whitehead's case, it was not just a few bad guys who cheered her rapists on. It was the entire country.

Some feminists said, "We must have a right to make contracts. It's very important. If a woman can change her mind about *this* contract—if it isn't enforced—we'll lose that right! And we'll lose the Equal Rights Amendment." They didn't consider that a contract that is both immoral and illegal isn't and shouldn't be enforceable. They didn't consider that businessmen make and break contracts every second, renegotiate them, buy themselves out—with only money at stake. Only a woman who, like all women, is seen as nothing but a surrogate uterus, is supposed to live up to—or be held down for—the most punitive, most dehumanizing of contracts. No one else. Certainly no man.

Judge Sorkow ruled that the contract was enforceable and awarded the Sterns custody "in the best interests of the child." Indeed, this was just one of many contemporary custody battles between a legally married man and woman or between an adoptive couple and an impoverished birth mother. The child is usually awarded to the highest bidder. Whoever earns more money is seen as "better" for the child. How can a stay-at-home mother, like Mary Beth Whitehead, who earns no money ever be seen as the better parent? Even when the mother has a comparatively lucrative career she is usually seen as a selfish career-monster and therefore bad for the child.

Judge Sorkow ruled that the contract was not baby selling. However, if the baby were stillborn, or the mother miscarried, contractually the mother only gets $1,000. But if she delivers a perfect, whole, living baby, which she surrenders for adoption, then—and only then—is she entitled to the $10,000. Is that baby selling or not?

Judge Sorkow also rejected the idea that surrogacy contracts exploit women and create an underclass of breeders. He reached this conclusion even though, under the contract, the surrogate mother gets approximately fifty cents an hour. (Mary Beth refused the $10,000. It was put in escrow and the interest that accrued contractually went to William Stern.) Now think: who is going to be so economically desperate that she will be happy and grateful to get fifty cents per hour? It will probably be working-class women, impoverished women, and/or Third World women—whose fertility is seen as a resource to be plundered by men who want genetically perfect babies in their own spermatic image. This kind of genetic narcissism means that already living children who need to be adopted — poor, black, minority, disabled, abused, abandoned, neglected children — are not being adopted. As a society, none of us is adopting such children *before* we sign surrogacy contracts, and *before* we decide to reproduce ourselves biologically.

As a start, we planned a feminist press conference at the Courthouse. And we kept going back. We demonstrated with whomever came to the courthouse to join us, with whomever called to offer their support. Local mothers of young children. Outraged mothers and fathers of grown children. I called at least two hundred feminists to join us. One liberal feminist expert in reproductive rights and motherhood said that she couldn't jeopardize her new-found celebrity as a neutral expert on network talk shows by joining us and appearing to "take sides." Another liberal feminist said that Mary Beth was too tarred and feathered and would only hurt our need for "main-stream respectability." A third liberal feminist said that Mary Beth was causing a lot of "anxiety" among lesbian co-mothers and infertile women who might themselves want the option of hiring someone just like her.

Eventually, the case was appealed to the New Jersey Supreme Court. The Court overturned Judge Sorkow's decision upholding the contract. It ruled that the contract was against public policy (in terms of baby selling and baby buying and in terms of the birth mother's right to change her mind) and could therefore not be enforced. And although it affirmed the lower court decision granting custody to the Sterns the court nevertheless acknowledged Mary Beth Whitehead's status as the mother and awarded her visitation rights. (Of course, why reward those who kidnap children?)

A partial victory at last. But New Jersey is just one state. Many courts in other states are hearing cases just like Mary Beth Whitehead's. They could rule in other ways.

Mary Beth Whitehead—the woman is brave. She went after what belongs to all of us. And we must not let her and others like her fight by themselves for our collective rights.

I call on everyone to join us at a rally tomorrow outside of Noel Keane's Infertility Center in NYC.

Sexual and Reproductive Liberalism

Janice G. Raymond

Once upon a time, in the beginnings of this wave of feminism, there was a feminist consensus that women's choices were constructed, burdened, framed, impaired, constrained, limited, coerced, shaped by patriarchy. No one proposed that this meant women's choices were *determined*, or that women were passive or helpless victims of the patriarchy. That was because many women believed in the power of feminism to change women's lives, and obviously, women could not change if they were socially determined in their roles or pliant putty in the hands of the patriarchs. We even talked about compulsory motherhood and yes, compulsory heterosexuality! We talked about the ways in which women and young girls were seasoned into prostitution, accommodated themselves to male battering, and were channeled into low-paying and dead-end jobs. And the more moderate among us talked about sex role socialization. The more radical wrote manifestos detailing the patriarchal construction of women's oppression. But most of us agreed that women were not simply "free to be you and me."

Time passed, and along came a more "nuanced" view of feminism. It told us to watch our language of women as victims. More women went to graduate and professional schools, grew "smarter," were admitted to the bar, went into the academy, and became experts in all sorts of fields. They partook of the power that the male gods had created and "saw that it was good." They started saying things like "great care needs to be taken not to portray women as incapable of responsible decisions" (Lori Andrews, 1988: 293).

Some women thought these words were familiar, that they had heard them before, but the feminist discourse analysts didn't seem particularly interested in tracing this back to what "old-fashioned" feminists labeled liberal patriarchal discourse. They said this was boring and outmoded and, besides, women had already heard enough of this and it was depressing. Let's not be simplistic and blame men, they said, since this analysis "offers so few leverage points for action, so few imaginative entry points for visions of change" (Ann Snitow et al., 1983: 30). Instead, they began to talk about the "Happy Breeders," and the "Happy Hookers" and the "women who loved it" and those who would love it if they could only have "the freedom and the socially recognized space to appropriate for themselves the robustness of what traditionally has been male language" (FACT, 1985: 31).

This was familiar, too, but then something strange happened. Those women who had noted the thread of continuity between liberal patriarchal discourse and FACT feminism, for example, began to notice that instead of women mimicking male speech, men began to mimic women. Gary Skoloff, the lawyer for Bill Stern in the New Jersey surrogacy case, summed up his court argument by saying: "If you prevent women from becoming surrogate mothers and deny them the freedom to decide . . . you are saying that they do not have the ability to make their own decisions. . . . It's being unfairly paternalistic and it's an insult to the female population of this nation" (Sarah Snyder, 1987). Some women felt that "imitation is the sincerest form of flattery." They began to testify in favor of things like pornography and surrogacy so that they could imitate all the men who imitated them. It became difficult to tell who was imitating whom.

And state legislators began to submit bills advocating surrogate contracts—with proper regulations, of course—that mostly protected the sperm donor and the brokerage agencies, because feminism was in the best interests of men, and finally men had realized this. It was as the feminist humanists had always said: women's liberation means men's liberation.

Harvey Sorkow, the judge in the initial "Baby M" decision, saw that Bill Stern, the sperm donor, was overwhelmed with the "intense desire" to procreate and even said it was "within the soul." He said the feminist argument, that an "elite upper-economic group of people will use the lower-economic group of women to 'make their babies,' " was "insensitive and offensive" to the Bill Sterns of this world. A man of feeling himself, he said that Mary Beth Whitehead was a "woman without empathy." He was very concerned that Mr. Stern experience his "fulfillment" as a father, and so he gave him Baby Sara whom Mr. Stern called Baby Melissa ("In the Matter of Baby 'M'," 1987: 72, 73, 106, 96).

Shortly before this, the Attorney General convened a Commission on Pornography which heard testimony from women who had been abused in pornography—"a parade of *self-described victims* who tell their *sad stories* from behind an opaque screen. . . . Many experts on both sides of the question say such anecdotal tales of woe prove nothing about the effect of sexually explicit materials" (Howard Kurtz, 1985: A4, emphasis mine). This was reported by Howard Kurtz of the *Washington Post,* another man of feeling. Not to be outdone in feeling, Carol Vance poured scorn on the testimony of these same women by quoting with approval a male reporter who would nudge her during the hearings and say "phony witness" (Lal Coveney and Leslie Kay, 1987: 12).

Victims of pornography choose their own beds to lie in. Mary Beth Whitehead chose to sign her contract. All men and women of feeling understand this. It's our right to choose which is at stake. Pornography and surrogacy protect that right of choice. Feminism is FACT; feminism is "procreative liberty." Liberty is liberalism.

Within the "coming of age" of this particular wave of feminism, we have seen a shift from feminist radicalism to feminist liberalism. This feminist liberalism is both cause and effect of the so-called feminist pro-pornography and feminist sexual libertarian movements. The sexual liberalism that has come to be defined as "feminism" we are now witnessing again in the reproductive realm. There are several comparisons that can be made between the sexual and reproductive liberals, especially in their vindications of pornography and the new reproductive technologies. I want to illuminate one of these comparisons here, specifically how both groups use the rhetoric of a woman's "right to choose." Both the sexual and reproductive liberals have invested an old, liberal discourse about choice with a new and supposedly feminist content.

The sexual liberals are uncomfortable with focusing on women as objects and victims of male supremacy. They invoke a language of going beyond the ways in which men objectify, exploit, and victimize women (not to any reality of how women survive because of their bonds with other women, however). They would have us take a "great leap forward" to the ways in which women are agents, for example, of their status in pornography or their role as surrogates in reproduction. Reasoning that because women choose pornography or surrogacy, women need these "choices" to be free.

Feminist sexual and reproductive liberalism calls for a more "nuanced" view of women and the world. This is a feminism that represents many women as "choosing" prostitution, pornography, and surrogacy, while paying perfunctory attention to the ways in which those "choices" are burdened by the male construction of women's reality. Further, the liberals maintain that because women supposedly make these choices, feminists should reconsider the ways in which prostitution, pornography, and surrogacy are not monolithically oppressive but can be liberating to women. While feminist liberal discourse often pays

lip service to women's victimization by male supremacy, it is "turned
on" by the fantasy that women initiate, or at least mediate, the culture
of male supremacy. Constant focus on the ways in which that culture
uses and exploits women, they say, perpetuates a view of women unable to make choices.

We all know that because women have been *constrained* or *influenced*
by a social context that fosters pornography, prostitution, and surrogacy does not mean that women are *determined* by that social context.
But the sexual liberals caricature the antipornography and antisurro-
gacy feminists as subscribing to a brand of social determinism. The
liberals would have it that one can no longer talk about constraints or
influences without lapsing into determinism. This is a convenient re-
ductionism achieved by liberal discourse for the purpose of valorizing
both the sexual and reproductive trade and traffic in women's bodies.

Lori Andrews sounds the new/old liberal discourse of choice in her
writings for both the American Fertility Society, in its report recom-
mending surrogacy as a "treatment" for infertility, *and* in her policy
recommendations and legislative proposal on surrogacy for the Rutgers
Reproductive Laws for the 1990s Women's Rights Litigation Project.[1] Note
that there is a blatant conflict of interest here. In crafting the case in
favor of surrogacy for the American Fertility Society, Lori Andrews has

---

[1] The American Fertility Society Report entitled "Ethical Considerations of the New Reproductive Technologies" (Special Issue of *Fertility and Sterility*, Supplement 1, September 1985. Vol. 46, No. 3), was authored by "The Ethics Committee" of the American
Fertility Society. This group counts among its membership many of the reproductive
endocrinologists and surgeons who are now engaged in research and practice of the new
reproductive technologies. Among the members of its "Ethics Committee" of eleven, for
example, were Clifford Grobstein, Gary Hodgen, Howard Jones, and Richard Marrs who
are all prominent research scientists and/or practitioners of the new reproductive technologies. In addition, John Robertson and Lori Andrews who were the lawyers on the
committee both validate the technologies as "procreative liberty." The document reads
like a brief for the technologies with all members in agreement as to their real and potential benefits. The only dissenting voice from this chorus of approval came on the use
of third parties in reproduction, specifically on surrogate reproduction. One member
argued that third parties were "ethically inappropriate." Lori Andrews was the principal
author for the sections on surrogacy.
Lori Andrews was also the principal author of "Alternative Modes of Reproduction"
(in one draft called "Feminist Perspectives on Reproductive Technologies"), a position
paper which is part of a larger project entitled "Reproductive Laws for the 1990s" (See
Andrews, "Alternative Modes of Reproduction"). This "Briefing Handbook" is a joint
effort of the Rutgers Institute for Research on Women and the Women's Rights Litigation
Project of the Rutgers Law School. Part of the Project's goal is to seek consensus "among
those committed to reproductive autonomy and gender equality" by developing briefing
papers and specific legal proposals. Much of the thinking that is contained in Andrews'
American Fertility Report segment is repeated—in places, almost verbatim—in the Rutgers *Reproductive Laws for the 1990s* piece.

justified the inhouse interests of a medical group that promotes the new reproductive technologies as part of its research and livelihood. In writing for the Women's Rights Litigation and Reproductive Rights project, she is representing a women's group that should address feminist concerns unaffected by the priorities of the medical establishment.

This collusion and conflict of interest is not surprising, however, when we note that the major author of the FACT brief, which opposed the antipornography ordinance and supported pornography as necessary to women's sexual freedom, works for the ACLU. Hugh Hefner's Playboy Foundation has been a major contributor to the ACLU. Like the feminist pro-pornography forces which were funded with pornography money, some of those who represent "women's rights" policies in defense of the new reproductive technologies, especially surrogacy, have the same double agent status.

As for the rhetoric of choice, Lori Andrews in the Rutgers Briefing Handbook sounds the theme that "great care needs to be taken not to portray women as incapable of responsible decisions" (Lori Andrews, 1988: 293). Her emphasis mimics legal scholar John Robertson's notion of "procreative liberty." She caricatures the basic radical feminist tenet that choice occurs in the context of a society where there are serious differences of power between men and women as "a presumed incapacity of women to make decisions" (Lori Andrews, 1988: 269). In contrast, Andrews fosters "enhanced decision making" to ensure that women make "informed, voluntary choices *to use* reproductive technologies," and also to ensure "enhanced participation of women in the development and implementation of reproductive technologies . . ." (Lori Andrews, 1988: 269). In one sentence, she has let the new reproductive technologies (NRTs) in the social door as necessary to enhanced decision making. With women participating in the development and implementation of the NRTs, with greater access to information and resources, and with greater control over the use of the technologies, the goal of full procreative liberty can be reached, she says.

If this rhetoric of choice sounds familiar, it is. We've heard it before in the FACT brief, which was written specifically to oppose the Dworkin-MacKinnon antipornography law. For example, the brief attacks the antipornography ordinance because "it implies that individual women are incapable of choosing for themselves what they consider to be enjoyable, sexually arousing material without being degraded or humiliated" (FACT, 1985: 4). It goes on to say that the antipornography ordinance "perpetuates beliefs which undermine the principle that women are full, equal, and active agents in every realm of life, including the sexual" (FACT, 1985: 18). Thus it attacks the first legal definition of pornography that was developed specifically to address the real ways in which pornography harms women. It does so on the basis that the *proposed* definition of pornography harms women more than the pornography itself because it implies that women are incapable of choice.

In her briefing paper on surrogacy, Lori Andrews echoes the same theme. She caricatures feminists who point to "societal pressures" that constrain women's so-called choice to mother as denying women the faculty of choice. Like the authors of the FACT brief, Andrews cautions that the feminist arguments against the NRTs offer a protectionism that, instead of helping women, ultimately results in harming them. This amounts to stereotyping women as powerless victims, in the opinions of both Andrews and FACT.

To expose the victimization of women by men is to be blamed for creating it and for making women into passive victims. The liberals fail to recognize that women's victimization can be acknowledged without labeling women passive. Passive and victim do not necessarily go together. It is the liberals who equate victimization with passivity. It is they who devise this equation. Jews were victims of the Nazis, but that did not make them passive, nor did the reality of victimization define the totality of their existence. It seems obvious that one can recognize women as victims of surrogacy, pornography, and prostitution without stripping them of agency and without depriving them of some ability to act under oppressive conditions.

The FACT brief went so far as to say that women have been stereotyped as victims by the statutory rape laws. "Such laws reinforce the stereotype that in sex the man is the offender and the woman the victim, and that young men may legitimately engage in sex, at least with older people, while a young woman may not legally have sex with anyone" (FACT, 1985: 6). Along these same lines, it faults the Mann Act, contending it "was premised on the notion that women require special protection from sexual activity" (FACT, 1985: 7). The Mann Act was enacted to prohibit the abduction of women into sexual slavery and specifically forbids interstate transportation of women for purposes of prostitution. The FACT brief finds this to reflect "the assumption that women have no will of their own and must be protected against themselves" (FACT, 1985: 7).

As Andrews's "Alternative Modes of Reproduction" went beyond attacking those who oppose surrogacy to defending surrogacy, the FACT brief goes beyond attacking the feminist antipornography position to defending pornography. Compare these two statements:

> Women need the freedom and the socially recognized space to appropriate for themselves the robustness of what traditionally has been male language. (FACT, 1985: 31)

Traditionally, people have been allowed to participate in risky activities (such as firefighting) based on their voluntary informed consent. The risks of participating in alternative reproduction do not seem to be greater than risks women take in other areas of their lives. (Lori Andrews, 1988: 267)

The sexual and reproductive liberals reiterate, almost as an incantation, that women are not merely the passive victims of surrogacy or the passive recipients of pornography, but are the agents of many different motives and practices in these contexts. New approaches, they say, must give prominence to women as agents in this "culture" and the ways women create, use, and infuse pornography and surrogacy with meanings unintended by the patriarchs. Women may be used, but women in turn use surrogacy and pornography in their own interests. The key word in the liberal lexicon is women's *agency.*

There is one thing very wrong with this emphasis. It finds evidence of women's agency *within* the very institutions of pornography and surrogacy. It locates women's agency primarily within the "culture" of male dominance. It shifts attention from an analysis and activism aimed at destroying these systems to a justification of them. By romanticizing the victimization as liberating, it puts women's oppression in surrogacy and pornography on a pedestal. And in doing so, it encourages more women into these systems. It accommodates women to a sexual and reproductive freedom which consists of their giving up their freedom. *How* women come to want, desire, choose what men want and desire us to choose is not part of the liberal agenda. It is this complexity that the more "nuanced" feminist liberalism would simplify.

Radical feminists have never denied the agency of women under conditions of oppression. But radical feminists have located women's agency, women's making of choices, in *resistance* to those oppressive institutions, *not* in women's *assimilation* to them. Nowhere in the more "nuanced" feminist liberal literature on choice is women's resistance to pornography and surrogacy stressed as a sign of women's agency. What about the agency of women who have testified about their abuse in pornography, risking exposure and ridicule, and often getting it? What about the ex-surrogates who choose to fight for themselves and their children in court, against the far greater economic, legal, and psychological advantages of the sperm donor? If we want to stress women's agency, let's look in the right places.

Feminist liberals are demanding that women be credited with a capacity for choosing pornography or surrogacy, because without this gloss on women's reality, they could never vindicate these institutions. If they really cared about how women break out of oppressive and traditional patterns of sexual and reproductive slavery, duty, and roles, then they would not find the evidence in behavior and actions that keep women's agency restricted to the states of pornography and surrogacy.

It is interesting to see where our right to choose gets defended and where it doesn't. It is more than coincidental that the liberals have not defended women's agency in the creation of a culture that defies patriarchy, but have chosen to restrict their defense of women's agency to those very institutions of pornography and surrogacy that uphold male supremacy.

The choice that radical feminists defend is substantive. We ask what is the actual content or meaning of a choice that grows out of a context of powerlessness. Do such choices as surrogacy foster the empowerment of women as a class and create a better world for women? What kind of choices do women have when subordination, poverty, and degrading work are the options available to most? The point is not to deny that women are capable of choosing within contexts of powerlessness, but to question how much real power these "choices" have. To paraphrase Marx and apply his words here, women make their own choices, but they often do not make them just as they please. They do not make them under conditions they create but under conditions and constraints that they are often powerless to change. When Marx uttered these thoughts, he was acclaimed for his political insight. When radical feminists say the same, they are blamed for being condescending to women.

The sexual and reproductive liberals would convince us that our freedom is in abdicating our freedom—in the case of surrogacy, the secured liberty of a contract which "frees" the so-called surrogate to be artificially inseminated, to be constantly monitored medically, to be paid only partially if she miscarries, to submit to amniocentesis, to undergo an abortion if the test reveals the fetus to be genetically or congenitally abnormal or, conversely, to refrain from aborting if the fetus is normal, to follow doctors' orders faithfully, to abstain from smoking, drinking, and drugs not authorized by the physician. Are these the freedoms that women have died for? Is this the final absurdity of a word and reality of freedom that has lost all depth and power of meaning?

If this is what female freedom reduces to, we are not far from the world that Orwell described in 1984 where, in pointing out how thought is dependent on words, he gave the example of the word "free" which had been stripped of all political meaning. Thus "free" could only be used in such statements as "This dog is free from lice" or "This field is free from weeds." "It could not be used in its old sense of 'politically free' or 'intellectually free,' since political and intellectual freedom no longer existed even as concepts" (George Orwell, 1949: 247). Judge Sorkow and the liberal lawyers, such as John Robertson and Lori Andrews whom he echoes in defending surrogacy as "procreative liberty," serve only to further strip the concept and reality of freedom of any real political meaning for women. For they help to reinforce the notion that female freedom is in having "the right" to give up our freedom, our control over our bodies.

There's a lot of pseudo-feminist rhetoric of freedom and choice that masks the essential slavery of surrogacy. And there's a conscious manipulation of language and reality that happens when defenders of surrogacy use the rhetoric of "procreative liberty," knowing that many women will resonate with this phrase because of the feminist emphasis on reproductive choice articulated around the abortion issue. Judge Sorkow himself equated the "right" to be a surrogate mother with the right to have an abortion. The feminist fight for legal abortions was the right to control over our bodies. Let there be no mistake about it— surrogacy is the "right" to give up control of our bodies. And anyone who doesn't understand this should read the surrogate contracts carefully, even the ones that have been legislatively laundered to omit the grosser inequities of the Whitehead-Stern agreement.

REFERENCES

Andrews, Lori. "Alternative Modes of Reproduction." In *Reproductive laws for the 1990's, A briefing handbook*. Newark, New Jersey: Women's Rights Litigation Clinic, Rutgers Law School, 1988.

Coveny, Lal and Kay, Leslie. "A Symposium on Feminism, Sexuality, and Power." *Off Our Backs* (January 1987).

FACT (Feminist Anti-Censorship Taskforce et al.). Brief Amici Curiae, No. 84-3147. In the U.S. Court of Appeals, 7th Circuit, Southern District of Indiana, 1985.

"In the Matter of Baby 'M'." Superior Court of New Jersey, March 31, 1987.

Kurtz, Howard. "Pornography Panel's Objectivity Disputed." *Washington Post*, October 15, 1985.

Orwell, George. *1984*. New York: New American Library, 1949.

Snitow, Ann, Stansell, Christine, and Thompson, Sharon, eds. *Desire: The Politics of Sexuality*. London: Virago, 1983.

Snyder, Sarah. "Baby M Trial Hears Closing Arguments." *Boston Globe*, March 13, 1987.

In the Best Interest of the Sperm: The Pregnancy of Judge Sorkow

Pauline B. Bart

Having learned libel law from Kitty MacKinnon I specify that the following is my opinion, hyperbole, and came to me in a dream.

Once upon a time, the Goddess of Gender Neutrality, Pregnant Person's Mode, who was made a Goddess by Zeus as a reward for signing the FACT brief,[1] flew into the chambers of Judge Sorkow[2] and landed on his Bible which was open to the "begats" part, where Abraham begat Isaac, Isaac begat Jacob, and on and on, with not a woman around. The goddess said, "Judge, have I got a deal for you! You can experience what you have been talking about, see what pregnancy really is. I have a client who wants to father a child, but he doesn't want a woman to have anything to do with it. I can arrange for you to carry the baby; and, of course, you will have your expenses paid and receive 'consideration[3] for your effort.' "

After several inseminations with a rooster baster, the Judge began to feel tired all the time. Frequently he had to rush back to chambers, barely making it, to throw up. He was pleased, however, that he was going to be a birth-father. By the second trimester, he started feeling better, and he was excited to feel the baby moving inside him. But the

---

[1] Feminist Anti-Censorship Task Force brief opposing the MacKinnon—Dworkin anti-pornography ordinance passed in Indianapolis.

[2] The New Jersey judge who upheld the contract awarding Mary Beth Whitehead's daughter Sara to William Stern, the sperm donor. The contract was later held to be against public policy and was voided by the New Jersey Supreme Court.

[3] Legal term for remuneration in a contract.

amniocentesis, which the contract required, was painful and dangerous, and when he had ultrasound he liked watching his child moving around on the screen. He hoped the needle that was inserted through his navel didn't hurt the baby. By the third trimester, he was grateful that his robes covered his protruding abdomen. He had trouble getting out of chairs and couldn't find a position in which to sleep comfortably. His feet swelled, he was constipated, and he developed hemorrhoids. Nevertheless he liked to watch his belly and see the baby moving around. He even enjoyed the kicking.

At last, he went into labor, which felt as if he had the stomach flu, for hours and hours. But when he went to the hospital they told him to go home, since it was just "false labor." He waited until he was sure the baby was about to come out before he returned to the hospital. They sat him on the operating table and told him to pant to delay the labor and keep his legs together hanging over the end of the table so that they could give him his anesthetic shot. It wasn't an easy thing to do. As the baby began to crown, he felt as if his urethra would burst. The doctor gave him an episiotomy, which in his case was a subincision. He was told, "At least in your case we don't have to take an extra stitch for your husband."

The baby emerged, and the Judge discovered that it looked just like him. He wanted to hold it and cuddle it, but they took it away because, after all, he had signed a contract of his own free will. He cried, saying, "I carried this baby. I had it in my body for nine months. I gave it life."

"Pathological narcissistic symbiosis," they said. "He'd probably flunk patty-cake," they said. "He buys panda bears," they said. And they knew because they were experts.

As consideration for his work, however, Judge Sorkow was given a review course in contract law. And because he once implied that there was no difference between jerking off and carrying a baby for nine months and birthing it, they gave him a free pass to Headstart classes, where they learn to make distinctions on that level.

Abortion and Pornography: The Sexual Liberals' "Gotcha" Against Women's Equality

Twiss Butler

In 1971, Professor Thomas I. Emerson of Yale University produced with women students a paper intended to define the meaning of the Equal Rights Amendment then being considered by Congress. In this paper, Emerson wrote:

> Any plan for eliminating sex discrimination must take into account the large role which generalized belief in the inferiority of women plays in the present scheme of subordination. (Barbara Brown, et al., 1971: p. 883)

Institutional discrimination relies for justification on *gotchas* — the reasons why the discrimination is necessary for the welfare of its victims, the reasons why ending the discrimination would do its victims "more harm than good." Forced pregnancy and maternity is the central gotcha that is used by patriarchal men to defeat legislation for women's equality.

This commentary looks at a new gotcha: Harvard University law professor Alan Dershowitz's claim that women's access to abortion (which is limited) depends upon men's access to pornography (which is unlimited). It argues that men's perception of pregnancy as pornography — that is, the sexually explicit subordination of women — creates a "causal link" between liberal men's cooperation with patriarchal men in the legal control of abortion and their legal defense of pornography.

THE "WOMEN WILL BE HARMED BY SEX EQUALITY" GOTCHAS

Public arguments for preservation of sex discrimination have always flaunted the gotchas of equality. ("You want equality? *We'll* give you equality!") Now that we are supposedly wallowing in the ill-got gains of the women's movement, these self-serving paradoxes are often signalled by a prefatory "ironically." Ironically, economists say, the deterioration of women's economic situation after divorce results from reforms in divorce law demanded by feminists. Ironically, insurers warn, women will have to pay more for auto insurance if feminists win their demand for unisex premiums. Ironically, say spokeswomen for liberal organizations, women's books will be the first to be censored if radical feminists are able to attack pornography under the guise of protecting women's civil rights. And, from an op-ed commentary on "The Baby M Verdict" in *The Washington Post*, "Ironically . . . Whitehead's position was undermined by two cherished and widely accepted feminist principles. The court's verdict represents, in fact, a perverse triumph of feminist ideology" (Charles Krauthammer, 1987).

It seems, then, that the difficulty with feminist remedies is not merely that, as defined by their enemies, they fail to identify the "real" harm to women which, if it is even admitted to exist, has its "root cause" in some non-gender-specific social problem which legal measures are either inadequate or overqualified to address. Rather, the most public-spirited reason to block feminist efforts for the benefit of women is the awful prospect of harm—first to women, then to everyone else—if feminist initiatives are allowed to succeed. Whether malign or well-intentioned, it is agreed, feminists can only do more harm than good when they insist—and they always insist—on trying to open a can of worms, trying to open Pandora's box, or trying to use an atomic bomb (such as the ERA or the antipornography ordinance) to swat flies.

PREGNANCY AS THE ULTIMATE GOTCHA

For those determined to maintain sex discrimination, the ultimate gotcha is pregnancy—a condition impossible to achieve without, as it were, male input, but one which assigns virtually the entire physiological burden to women. Thus, pregnancy discrimination cuts clean, controlling women without penalty to men. "Men can't get pregnant, you know," chuckles an insurance executive, justifying maternity surcharges on women's health insurance and easily ignoring the actuarial certainty that every baby has a male parent. As biologist Garrett Hardin said in 1970, when explaining a scheme for sterilizing women, but not men, as a population control measure, "Biology makes women responsible" (Garrett Hardin, 1970).

It is pointless to talk about avoiding entirely that which is generally mandated by nature and society. A subordinated class experiences countless ways of being unable to refuse the demands of the class that dominates it. Moreover, the natural bias toward pregnancy is further culturally enforced by making the best contraceptives, those for men, aesthetically undesirable except when men perceive themselves to be the ones for whom sexual intercourse involves a risk of undesired results.

For some years, an "epidemic" of teen pregnancy has been responded to with journalistic handwringing and slyly pornographic photographs of girl children with downcast eyes and big bellies. When, however, the surgeon general woke up one morning and realized that the AIDS epidemic could kill heterosexual men, condoms became respectable[1] and abortion became a "possibility" to be tactfully mentioned to a pregnant AIDS victim (*Washington Post*, 1987). This strikingly disparate response to sex-related epidemics has passed without public comment, prompting a suspicion that any side benefit to women and girls from this abrupt policy change is supposed to be accepted with silent gratitude and no sense of entitlement whatever.

Pornography is subordination seen as an invasion of privacy. It relies on the existence of an idea of privacy in order to demonstrate power and dominance by violating it. There must be limits so that limits can be overrun. Physically, it uses the most elemental imagery of human vulnerability—the naked body and particularly the naked woman among clothed men. Dominance and the threat of violence are thus made flesh.

It is hard for a pregnant woman to look and feel like a person in full command of her own body and destiny (Twiss Butler, 1976). Preg-

---

[1] Why was it censorship when the Southland Corporation, responding to public pressure, made a commercial decision not to sell pornography, and yet it was not censorship when broadcasting networks, responding to pressure, made a commercial decision not to sell condoms? Is there really a constitutional difference between being dictated to by religious fundamentalists on the one hand, and by religious traditionalists on the other? Or was it that men who saw pornography as a sexual entitlement for themselves did not want women to see effective male contraceptives as a sexual entitlement for themselves? Yielding to the overwhelming power of the Catholic Church makes a nice excuse for network executives, but it is hardly consistent with indignant denials that networks allow themselves to be censored with the obvious failure of the Catholic Church to force network compliance with its wishes on any other issue.

nancy is a physical fact which precludes privacy. It "shows." What? That a woman is manifestly not a virgin. Moreover, that she has been invaded by a man and visibly subjugated and colonized (Twiss Butler, 1976). In traditional terms, she is "in a fix," a description which underscores her lack of autonomy. There is, they say, "no such thing as a little bit pregnant."

But suppose that there were a way to be only a little bit pregnant and then not pregnant at all. Women, including little girls, from time to time need, want, and, to a lesser extent because of pressures to the contrary, will have abortions. The only question, as we know, is what kind of abortions they will be able to have.

Thanks to physicians who wanted to be able to engage in this branch of medical business without running afoul of the law, and thanks to population planners who saw a need for limiting reproduction of some populations, and thanks to liberal men who put a higher priority on sexual access to women in general as a method of control and subordination than on patriarchal control of specific women, and thanks hardly at all to the considerable efforts of women, a way was found in *Roe v. Wade* to legalize abortion without acknowledging women's right to autonomy in reproductive decision making.

PRIVACY, NOT EQUALITY

For any woman who has been able to get the abortion she needed, the benefits of the reform are obvious and genuine. Not at all ironically, however, but quite as intended by the men who devised it, granting women a sex-neutral right to privacy in reproductive matters was like granting women expensive, limited, and easily revokable guest privileges at the exclusive men's club called the Constitution. In contrast, men's membership in this club is a birthright, possibly retroactive to conception.

Between the "creation" (Lawyers, 1985), as he termed it, of the constitutional right to privacy in *Griswold v. Connecticut* (1965) and its application to team decisions about abortion in *Roe v. Wade* (1973), Professor Emerson pondered its relationship to the proposed Equal Rights Amendment in the 1971 *Yale Law Journal* article mentioned above (Barbara Brown, et al., 1971: p. 871).

In this article, Emerson criticized earlier efforts to gain congressional approval of an equal rights amendment for yielding to political pressure in failing to uphold an absolute standard of equality between the sexes. In the same article, however, he proceeded for the same reason to replicate the failure by allowing the only exceptions needed to render the ERA ineffective, those for "compelling social interests, such as the protection of the individual's right to privacy, and the need to take into account objective physical differences between the sexes" (Barbara Brown et al., 1971: p. 887).

Abortion is not mentioned in this article[2] which was intended to guide the legislative history of the ERA. Still, we are to understand that it was not just police searches that were to be handily taken care of elsewhere in the Constitution by the right of privacy, even though it was admitted that "the position of the right of privacy in the overall constitutional scheme was not explicitly developed by the Court" in the 1965 *Griswold* decision (Barbara Brown, et al., 1971: p. 900).

Perhaps this assurance of the vagueness and elasticity of the new abortion-privacy constitutional right, "derived from a combination of various more specific rights embodied in the First, Third, Fourth, Fifth and Ninth Amendments," tempted liberal women to hope that they could get by stealth what they dared not demand as a fundamental right to be secured by the ERA as a requisite for equal treatment under the law. Certainly, liberal men must have been satisfied with the prospect of having abortion legally available, but isolated from any woman's claim to bodily integrity or equal protection, and thoroughly under male control. Then as now, political supporters of the Equal Rights Amendment could be counted on to welcome a solution that simply shunted an awkward issue onto another track. Their instincts could hardly have differed from those of their predecessors of whom Emerson wrote, "The proponents may have wisely refused to be too explicit about the laws and institutions the Amendment would reach" (Barbara Brown et al., 1971: p. 886).

In evident delight at the versatility of his new invention, Emerson speculated on the many ways in which the right of privacy might be applied. His 1971 comments clearly suggest the legal basis for its later use in defending pornography: "This constitutional right of privacy operates to protect the individual against intrusion by the government upon certain areas of thought or conduct, in the same way that the

---

[2] In a 1974 letter, Emerson explained why the article did not address abortion:

> The main reason we did not discuss the abortion problem in the article was that abortion is a unique problem for women and hence does not really raise any question of equal protection. Rather the question is one that is concerned with privacy. (Senate Subcommittee, 1983 & 1984: p. 635)

If abortion is "a unique problem for women," so is pregnancy. Under this standard of equal protection defined by men's needs rather than human needs, women would not be protected from discrimination on the basis of pregnancy, the quintessential form of sex discrimination.

First Amendment prohibits official action that abridges freedom of expression" (Barbara Brown, et al., 1971: p. 900).

Moreover, the right of privacy could be developed to meet new challenges. Although its exact scope conveniently "was not spelled out by the Court in the *Griswold* case," nevertheless "it is clear that one important part of the right of privacy is to be free from official coercion in sexual relations" (Barbara Brown, et al., 1971: p. 901).

Lastly, concerning "the impact of the young, but fully recognized, constitutional right of privacy," Emerson said that its scope "is dependent upon the current mores of the community. Existing attitudes toward relations between the sexes could change over time—are indeed now changing—and in that event, the impact of the right of privacy would change too" (Barbara Brown, et al., 1971: p. 902).

And so it has. In 1983 Catharine MacKinnon observed that, in *Roe v. Wade*, women got a constitutional right to abortion "as a private privilege, not as a public right" (Catharine MacKinnon, 1984: p. 52). In 1985, twelve years after *Roe v. Wade*, Emerson admitted that it had been difficult to argue for a constitutional right unmentioned in the Constitution and "thinks that it is more likely that the right to have an abortion might become so hedged in by bureaucratic regulations that it would be difficult to exercise the right" (Lawyers, 1985).

Professor Laurence Tribe of Harvard Law School mused in 1985 on what he called "the always difficult problem of abortion," and wondered if the "somewhat obscure 'privacy' rationale" of *Roe v. Wade* and its ranking "the rights of the mother categorically over those of the child" did not perhaps mean that the Court "forsook a more cautious sensitivity to the mutual helplessness of the mother and the unborn that could have accented the need for affirmative legislative action to moderate the clash between the two" (Laurence Tribe, 1985: p. 336).

THE RIGHT TO CHOOSE—
PORNOGRAPHY

These speculations about an obscure, contested, and sometimes unavailable right which probably cannot claim public entitlement suggest that legal scholars understand it is now open season on "women's constitutional right to abortion."

When the patriarchal use of pregnancy to enforce women's subordination is combined with privacy theory's potential for creating sexual harassment, and both are emotionally associated with pornography's view of a pregnant woman as sex in bondage (Andrea Dworkin, 1970: p. 218), it is hardly surprising that it occurred to Professor Alan Dershowitz that abortion could be held legal hostage for pornography. The rapidity with which Dershowitz made the connection suggests that he and others envisioned the pornography of pregnancy as well as the sexual accessibility of women when they championed abortion. Its manipulation against the civil rights antipornography ordinance is like a promise redeemed, a latent possibility realized.

Dershowitz's clever idea seems to have appeared first in July, 1984, in a syndicated version of his monthly *Penthouse* column on the law. Commenting on the Indianapolis antipornography ordinance, he said:

> In the end, the issue is one of choice and freedom—much like the debate over abortion. On one side of the scale are practices that some regard as immoral and dangerous (pornography and abortion). On the other side is the right of individuals to choose to engage in such practices. No one would deny either side the right to try to persuade the other that its practices are terrible. The real question is whether we are willing to give one side the prohibitory power of the government to enforce its views against the other. (Alan Dershowitz, 1984: p. 19)

The argument is that, by becoming gatekeepers to women's reproductive rights, Dershowitz, the American Civil Liberties Union, and other civil libertarians also became gatekeepers to women's right to a legal defense against pornography. The more vigorously they defend the "right of privacy" for abortion, the more legitimacy accrues to such other "privacy rights" as unlimited access to pornography and other behavior characterized, however harmful to women, as "sex" and therefore as "private."

But who is that "we" who make decisions about applying the prohibitory power of government? Certainly not women, who have no claim to the constitutional protection of the First Amendment when they are harmed as women. When *Playboy* magazine can sue to suppress testimony given in a U. S. Justice Department hearing, win, and have its censorship hailed as a victory for freedom of speech, there does not seem to be a "real question" any more about which side has already been willingly given the prohibitory power of the government to enforce its views against the other.

Having made his argument, Dershowitz springs his gotcha:

> In the abortion debate, most feminists insist on the right to choose. In the current debate over the Indianapolis statute, some feminists would deny that right to those who choose pornography. (Alan Dershowitz, 1984: p. 19)

Thus, any limitation on pornography would cause the loss of "women's constitutional right to abortion" and feminists would be to blame. This is logic, we are to understand, not retaliation. Although it certainly assumes a causal link between legal restraints on pornography and a negative effect on abortion, Dershowitz seems to regard himself as exempt from the sexual liberals' requirement, for women at least, that "scientific proof" be provided for assertions of causality in relation to pornography.

If further assurance is needed that women's right to make autonomous decisions about pregnancy is not secured by the right to privacy, recall the New York hearing of the Attorney General's Commission on Pornography in January, 1986. Outside the building, pro-pornography women picketers waved their signs begging "Don't take away our right to choose." And in the hearing room, representing *Penthouse* and with a former *Penthouse* Pet at his side, Alan Dershowitz testified as follows:

> I am not sitting here telling you what my views on pornography are. I am not going to demean myself . . . by telling you I am for or against it any more than I would tell a hearing on abortion whether I was for abortion or against it. I am for choice. Let me add one personal word. It is a disgrace to the memory of *Roe versus Wade* whose thirteenth anniversary we celebrate today and which celebrates choice by women as to how to deal with their bodies, that so many women purported to speak for the women's movement, which they do not speak for, came into this Commission today and urged this Commission on the thirteenth anniversary of *Roe versus Wade* to cut back on freedom of choice as to what women and men shall be able to do with their minds, their eyes, their ears, and their bodies. (Alan Dershowitz, 1986: p. 291)

Ironically, I think that Professor Dershowitz is owed a vote of thanks for making one thing entirely clear. A legal right of privacy that depends on violation of the privacy of those whom it is supposed to protect is not a right at all but a gotcha, a demonstration of what Emerson called "the large role which generalized belief in the inferiority of women plays in the present scheme of subordination" (Barbara Brown et al., 1971: p. 883).

I fully agree with Emerson that no "plan for eliminating sex discrimination" can hope to succeed without directly attacking this belief and every institution that supports it.

End note: Since this paper was presented, the U.S. Supreme Court's 1989 decision in *Webster v. Reproductive Health Services* has reconfirmed the inherent instability of the constitutional right to privacy as applied to a class of persons whose constitutional right to equal protection under the law has repeatedly been denied. The journalistic frenzy anticipating the decision and the legislative and electoral furor following it show the significance of pregnancy as a prime opportunity for harassing and controlling women. Armies of legal scholars, politicians and pundits are pouring through the gap in federal boundaries hacked by

Webster and rushing into the states with the keen excitement of a gang attack in which men test themselves against each other in pursuit of a common enemy. The battle cries are "life" and "choice." The rhetoric on both sides is pornographic, but to speak of sex discrimination is treason.

REFERENCES

Brown, Barbara A., Emerson, Thomas I., Falk, Gail, and Freedman, Ann E. (1971, April). The equal rights amendment: A constitutional basis for equal rights for women. *Yale Law Journal 80*, 5.

Butler, Twiss. (1976, April 22). A few things Frances didn't tell. Letter to *Houston Post* columnist Leon Hale.

Dershowitz, Alan. (1986, January 22). Testimony before the Attorney General's Commission on Pornography.

Dworkin, Andrea. (1979). *Pornography: Men possessing women.* New York: Putnam.

Dershowitz, Alan. (1984, July 8). Feminist fig leaves. *This World.*

Hardin, Garrett. (1970, July 31). Parenthood: Right or privilege. *Science,* 169, p. 3944.

Krauthammer, Charles. (1987, April 3). The Baby M verdict. *Washington Post.*

Lawyers in birth control case honored by NOW. (1985, February 11). *New Haven (Connecticut) Register.*

MacKinnon, Catharine. (1984a). *Roe v. Wade:* A study in male ideology. In Jay L. Garfield and Patricia Hennessey (Eds.). *Abortion.* Amherst, Massachusetts: University of Massachusetts Press.

Senate Subcommittee on the Constitution, Committee on the Judiciary. (1983 & 1984). *The impact of the equal rights amendment: Hearings on S. J. Res. 10.* 98th Cong., 1st & 2nd sess. Serial No. J-98-42. 635.

Tribe, Laurence H. (1985). The abortion funding conundrum: Inalienable rights, affirmative duties, and the dilemma of dependence. *Harvard Law Review,* 99.

Washington Post (United Press International). (1987, March 25).

Part IV

SEXUALITY

When Women Defend Pornography[1]

Dorchen Leidholdt

I'd like to talk about the theory underlying the thinking and action of that part of the contemporary women's movement that identifies itself as "pro-sex." It includes FACT (the Feminist Anti-Censorship Task-force), No More Nice Girls, the veterans of Samois, and the editors and writers of *On Our Backs*, *The Powers of Desire*, *Coming to Power*, and *Pleasure and Danger*. I'm talking about all those groups and individuals who have labeled the antipornography feminist movement "antisex."

The antisex label is in large part an age-old antiwoman slur, originated by men to punish rebellious women for not doing what they wanted us to do. It's the flip side of that other time-honored slander, "whore," which is the way men punish women for doing what they force us to do.

But there is a partial truth in the antisex gibe. If you understand that sex is socially constructed—which we do—and if you see that male supremacy does the constructing—which we see—and if the sex in question is the sex men use to establish their dominance over women, then yes, we're against it. We argue that this sex puts women down, that it keeps us there, and that in this society, pornography is central to its construction. I'm saying the antisex label that has been attached to us really should read: "against the sexual oppression of women." I'm also suggesting the converse: that knowingly or not, the "pro-

---

[1] This essay is based on a speech given at the National Conference on Women and the Law, 1985.

125

sex" people are supporting and defending the sexual oppression of women.[2]

At the core of pro-sex theory are ideas about restriction, repression, danger, and pleasure. These ideas are neither new nor unpopular. Their champions over the centuries have included the sex researchers, especially the Kinsey Institute; Hugh Hefner along with the less socially acceptable pornographers; left and liberal writers, lawyers, and political activists; Havelock Ellis; and the Marquis de Sade. In fact, the radical part of the second wave of feminism was sparked by opposition to these ideas and the practices they embody.

The problem with the ideas of the pro-sex people is that they beg important political questions—like how, why, and in whose interest. They fail both to look at sexuality as a political system and to examine women's position in that system. They make sense in the abstract, but are revealed as critically flawed when measured against women's actual condition in society. They are not feminist but "sexual liberationist." And I put "sexual liberationist" in quotes because it has never included the liberation, sexual or otherwise, of women.

Central to pro-sex thought is the idea that there is a plethora of sexual preferences and practices which profoundly violate societal restrictions. Among these restricted sexual activities—which are seen as wildly divergent—are cross-generational sex (to use their euphemism for child sexual abuse), fetishism, sadomasochism, and the making and use of pornography. Such deviant sexualities, so the theory goes, are at the bottom of a hierarchy of sexual privilege, which has heterosexuality, marriage, and procreation at its pinnacle, and "vanilla" homosexuality somewhere in the middle. "Those engaging in these privileged acts," Carol Vance writes in her introduction to *Pleasure and Danger*, "enjoy good name and good fortune."

All of this sounds logical and persuasive until you move beyond society's pieties and look at what it actually practices. Then it becomes clear that, instead of being forbidden or persecuted, these frowned upon sexual activities are, in the case of men, promoted, encouraged, and

---

[2]There is a small group of women within the feminist movement against pornography that rejects all sexual expression as oppressive to women (see A Southern Women's Writing Collective, "Sex Resistance in Heterosexual Arrangements" p. 140). Most feminists fighting pornography, however, believe that although male supremacy has turned sexuality into a weapon against women, sex is not inherently male supremacist and can be transformed through feminist consciousness and action (see Wendy Stock, "Toward a Feminist Praxis of Sexuality," p. 148). I, for one, find the contention of the Southern Women's Writing Collective—that sex by definition is what the pornographers make of it—both reductive and deeply pessimistic, and ultimately a capitulation to a culture that denies women our sexual potential and power.

rewarded, and, in the case of women, imposed and enforced. More-over, instead of being incredibly different from one another, they all have a common denominator: a power relationship that replicates in miniature the power relations of society.

How deviant is cross-generational sex, for example, when, laws against child sexual abuse notwithstanding, the activity is so popular that more than a quarter of all females are sexually abused as children? How nonconformist is fetishism when "regular guys" proudly identify themselves as "tit men" or "ass men," and the best-selling men's entertainment magazines devote whole glossy pages to just our genitals, just our breasts? How taboo is sadomasochism when *Penthouse* boosts sales by displaying Asian women tied up like slabs of meat and strung up from trees[3] and trendy sportswear manufacturers successfully promote their products by showing battered-looking models in torn clothing?[4] How forbidden is pornography when, aided by antiobscenity laws, the industry rakes in more than the film and record industries combined?[5]

As for the hierarchy of sexual privilege, it too sounds convincing, until you examine the position of women in this hierarchy. Heterosexuality, procreation, and marriage may mean privilege for men, but they mean something very different for the married woman. Her "good fortune" is a one out of three chance of being a battered wife, a one out of seven chance of being raped by her own husband, and a statistically undetermined probability that she will be her husband's domestic servant and that her identity will be subsumed in his. The so-called good fortune of lesbian feminists is either public denigration or invisibility and often loss of jobs and family.

It's not that "cross-generational sex," fetishism, sadomasochism, and trafficking in or using pornography are never punished. Sometimes they are, but never enough to dampen their popularity. Just enough to make them seem forbidden and keep them exciting. It's not that there are no sexual choices that truly violate society's rules. What I am suggesting is that the "deviant" sexual practices defended and promoted by the pro-sex people aren't really *pro*scribed by society; they're *pre*scribed. They're not really deviant at all. They're good soldier conformity.

Another related idea in pro-sex theory is the notion of sexual repression. Whereas restrictions are real prohibitions, according to this school of thought, repression is restriction internalized—the thought police

---

[3] See the December 1984 issue, in particular.
[4] Georges Marchiano is the current leader of this trend.
[5] Experts estimate the industry's profits to be approximately 10 billion dollars a year. See Report of the Attorney General's Commission on Pornography.

that keep people from acting on or even knowing about their inner-most sexual desires. Unquestioned is the belief that society is unrelent-ingly hostile to sexual expression, especially to sex that centers around dominance and submission. "Erotophobic" is the adjective that crops up again and again in pro-sex writing.

I confess that I find this theory perplexing. It sounds fine in the abstract. It just doesn't apply to the world in which I live. When I walk down the street on my way to work in the morning, I pass newsstand after newsstand in which pornography magazines outnumber nonpor-nographic publications ten to one; I get ogled by businessmen with briefcases and construction workers in hardhats; I pick up the *Daily News* waiting for the Number 1 train, and, while trying to ignore the *Penthouse* subway advertisements undressing Princess Diana, I con-front *New York Post* headlines about the rape and murder of a Harlem mother of six. I'm beginning to think that there's been a time warp, and the pro-sex people really inhabit America circa 1955.

Instead of being repressed, sex is being expressed and expressed and expressed. And it's not the sex of intimacy, mutuality, and equal-ity, which the pro-sex people deride as "vanilla," that's being pro-moted and acted out. It's the supposedly kinky variety—the sex of dominance and subordination. How prevalent is this kind of sex? Con-sider John Briere and Neil Malamuth's 1983 study, which found that 60 percent of a sample of 350 ordinary male students indicated a like-lihood of sexually coercing (read *raping)* a woman, and Diana Russell's 1978 study, which found that only 7.8 percent of a probability sample of 930 women had *not* been sexually harassed or assaulted. If you put these together, you realize that sexual dominance and subordination are a majority experience. Obviously the thought police are falling down on the job.

To be fair, not all the pro-sex people contend that male sexuality is repressed. Some believe that sexual repression is the peculiar plight of women, indeed the only noteworthy problem of women. The argu-ment goes like this: Because of our sexual repression, we must unques-tionably make use of any means available to stimulate our desires—sex roles, pornography, whips and chains, swastikas, you name it. It is suggested that the more our desires and fantasies are like those of sexist men, the better. If only women can uncover our repressed sexual fantasies and give free reign to them, so it goes, then we will be liber-ated, too.

This apparently was the rationale behind an exercise Paula Webster conducted in a workshop at the 1982 Barnard conference on sexuality, organized by "pro-sex feminists." There she asked the women partici-pating to write down, anonymously, their most forbidden sexual fantasies. Some of them went like this: "I want to buy a strap-on dildo"; "I want to fantasize about being a porn star"; "I want to rape a woman"; "I want to sleep with a young girl"; "I want to be fucked into insensibility every which way."

I'd like to break a real taboo at this point, and raise a few questions that the pro-sex people consistently evade. Where do these sadistic and masochistic fantasies come from? To borrow from Simone de Beauvoir, are they born or are they made? Are they really agents of our liberation? If we are aroused by them, does it automatically follow that we are empowered by them?

To begin to answer these questions, we have to look beyond the fantasies themselves to the culture in which they develop. It is not just coincidence that they imitate the violence men do to women and girls. Think about the implications for our sexuality of the following statistics: More than a third of us were sexually abused as children (Russell, 1984). For many of us, our first sexual experience was a sexual assault. Forty-four percent of us will be raped (Russell, 1984). The environment in which we learn about and experience our bodies and sexuality is a world not of sexual freedom but of sexual force. Is it any surprise that it is often force that we eroticize? Sadistic and masochistic fantasies may be part of our sexuality, but they are no more our freedom than the culture of misogyny and sexual violence that engendered them.

The inescapable fallacy of the sexual repression thesis, as applied to women by the pro-sex people, is that it looks at sexuality within a context of largely mythical sexual restrictions and outside an environment of real, ongoing male sexual exploitation and abuse. In doing so, it turns what is done to women's sexuality by external oppression into something we do to ourselves in our heads. It suggests that if only women can break through internal "taboos," we will have sexual freedom, indeed we will be free. It ignores the real political lesson of women's sexual experience: women cannot have sexual freedom, or any other kind of freedom, until we dismantle the system of sexual oppression in which we live.

The failure to recognize and confront this system is most evident in pro-sex thinking about pleasure and danger. It is significant that the pro-sexers use the word "danger" to describe the less-than-rosy side of women's sexual experiences. *Danger* connotes the threat of something harmful. It does not describe the *actual* denigration, exploitation, and violence that are done to women daily. Danger is the boogeyman in the dark. It is not the continuous insults, the leers and entreaties, the chattel status of our bodies, the real brutal fucks, the rapes, and the beatings.

By making the sexual use and abuse of women into just a scary game, the pro-sex people can locate pleasure for women squarely in its midst. "Pleasure and danger" really mean "pleasure *in* danger"; "coming to power" means "orgasm within a system of power over and power against women." What is ignored is that the governing sexual system *exists* to keep women from exercising real power and experiencing authentic pleasure. Within its perimeters, there is no meaningful choice, real agency, or genuine pleasure.

Acting out the roles of dominance and submission that the system forces on us is not the same as choosing them. Experiencing arousal and orgasm in the course of acting out these roles is not defining our own sexuality. I've come to believe that a human being can learn to eroticize anything—including banging one's head against a brick wall. I think that this is pretty much what sex has been for women—except that it's often more like being banged against a brick wall. Women learn to eroticize this abuse in spite of our bodies and against our interests. The sexuality our culture offers women today through pornography is not new, not avant-garde, not revolutionary. It's the same sex male supremacy has always forced on us: being used as the instrument of someone else's sexual agency—the instrument of someone socially male.

False assumptions of choice, agency, and pleasure have led the pro-sex people into mindboggling doublethink and utter callousness to women's condition. I offer two examples. In an article called "Pornography and Pleasure," which appeared in the 1981 *Heresies Sex Issue*, Paula Webster took issue with Women Against Pornography for interpreting a picture in its slide show as the documentation of a rape. Webster wrote, "I thought this [characterization] indicated certain biases about pain and pleasure and preferred positions. Yet the most important misunderstanding was that a mere representation was spoken of as a reality." The representation in question was an actual photograph of a prepubescent girl being anally penetrated by an adult man.

The second example is a quote from Kate Ellis in an article that appeared in *American Film*. She said, "There were always certain kinds of sex that took place out of the home and certain kinds in the home. Good women were in the home; bad women were someplace else. If a man wanted to do 'that,' he'd go to a prostitute. Cable porn can feed women's imaginations so that 'good girls' will feel free to do what only 'bad girls' used to do." By holding up the condition of the prostitute as the model of sexual emancipation for all women, Ellis is operating in the great liberal tradition. She is also utterly denying the reality of prostitutes' lives. A 1984 study of San Francisco street prostitutes got at some of it (Mimi Silbert and Ayala Pines, 1984). Of the 200 girls and women studied, 60 percent reported sexual abuse in childhood and 73 percent reported having been raped since entering prostitution. That's about double the rape rate arrived at by Diana Russell in her study of mostly nonprostitutes. As for all the good sex, listen to Connie in *Chicken Ranch*, Nick Broomfield and Sandi Sissel's documentary about life in a legalized brothel in Nevada: "The old guys who can hardly move are good tricks. The young guys I hate. . . . I tell them, 'Please don't do that!' They think they can fuck you as long and as hard as they want. I say, 'You're hurting me!' "

In both examples the pro-sex people turn the tables on women's reality as surely as does pornography. Child sexual abuse becomes a child's sought-out pleasure. The woman who is bought and sold is the woman who is most free.

The stated goal of the organizers of the 1982 Barnard sexuality conference was "to create a movement that speaks as powerfully in favor of sexual pleasure as it does against sexual danger." The issue that this movement has yet to recognize or grapple with is the fact that under male supremacy, sexual danger—women's reality of denigration and abuse—*is* sexual pleasure. To speak powerfully in favor of sexual pleasure while blithely ignoring the fact that this pleasure is usually achieved through women's subordination and violation is to speak powerfully in favor of a system that keeps all women down.

In *Pleasure and Danger*, Carol Vance concludes her introduction by raising the sexual liberationist colors: "Feminism must insist that women are sexual subjects, sexual actors, sexual agents." But feminists who insist that this is true within the system of pornography insist on a felicitous lie. Within the predominant sexual system, articulated and reproduced in pornography, women are defined and acted upon as sexual objects; our humanity is denied and our bodies are violated for sexual pleasure; the bodies of our sisters are literally marketed for profit. We can't think away this system: it is practice as well as ideology, out there as well as inside. What we can do is analyze it, challenge it, fight it, and ultimately change it. In this struggle there is real subjecthood, action, and agency. The option is pro-sexism: to embrace pleasure in our degradation and pacifying lies.

REFERENCES

Russell, Diana E. H. (1984). *Sexual exploitation*. New York: Macmillan.
Silbert, Mimi H. and Pines, Ayala M. (1984). Pornography and sexual abuse of women. *Sex Roles* 10, Nos. 11/12.

Eroticizing Women's Subordination

Sheila Jeffreys

I want to talk about the construction of women's sexuality around our subordination, and what, if anything, we can do about it as lesbians and as heterosexual women.

This has become a crucial issue because of the backlash, developed by women describing themselves as feminists, against those of us who fight pornography. In the early days, when we were first fighting pornography and male sexual violence, it appeared to be a straightforward struggle.

It was never really a straightforward struggle, since those of us involved in the British feminist movement against pornography often sat around in groups and admitted, though not at first since it was not easy, that even the most antiwoman material with which we were dealing could cause us to be turned on. Individual feminists who had that sort of reaction to the pornography we were analyzing and trying to do something about, would feel individually guilty and individually isolated. We especially would feel so when other women in the group would say they couldn't imagine how anybody could possibly be turned on to this material.

After this situation had existed for a few years and we had not made very much progress in understanding sexual reactions to pornography, a backlash developed against us. This backlash came from women who described themselves as feminists and who said they wanted to create a new feminist erotica. Not surprisingly, the new feminist erotica looked a lot like the old antifeminist pornography: it eroticized dominance and submission.

Some of those women involved in fighting the feminist activists against pornography, some of those involved in creating the, supposedly new, dominance-and-submission erotica, are feminists who at one time were involved in fighting pornography and male violence themselves.

What I think happened is that as feminists started putting out slide shows analyzing pornography, and as women started having reactions to those slides—at times becoming turned on by those slides themselves—there were two choices that women could make. They could say: "I am turned on by these slides. Isn't it absolutely horrifying how my subordination as a woman has been eroticised and gotten into what is the most intimate and personal part of me—the middle of my heart and my body—and appears to be part of what is most personal and most mine?"

They could say that, and become absolutely furious about the extent to which women's oppression can actually enter into our hearts and minds. That is the choice I have made and other feminists have made. And therefore it motivates us even more to fight pornography and male violence.

Alternatively, women who are turned on by such slides could think: "I am aroused by this material. Therefore, I am angry with the feminists who are showing it to me. I am angry because they are making me feel guilty and ashamed. Therefore, I will fight them." I think this is why some feminists are fighting the antipornography activists, are fighting us.

What I'm suggesting is that we all have the same problem: the way in which our subordination has been eroticized. But there are two ways of dealing with that injury: one is the feminist direction, and the other is fighting feminists on this issue.

So it seems to me that the most important thing we have to do in order to move on is to talk together as women, consciousness-raise, about the construction of our sexuality. We've got to talk about those things that have been so hard to talk about, such as the fantasies we have had inside our heads, how we get turned on, what all of this is about. Then we can start discussing the difference between negative sexual feelings and positive sexual feelings. We can work out where we're going to draw the line for ourselves. I think there is a line to be drawn, and as yet there is a lot of confusion as to where it should go.

When we do that, when we are able to talk together about these things, we will be able to come to grips with the extent to which we have internalized our oppression, and how it has affected us. Then and only then will we be able to get together again, reconnect, unify, direct our anger out there at pornography and male sexual violence.

You probably know that some of the libertarians who have been eroticizing dominance and submission have been promoting practices among lesbians such as butch and femme role playing in relationships, as well as sadomasochism. Butch and femme is beginning to take over any kind of possible analysis of lesbian sexuality right now, and I find this very alarming. (For a discussion of the implications of the revamping of role-playing for lesbians, see Sheila Jeffreys, 1987.) An example of the eulogizing of role playing is an article called "What We're Rolling Around in Bed With" by Cherrie Moraga and Amber Hollibaugh (Amber Hollibaugh and Cherrie Moraga, 1984). In that article, Amber Hollibaugh identifies as a femme and says that you must not injure the sexual identity of a butch because it is fragile. Where have we heard this before? Therefore, she says, she would just go and sit on the lap of a butch rather than make an approach to a butch in any way more obvious.

Her co-author, Cherrie Moraga, identified as a butch in this article, talks about how—because she is butch—she doesn't just go and sit on somebody's lap; she goes for the throat. Now the part played by the femme here is terribly similar to the role of the heterosexual femme in Marabel Morgan's antifeminist classic, *The Total Woman* (Marabel Morgan, 1975).

A problem with raising these issues is that it can look as if it is only or mostly lesbians who are eroticizing dominance and submission. That, of course, is far from the truth. However, it is necessary for lesbians to confront role playing in order to work toward an egalitarian sexuality. When I came out as a lesbian, for the first time I wasn't playing games, and I wasn't imagining that the person I was with was somebody completely different with incredible powers that she actually didn't have. For the first time, I was able to have an egalitarian sexual experience.

I do believe that it is possible for women to transform our sexuality and to move toward egalitarian ways of relating sexually. But I think this transformation may be more difficult for heterosexual women than for lesbians.

Role playing is endemic to heterosexuality, of course, but women with raised consciousnesses often see themselves as exempt. If you look at any pro-feminist, nonsexist couple, you will find that the disparity between the ways in which they sit, move, and dress is extreme. The eroticizing of inequality is not necessary to lesbianism since the inequality of sex class is not the basis of the sexual relationship. It is difficult to imagine how heterosexual desire—considering the role playing in just about every relationship—could possibly be egalitarian.

So, I think that as lesbians and as heterosexual women we all have a problem to confront and try to solve. I think we've got to do something about the eroticizing of our own subordination. It's undermining to us personally, and it's undermining to our relationships. It's also undermining to us politically because it makes it difficult to fight male supremacy. Only by attacking the construction of our sexuality can we move forward and actually make an impact upon the hetero-patriarchal society in which we live. So perhaps we can begin a dialogue, as lesbians and heterosexual women, about how we go further toward an egalitarian sexuality.

REFERENCES

Hollibaugh, Amber, and Moraga, Cherrie. (1984). "What we're rolling around in bed with: Sexual silences in feminism." In Ann Snitow et al. (Eds.). *Desire: The politics of sexuality*. London: Virago.

Jeffreys, Sheila. (1987). Butch and femme now and then. *Gossip*, 5. (Gossip is a British Lesbian Journal published by Onlywomen Press, 38 Mount Pleasant London WC1X OAP, UK.)

Morgan, Marabel. (1975). *The total woman*. London: Hodder and Stoughton.

Resistance

Andrea Dworkin

It's been an incredible pleasure to be here today because it had begun to seem that the women's movement had become a kind of sexual protection racket, and that our only purpose on earth was to make sure that nobody hurt sex, that nobody talked bad about it, that nobody had any bad attitudes toward it, that no nasty political thinkers began to make any of us feel uncomfortable about it. And, of course, in the most material way, that has meant consistent defenses of the pornography industry. And where there hasn't been an aggressive political defense of the pornography industry, there has been the most astonishing passivity and apathy and indifference on the part of women who deeply in their hearts are feminists but who will not get their asses out on the street to do something for the women who are being hurt.

And it had begun to seem, truly, that the pornographers were winning. And what is so exceptionally peculiar about that is that for the first time, they're scared. And they have reason to be, because we have hurt their business. They never thought we could. They are the emperors of profit and pain. Nothing can touch them.

In the early days, when the women's movement began to take on the pornography industry, people said: "It's pointless. It's hopeless. You can't go up against them. There's nothing we can do." Their power seemed so overwhelming because their money was overwhelming. The fact that they owned media made them a formidable kind of opponent. We didn't own very much. Their access to legitimacy—the stables of lawyers that they have to protect their interests; what were we going to do in the face of all of this?

And we would take our raggedy little signs and we would march 10,000 miles in a circle. And we'd be tired and dead and defeated, and we would say, "We're not getting anywhere." And the next day we

would go out again, and we would march another 10,000 miles in another circle somewhere. And all over this country, in cities and in towns,
everywhere, women were activists against pornography.

The media never reported it. Whole bunches of people didn't care
about it. But feminism was alive and well throughout the country because women were activists on the issue of pornography and, at the
same time, were using pornography to build a very sophisticated and
new understanding of the reality of sexual abuse: how all the sexual
abuses cohere to hurt us, to put us down, to turn us into commodities.

Then in Minneapolis we developed a civil-rights law, and suddenly
the pornographers understood that we were trying to take their money
away from them. Not only were all these strange little women marching in circles and making themselves dizzy, but we actually thought
we were going to walk into a courtroom and say: "We're breaking your
piggybanks open, and we're taking all your change, and we're using it
for women. That's what we're going to do."

Their reaction, their mobilization against the civil-rights ordinance,
has been spectacular. It hasn't been spectacular because they think the
ordinance isn't going to work. Their anger, their hostility, their frustration, their aggression, is because finally they take us seriously as a
political presence that can hurt them.

And, horribly, at exactly the same moment, the ground collapses
out of the women's movement. And everybody turns into chicken shit
and runs. Now we try not to tell them that. We try to keep it to ourselves as much as we can and we don't say, "Well, you know, really,
we use mirrors." We have approached them as if we know what we're
doing, as if we know what they're doing, as if we know what they're
going to do tomorrow the same way that we figured out what they did
yesterday.

But the reality is that the will to destroy them has gone out of fashion, because destroying them is a bad thing, because destroying them
is censorship. And if little Bob Guccione can't say what he wants to
say—even though he happens to need a woman's body to say it—
then the country is poorer in ideas, in political freedom—*our* political
freedom, we're told. We have to protect him in order to protect our
political freedom. Our bodies are his language that he's expressing
himself in, and our responsibility is to make sure that he keeps doing
it.

And the horror has been that women have fallen for it, women have
bought into it, women have been intimidated, women have been shut
up in defense of this First Amendment that is not even ours to use.
You have to be able to express your communication before it's entitled
to First Amendment protection and you can't express it if you are too

poor, not to mention if you are too crazy, which a hell of a lot of women are after what we have all been through, not to mention if you have been silenced by sexual abuse, not to mention if it began when you were a child, and you have been fighting, and fighting, and fighting for your identity and your integrity because somebody tried to destroy it back then before it was even fully formed. This silence that we live in is supposed to be okay. We're supposed to accept it.

Then the reality—the hard thing, the difficult thing—is that men use sex to express their dominance over us. And that is a very nice way of putting it. Sex is constructed, as people have said, specifically to be male dominance. That is what it is in a society that men run and control and in which we are unequal and sexually subordinated.

I think it is not a surprise in this system that women have learned to eroticize being powerless. It is a tragedy, but it is not a surprise. And the beautiful benefit to male dominance of women's learning to feel sexual pleasure in being powerless is that it makes it a lot easier to be dominant. The police force isn't what keeps this subject population subjected.

I don't know why we don't think that we have a right to exist, just to exist. The pornographers can feel safe walking down the streets. I don't know why all the stores that sell pornography feel safe day in and day out, but they're safe. I don't feel safe but they're safe. They're not worrying about anyone. They're not worrying about us. What are we going to do to them? We could do plenty but we don't do anything.

Now what I am asking for, pleading for, is a consistent and militant activism against those institutions and systems of exploitation that hurt women. I would beg you to consider pornography a primary one of those institutions. But wherever it is that you want to put your heart and your spirit and your body in fighting for women's freedom, you've got to tell someone or show someone. You can't just have it in your head and be good at heart. You have to be willing to be a little bit heroic, to take the blows that come when you are, to take the punishment—you're going to get punishment for being a woman anyway, you're going to get hurt anyway.

The difference is that when you become politically active, as I'm sure many of you know, they learn your name. And then they say: "Get her. Pick that one. Get that one. Make sure." They write down your name. They understand. They have a list of priorities. And if they know your name, you're at the top of the list, and not just at the bottom. And so you risk something, because you can get punished more.

I am asking you not to let us lose what we have gained through fifteen years of an effort to understand sexual abuse, an effort to understand the way sexual violation becomes normative in this society,

every effort that we have made to fight the people who are purpose-
fully trying to hurt us. There's no ambiguity about it. They're not lying
about it. They're really not. They admit it. They just don't want you to
care about it, or do anything about it, or think you can do anything
about it.

We've made tremendous gains. If there is no women's movement—
no real, political, organized resistance, active and militant—we will not
make more gains. Mirrors can only take you so far. I plead with you
to find some way to reinvigorate your activism against woman-hating,
against sexual violation of women, and not to be part of the women's
movement as a protection racket for sex, and especially for all kinds of
sexual practices that specifically and clearly hurt women.

Sex Resistance in Heterosexual Arrangements

A Southern Women's Writing Collective

This paper was collectively produced by the women of A Southern Women's Writing Collective. In contrast to the pro-sex movement, we are calling ourselves Women Against Sex (WAS).[1] We are offering a theory which describes the practice of sexuality at the level of class interaction, struggle, and conflict; that is, at the political level. We take seriously the overwhelming statistics that scientifically document the harm done to women by men for sex. The statistic that most clearly shows the staggering amount of sexual assault or sexual harassment done against women is Diana E. H. Russell's findings from a random sample of 930 San Francisco households: only 7.8 percent of women reported experiencing *no* sexual assault or sexual harassment. (We must assume that the reported number of incidences were lower than actual experiences because we know that women frequently fail to recognize, name, or report abuse, including rape.) These sexual acts, done individually and one at a time, destroy women's lives, literally. They begin when we are infants, and never end, not even when we are corpses. Sex *is* what men say it is. It *means* what men say it means. Its practice is *how* men practice it. It is what has to remain in place no matter what. Otherwise, patriarchy will fall. As the systematic political practice of male supremacy—the concrete manifestation of male power over women—sex *is* our oppression. It is also how our oppression stays. Since we believe that the practice of sexuality politically subordinates women, we believe that the entire practice must be dismantled, taken apart, or deconstructed. Though we realize that many women, including WAS

---

[1] Our analysis has evolved from our work as radical feminists in the antipornography movement. Specifically, our analysis reflects the realization that pornography *is* sex. We accept the definition of pornography as written in the Dworkin/MacKinnon Civil Rights Law (model) against pornography.

members, have had self-described affirmative sexual experiences, we believe that this was in spite of and not because the experiences were sexual. We also recognize that, as women in this patriarchal culture, we have not escaped the socially constructed dynamic of eroticized dominance and submission; that is, dominance and submission is *felt* in our bodies as sex and therefore "affirmative."

We believe that homosexuality, pedophilia, lesbianism, bisexuality, transsexuality, transvestism, sadomasochism, nonfeminist celibacy, and autoeroticism have the same malevolent relationship to conceptual and empirical male force as does heterosexuality. These activities represent only variations on a heterosexual theme, not exceptions. There is no way out of the practice of sexuality except *out*. All these erotic choices are also a part of sexuality as constructed by male supremacy. *We know of no exception to male supremacist sex.* The function of this practice permits no true metamorphoses; all gender permutations remain superficial. We therefore name intercourse, penetration, and all other sex acts as integral parts of the male gender construction which is sex; and we criticize them as oppressive to women. We name orgasm as the epistemological mark of the sexual, and we therefore criticize it too as oppressive to women.

We wish to emphasize that we are not attempting to describe or redescribe the lived sexual experiences of all women. We realize that these experiences are lived out in various ways, ranging from the joyous to the humiliating to the murderous. Though we believe that political reality "connects up" with each individual woman's personal experience and psychology, we do not believe there is any static formula that neatly captures this connection. We offer to the radical feminist community our beginning analysis of a practice—sexuality—which we believe is the root cause of women's political subordination.

The practice of sexuality is everything that makes socially possible the having of sex. That is, the practice of sexuality is everything that makes sex socially happen, that makes it socially real. The practice of sexuality includes gender roles, or social identification with femaleness and maleness; these roles function to make sex acts seem natural and inevitable, even though they are neither. Sex acts are central to the practice of sexuality; they are to sex what sex is to the subordination of women.

Historically, sex acts have included rape, marital rape, footbinding, fellatio, intercourse, autoeroticism, forced sex, objectification, child rape, incest, battery, anal intercourse, use and production of pornography, pimping and the use/abuse of prostitutes, cunnilingus, sexual harassment, torture, mutilation, and murder—especially by dismemberment, strangulation, and stabbing. Sexual torture is known to be a military tool of genocide, targeting women most horribly; it functions to make war into a sexual experience. Forced breeding of black women and men under slavery, the rape of black women by white men, and the lynching primarily of black men are also understood to be sex acts perpetrated by white male supremacy shaped by racism.

Sex acts are those acts that men as a gender class have constructed as genitally arousing or satisfying. The medium of this construction is that of social meaning; the method of construction is material, and both meaning and method rely on male force.

Material conditions are (a) direct force used by men as a gender class against women as a gender class, and (b) preclusion of women's rightful options. Thus, the empirical conditions under which women's sexual desire is socially incarnated are the autonomy-denying conditions of direct force and preclusion used by men against women. These conditions which construct our desire produce a sexual desire which is nonautonomous or "unowned." The desire to act as one is forced to act becomes nonautonomous. Since there is no phenomenological difference between those desires produced by preclusion or force and those not so produced, introspection alone is a poor guide for discovering the nonautonomous nature of unowned desire.

We have learned that we cannot trust our feelings as the litmus test for the truth about sex because—although sex is experientially about feelings—it is about constructed, manipulated feelings. At the social level, the coercion that produces unowned desires can be experienced as coercion only if the process fails. If the incarnation of the desire is successful, the coercion can only be found by looking at the social conditions under which the desire was produced. This is why we base our analysis on our observations of sexuality as practiced under male supremacy, not on our feelings—good, bad, indifferent or rapturous— about patriarchal sexual practices.

Preclusion and force play another role, which is the medium of social meaning. They are the elements which subjunctively define sex acts. A sex act can be operationally defined as an act which, if a woman does not choose it, a male *qua* male would find it genitally arousing to force her. Thus, even if a woman is not empirically forced into a sex act, male arousal is nevertheless a response to the element of subjunctive force, which remains in all instances definitional. While a woman might evade empirical force, she literally cannot evade conceptual or definitional sexual force. This truth about sex, like all conceptual truth, is beyond the reach of individual choice, cleverness, privilege, or negotiating ability. It is for this reason that male force which defines sex is inescapable. For this reason, lesbians or people of other sexual preferences cannot escape or redefine sexual practice inside male suprem-

acy. Thus, women are politically subordinated through sex, not because we do not ever choose it, but because the identity of what we
choose is a function of male political power, power that valorizes and
maintains itself through a process of genital arousal that is informed
by the denigration and violation of women's autonomy and equality.
Given this definition, genital arousal represents the literal incarnation
of women's political subordination. It is politics made flesh.

Our study of pornography has made it clear that because the male
is aroused through this medium of social meaning, pornography is as
arousing as "real-life" sex. In both life and art, the male responds to
the male-constructed meaning of woman. Thus the equation "pornography = sex" is literally true.

We believe that the practice of sexuality is entirely socially constructed by the power of men as a gender class. We do not believe it
is either a curse of biology or a gift from God. Neither do we believe it
is a joint-gender project of men and women. We believe the practice to
be animated by an eroticized dynamic of male dominance and female
submission. What makes this practice live and breathe, what sparks its
social life, is class hierarchy or social top-bottomism. We believe that
the function of this practice is to subordinate women to men. This dynamic and this function identify the practice at the political level. Any
act informed by a practice without this dynamic and function—any act
informed by a practice which did not subordinate women—would literally not be a sex act. More succinctly: *if it doesn't subordinate women,
it's not sex.*

As far as we know, no act experienced as sexual is this "something
else." The practice that could make this happen does not exist. In our
feminist future, an act outwardly identical to a sex act *might* be informed by an entirely different practice. That act would not subordinate women. But that feminist future is not now and that different
practice is not now. That is where we want to go/be after the defeat of
male supremacy, after dismantling the practice of sexuality.

The sexual experience of most women occurs within heterosexual
arrangements, and this experience is often lived out as an attempt to
escape from the practice of sexuality. It is the experience of avoidance.
In the past, it would have been said that a woman's avoidance of sex
represented a failure to fulfill her conjugal duty. Today, such talk is
outmoded. Now it would be said that she is avoiding intimacy in an
unhealthy way, that she is rejecting sexual agency, that she is rejecting
pleasure, short-circuiting emotions and needs that are natural and good.
In the past, failure to acquiesce may have resulted in rape or forced
sex. Today, the remedy for nonacquiescence is found also at the level
of desire. Women must learn to desire sexual pleasure by eroticizing

violation. The oddity is, women must *learn* to desire. To learn such "natural" desire, women are encouraged to engage in scripted masturbation, to create fantasies where none exist, to try "adventurous" and "new" sexual techniques, to accept pornography—in other words, to seek out as desire the disorientation that accompanies sex.

Attempting to achieve nonacquiesence to male-constructed "needs," women learn to recognize even the subtle signs of male desire. Enough women have learned how to avoid becoming available to it so that mention of women's headaches is a male joke. So women do have headaches, and dress and undress in closets, deliberately gain or lose weight, become alcoholic, develop other drug dependencies, carefully orchestrate schedules, and attempt to shut down all communications that might hint at intimacy.

There are some feminists who seem to believe that these activities of sex avoidance represent the quaint subterfuges of a long-dead past —but they are wrong. This dismissive view may be a function of some social privilege that most ordinary women do not have. We believe the life of sex avoidance is the reality for many women in heterosexual arrangements.

Women's historical sex avoidance can, with feminist consciousness, become an act of *sex resistance*. The sex resister understands her act as a political one. Her goal is not only personal integrity for herself but political freedom for all women. She resists on three fronts: she resists male-constructed sexual "needs," she resists the misnaming of her act as prudery, and she especially resists the patriarchy's attempt to make its work of subordinating women easier by "consensually" constructing her desire in its own oppressive image.

The patriarchy attempts to reach *within* women to fuck/construct us from the inside out. This attempt assumes many forms, such as sex "education" and sex advice. Popular advice columnists counsel women to use pornography, pornographic fantasy, and sex toys in order to "enhance" their sexual lives. Such advice, which relies on the patriarchy's account of sexual "normalcy," never questions the practice of sexuality and the ways in which this practice precludes women's rightful options, including the option of sex avoidance. The choice to avoid sex is never perceived as valid. Women are schooled to "choose" pornography and pornographic lives under the threat of losing their primary relationships with husbands or boyfriends. They are taught by male "experts" to desire male-constructed sexual pleasure.

The normalcy of such coercion of desire makes untrue the claim that our sexuality is our own. As long as the price of not choosing sex is what it presently is for any woman, sex is in fact compulsory for all women.

The compulsoriness of women's sexuality (not just heterosexuality) is hidden because it is sexual. We can try to expose this hidden force through thought, reflection, and action. If the conditions which construct women's desire were structurally reproduced in any nonsexual situation—consider the loyal Party Member's desire to support Stalinism—would we celebrate that desire as being in any way that person's own? When conditions of preclusion and force construct desire, we recognize that desire as being nonautonomous or unowned, unless it is sexual and is women's. We ask: In whose interest is it to make this exception? We believe that we can begin by and through the processes which we have identified as (a) sexual resistance, (b) deconstructive lesbianism, and (c) radical celibacy to expose and perhaps even unmake or undo the sexualization that is our subordination.

Through collective and personal struggle, the desires that were socially incarnated in us in order to effect our subordination to men can be named and disowned. After all, if we can teach pigeons to play ping-pong, incarnating in them desires they never thought they had, perhaps we can teach ourselves to prefer a nonsexualized woman-identification to the desire for subordination and for self-annihilation that is the required content and social paradigm of our sexuality. Though political, structural conditions must change before the practice of sexuality can be eradicated, this should not stop us from politicizing the content of our own individual sexual lives. While we do not know to what extent changes in the practice of sexuality can be accomplished through collectively determined but individually initiated changes, we do know—sexually speaking—that business as usual is not liberating. The content of the sexual is the content of our subordination.

For women, sex acts have sometimes been sought out in love and through desire, and sometimes avoided and resisted with perhaps a nascent awareness of their antiwoman political function. The material arena for adult women's orientation to sexuality in general and sex acts in particular has usually been heterosexual. Our focus in this paper is on women in such heterosexual arrangements. We want to mention very briefly both deconstructive lesbianism and radical celibacy before discussing sex resistance in heterosexual arrangements.

At the practical level, we see deconstructive lesbianism as a transitional political choice. Deconstructive lesbianism aims to de-construct or dismantle the practice of sexuality at the personal and experiential level. It attempts to unweave the pattern of dominance and submission which has been incarnated as sexuality in each of us. At its most basic level, deconstructive lesbianism means being who we are as lesbians, but without sex. It represents a woman-centered attempt to say no to male force at all its levels, including the level we have all interiorized as sexual response. We believe that many lesbians in couples are living out deconstructive lesbianism at the present time, in fact, but not in theory. Unfortunately, this practice has been criticized as a problem rather than part of a solution. Named antisex (which it is), it has been seen as similar to the situation of the "frigid woman" with similar prescriptions recommended (pornography, for one) as a way to get back on track with dominance and submission. We hope that these lesbians will begin to think and write about their experiences in political terms.

Radical celibacy differs from celibacy—whether done by feminists or others—because it contains the analysis discussed in this paper about the condition of women under male supremacy and sees that our subordination turns on the continuation of the practice of sexuality. Radical celibacy understands that sex has to stop before male supremacy will be defeated. We believe that many women practice radical celibacy, perhaps without naming it, but knowing that it is key to their personal integrity and frequently as part of "sexual healing" after assault. We urge these women to speak out. Sex resisters can struggle and act within heterosexual arrangements to dismantle the dynamic through which men self-identify as the subordinators of women and women self-identify as the subordinated, meanwhile keeping other nonsexual, nonsubordinating aspects of relationships that have value for them.

Sex resistance is not to be understood as what has been traditionally known as celibacy, as that which lacks an articulated radical feminist analysis of the subordination of women. Although celibacy can and does have positive effects (e.g., lessening a particular woman's direct, personal sexual exploitation), celibacy must be transformed by a radical feminist consciousness to become politically meaningful. Sex resistance has a historical claim to feminist authenticity. It is what many women have done when demonstrating our claims to integrity, to self-possession of our own lives and bodies. It makes speech of women's silent refusal to validate and valorize male-constructed desire. Sex resistance has been misnamed and ridiculed by most men and some women as "prudery," "frigidity," and "sexual incompatibility." By performing the political act of sex resistance, the power imbalance is challenged and the practice of sexuality is exposed. We believe that acts of sex resistance can be part of the process of transition that will dismantle the practice of sexuality.

Radical celibacy together with deconstructive lesbianism and sex resistance are the only practical political choices for women oppressed under male supremacy.

In conclusion, our analysis claims that sex is compulsory for women because the price of not choosing it is social worthlessness and exclusion. There is no esteemed place—or even a socially neutral place—for the women who will not put out to someone at some time in some way. By male design, the relationships that ground our social sense of self and self-worth are a package deal—with love, security, emotional support, and sex all going together. Your value as a piece of ass becomes clear when you stop being that piece. The sex resister understands that beneath the label of "sexual incompatibility"—beneath that mystification—is the truth of the political equation: Woman equals her capacity as a cunt. The sex resister brings this hidden equation into view, dragging the entire practice of sexuality into the light of feminist scrutiny. The sex resister refuses to accept the package deal of male design. She demands the right not to be forced to follow the cultural precept that says: PUT OUT or GET OUT.

Toward a Feminist Praxis of Sexuality

Wendy Stock, Ph.D.

The feminist movement is currently in a state of deep division over where to place sexuality within feminist theory and practice. The issue of pornography has highlighted this division, which has occurred on both political and personal levels for many women. Representing extreme ends of the continuum of the response to pornography and views of sexuality are the Feminist Anti-Censorship Task Force (FACT) and Women Against Sex (WAS). Although I am more sympathetic to the analysis of WAS, I find that the positions of both groups have inherent limitations and contain theoretical oversights. I am a feminist clinical psychologist specializing in research and treatment in the area of sexuality.

The major inadequacy of FACT's position lies in its tacit acceptance of sexuality as currently constructed by the patriarchy, and its belief that women need only appropriate their rightful piece of the pie to achieve sexual liberation (Gayle Rubin, 1984; Jessica Benjamin, 1983; Ellen Willis, 1983). This position is similar to that of some middle class feminists who believe that upward mobility for some women, while leaving the current political system intact, will lead to a just society. WAS, conversely, errs in the opposite direction, by assuming that *all* sexuality that occurs within the patriarchy is patriarchally constructed sex (Southern Women's Writing Collective, 1987a, 1987b). This viewpoint, by definition, does not allow for the existence of any current feminist vision or practice of sexuality, and assumes that absolute ubiquity of patriarchal control.

Both FACT and WAS believe that, currently, patriarchally constructed sexuality represents all sexuality, which must be either enthusiastically embraced and adopted (FACT), or rejected completely, by resisting engaging in sexual practices (WAS). The limitations of these views, respectively, indicate either a culture-bound and context-absent analysis of sexuality, or an overinclusive, absolutist, and static analysis of sex. What remains to be developed is a view of sexuality that allows for the possibility of feminist change, even before the overthrow of the patriarchy. This feminist praxis of sexuality must incorporate a radical critique of patriarchally constructed sex, and place at its forefront an awareness of the conditions of sexual subordination under which women live now.

The FACT position will be discussed first. By uncritically accepting sexuality in all its current manifestations, FACT errs in assuming that what we see in sex is the natural expression of sexuality. In adopting this view, FACT overlooks the ways in which patriarchal society has shaped and determined sexuality by eroticizing the hierarchy of power at every level of society. Ehrenreich et al., in *Re-Making Love*, erroneously disassociate sex from its political context: "For women, sexual equality with men has become a concrete possibility, while economic and social parity remains elusive" (B. Ehrenreich, E. Hess & G. Jacobs, 1987). Marx said that every social institution reflects the unequal distribution of power inherent in capitalism. Embedded within feminist analysis is the similar theorem that all social institutions, including sexuality, reflect the power that men have over women. As Catharine MacKinnon has pointed out, as work is to Marxism, sexuality is to feminism (Catharine MacKinnon, 1982).

Many women are currently embracing and defending a patriarchally constructed notion of sex. They believe, in keeping with psychoanalytic thinkers, that the erotic *necessitates* an imbalance of power, and that our "erotic scripts" are expressions of the fantasized reversal or the reenactment of thwarted infantile desires (R. Stoller, 1979). Thus, all eroticism is seen as governed by a fantasy of retribution, by an attempt to restore a balance of power by doing to others what has been done to the self as a powerless infant. Eroticism becomes defined in this view as the enactment of either dominant or submissive sexual behaviors which are endlessly repeated with supposedly cathartic effects. This model of sexuality presupposes this dynamic as *innate* and natural. Women identified as feminists who adopt this theory believe that the key to liberating women is to reverse or invert the oppressor-oppressed dynamic in sex, or to act out these roles within an eroticized context. As Ehrenreich et al. assert, "The suburban woman who gets her thrills from watching male strippers is paying, with her admission price, to invert the usual relationship between men and women, consumer and object. At a different end of the cultural spectrum, a practitioner of ritualistic sadomasochism confronts social inequality by encapsulating it in a drama of domination and submission" (B. Ehrenreich et al., 1987). Becoming a dominatrix and assuming a position of total control of a sexual partner or "choosing" to be subordinate in sex is supposed to heal us of our prior victimization.

Women's advocacy of patriarchal sexual relations is a part of the phenomenon of identification with the oppressor, much like that of some concentration camp prisoners with their jailors. Lenore Walker, in *The Battered Woman*, has observed that battered women sometimes plan when their abuse will occur by intentionally precipitating a battering incident (Lenore Walker, 1979). In a battering relationship, it is a given that violence will occur, and by choosing to precipitate when, the woman gains the illusion that she is exercising control over her situation. In a culture in which the majority of women will experience at least one form of sexual aggression (rape, 15–44%; childhood sexual abuse or incest, 38%; spouse abuse, 50%; and sexual harassment, 88%),[1] a culture in which sexual violence is normative, women develop psychological mechanisms to cope with the inevitable violence. This phenomenon can also explain the existence of the rape fantasies that some women are aroused by. To quote from an anonymous letter sent to *Off Our Backs*, a feminist newspaper reporting national and international political and cultural issues: "If women were capable of enjoying rape, this restored some dignity and equality to them, and was a source of strength. I saw enjoyment of rape as a victory over man because it foiled their attempts to hurt me. Often when women appear to be acquiescing in oppression, they are, in a misguided way, attempting to adjust to male violence and domination as best they can" (Anonymous, 1986).

I believe it is this phenomenon to which Sheila Jeffreys refers when she speaks of women learning to have "pleasure" in their own subordination. Such fantasies may be interpreted as attempts to establish a sense of subjective control over the threat or reality of sexual coercion. Women who enjoy pornography or rape fantasies are not rebels, as Ellen Willis maintains (Ellen Willis, 1983); rather, they are like slaves

---

[1] M. Koss, C. Gidycz & N. Wisniewski, 1987: In a national sample of 3,187 women, 27.5% had been raped. Authors cite other studies ranging from 14.5% to 44%. A. Johnson, 1980: A statistical analysis based on a sample of 250,000 females living in metropolitan areas, and assuming that only one in ten rapes are reported, a female living in a metropolitan area has a 40% chance of being raped between the ages of 12 and 60. C. Safran, 1976: Nine thousand readers of *Redbook* responded to a questionnaire on sexual harassment on the job published in the magazine. Eighty-eight percent said they had experienced sexual harassment on the job. L. Walker (1979) estimates that at least 50% of women will be battered in their relationships at some time. Diana Russell (1986) found that 38% of a sample of 930 women reported at least one experience of incestuous and/or extrafamilial sexual abuse before the age of 18 years. This figure is similar to rates reported in other studies involving large samples.

adjusting to the seeming inevitability of their position. By mislabeling and glorifying this internalized oppression as a celebration of the erotic by such doublespeak terms as "rebel," FACT grossly misinterprets and perpetuates the psychology of the oppressed.

When women defend pornography and patriarchally constructed sex and attempt to make it their own, they are "timing" sexual abuse in the same manner as do some women in battering relationships. We do not need to define our liberation as an acceptance of the erotic inequality that characterizes the turn-on of the patriarchy.

The seemingly dichotomous ways in which FACT and WAS deal with sexuality resemble the reactions of some survivors of incest and child sexual abuse. While some develop sexual dysfunctions and avoid sex, others respond by becoming very sexualized, initiating sex indiscriminantly, or becoming prostitutes. Several studies have indicated that as many as 50 percent of prostitutes have been sexually abused as children (J. James & J. Meyerding, 1977). FACT's position on sexuality seems to be in line with this second response, i.e., to identify with the oppressor and adopt his view of sex. In this vein, FACT members try to appropriate sex for themselves, but do so without questioning the dynamics of oppressor and oppressed and by eroticizing dominance and submission. The FACT creed seems to be, "O.K., you call us bad women, so we'll show you just how bad we can be." Ironically, this effort at self-definition and rebellion against sexual subordination is in reality conformity to the sexual paradigms of the patriarchy. FACT has lost its ability to distinguish between a positive sexuality for women and the patriarchally constructed practice of sex.

Another mode of response to incestuous abuse is the avoidance of sex and a diminished ability to distinguish between coercive and non-coercive sexuality. Some incest survivors find themselves involved in situations in which they continue to be hurt, feeling as if they deserve it or it is the best they can do or that ongoing abuse is an inevitable part of a sexual relationship. In treatment, a period of celibacy is often recommended to allow the woman to heal from her injuries. WAS contends that it is necessary to resist all sex practices within the current social structure, that none can occur outside the context of coercion, in either subtle or obvious forms. WAS emphasizes that we cannot trust our feelings, a statement common among incest survivors. It is true that the patriarchy may have eroded our ability to distinguish between sex that is consensual, mutual, and egalitarian, and sex that is exploitative and violent.

WAS claims that all sex is the same under patriarchy and assumes that nothing good can happen sexually under current conditions. If one accepts this premise, arguing for the possibility of healthy forms of sexual expression becomes totally irrelevant. It is this overarching assumption that constitutes the major flaw in the WAS position. Actually, the patriarchy is contested on a daily basis. While strikes or worker slowdowns are several very effective tactics used to bring management to the bargaining table, with sex resistance as a parallel, struggling for creative alternatives is at least of equal importance. This effort can take place as an ongoing dialogue among feminists, as we implement, critique, and restructure our sexual practice.

In incest we learn not to trust, because our trust has been violated. We also may learn to dissociate our bodily experience from sex acts, and to separate sex from any valid experience of love. Similarly, the meaning and practice of sex within patriarchal culture has become identified with subordination. In distrusting our ability to distinguish between desirable and undesirable sex, we are similar to incest survivors, who sometimes suffer from frightening flashbacks in which the past and the present become blurred. However, in therapy, it is possible for incest survivors to differentiate past abuse from present experience, to take control of sexual encounters, and to choose partners with whom they feel safe and honored. These changes are not accomplished by avoiding sex. I am raising the possibility that, even in an imperfect and misogynist society, even in the area of sexuality, healing and growth can occur.

Given that we all exist under patriarchy, it influences us at all levels of our being, including our sexuality. Changing these conditions cannot be accomplished in a vacuum or through withdrawal. We may choose to withdraw from individual relationships that are intrinsically unequal and oppressive, in which sexuality cannot occur without the burden of that inequality. Extrinsic to all sexual relationships is the context of gender inequality, which must be recognized and struggled against as it impinges on the relationship. In some situations it is survival to withdraw. In others, however, it is accepting disenfranchisement and ghettoization not to stand firm and demand change. Demanding change *within* institutions and *within* relationships is a crucial and effective way to push back the boundaries of patriarchy.

There are many other examples of social change implemented successfully on a massive scale. One, assertion training for women, has resulted in a more widespread and public acceptance of assertiveness as a normal and healthy quality for women. This training involves teaching actual skills and, more important, identifying basic rights and fostering a sense of entitlement, a belief in one's basic integrity. Although this change has occurred within a social context of gender inequality in which there are limitations on when and how assertion may be successful, it nevertheless has produced many significant changes in the individual and social behavior of women. We did not have to wait until the revolution to implement such change.

Sex-avoidant behaviors, including feigning or developing illness, changing clothes in the closet, staying up until one's partner is asleep, or making oneself unattractive, are used by women who do not feel they can legitimately decline unwanted sexual contact, or who are punished with physical or verbal abuse when asserting their right to control their bodies. In these cases, sex is not the primary concern in therapy; changing power distribution within the relationship or leaving the relationship if the partner will not change are more important concerns. Some relationships have the potential to recognize and realign unequal power dynamics, and in turn, to help the woman to experience and believe in her own bodily integrity, to discover what gives her pleasure, and to implement this within her relationship. This positive experience has been labeled negatively by WAS as "consensually constructing her desire in [patriarchy's] oppressive image."

WAS denies and/or grossly misrepresents the feminist practice of sex therapy, and has leaped to the conclusion that all sexual self-help books are pornography. This description could as easily apply to several excellent and sensitive books available for women with sexual problems such as *Becoming Orgasmic* (J. Heinman, L. LoPiccolo & J. LoPiccolo, 1976) and *For Yourself* (L. Barbach, 1975). These books encourage, in gradual stages, self-exploration and discovery of what specifically, uniquely is arousing to the individual woman. The exercises which WAS refers to as "scripted" masturbation are actually suggestions to explore the vaginal area visually, with the use of a mirror (something that many women have never done) and tactually, to identify sexually sensitive areas. The ultimate goal of these exercises is to bring the woman's sexual arousal and sexual knowledge under her own control, rather than her partner's. In both books, orgasm during intercourse is not the focus; instead, the emphasis is on discovering alternative pleasuring techniques that are more strongly associated with women's enjoyment of sex. Two more recent books, *The Courage to Heal* (E. Bass & L. Davis, 1988) and *Incest and Sexuality* (W. Maltz & B. Holman, 1987) are books sensitive to feminist issues and invaluable resources for incest survivors in addressing sexual problems, either within or outside the therapeutic context. This type of treatment represents a considerable departure from Freudian psychoanalysis, from the sexual myths of the 1950s, and from patriarchally defined sex in general. While these changes in sexuality are, of course, taking place within a social context of women's inequality, they are part of feminist activism against it. The actual changes feminist sex therapy effects in real women's lives that I have observed in my own clinical practice are welcome and empowering ones.

Whether we uncritically adopt the male-constructed model of sexuality and act on the assumption that all sex is good sex, or take the opposite tack, avoiding sex out of an aversion to the subordination under which we live and its construction as sexuality, we are acting in response to the reality of patriarchy. Other options are possible. Social change does not suddenly emerge from nothingness; it evolves often through a series of social mutations. Some of these mutations are feminist and some are not; we need to foster the feminist elements, and use them, discarding the rest as we redefine our practice of sexuality through analysis, application, and reanalysis. We cannot afford to wait and do not need to wait for the revolution. We have not waited to become assertive, to begin to analyze and change the politics of child-care and housework, and to organize women's groups to challenge and end pornography, battery, and rape. Sheila Jeffreys spoke about sharing sexual fantasies, including disturbing rape fantasies, with other feminists with the goal of examining these fantasies, understanding their origin, and ultimately transcending them. A consciousness-raising format might lend itself well to development of a feminist praxis of sexuality.

My own passionate opposition to pornography and commitment to the antipornography movement is fueled not only by my anger at men's rape, abuse, and sexual subordination of women, and their control of our lives and our sexuality. It is fueled *also* by my hope that women can evolve and develop our own model of sexuality based *not* on a submission/domination dynamic but on a mutual exchange between equals. Both FACT and WAS suffer failure of vision: FACT in its inability to imagine an alternative to patriarchal sex, and WAS in its inability to imagine that creating alternatives is a form of resistance to the patriarchy.

All feminists are "socialization failures." If the patriarchy functioned perfectly, we would not exist with our current consciousness. Somehow, some of us have managed to slip through the cracks and avoid the attempts of the patriarchy to brainwash us completely. Consequently, we have the ability to imagine a different sexuality and to struggle to create it. We must continue to question our assumptions and, through feminist analysis, to detoxify ourselves from a culture that hates women. Through these experiences we are formulating new ways of living and being. Deconstructing patriarchal sexuality and abstaining from patriarchal sex may be a stage in the articulation and creation of a feminist sexuality, in the same way that black separatism and lesbian separatism have helped these movements to define themselves apart from their oppressive context. But we cannot give up on sexuality; we cannot turn away from it as if sexuality itself was a patriarchal abomination.

By turning our backs on our own sexuality, we are admitting defeat to the same degree that we would if we accepted the patriarchy's constructed version of sex. We must sustain a vision of what the erotic can be. By nurturing our sexuality with a critical feminist awareness, we can resist the social structure that would take away this vital part of ourselves.

REFERENCES

Anonymous. (1986, August/September). Understanding rape fantasies. Letter. *Off Our Backs*, 16:8. p. 31.

Barbach, L. (1975). *For yourself: The fulfillment of female sexuality.* New York: Doubleday.

Bass, E. and Davis, L. (1988). *The courage to heal: A guide for women survivors of child sexual abuse.* New York: Harper & Row.

Benjamin, Jessica. (1983). Master and slave: The fantasy of erotic domination. In A. Snitow, C. Stansell & S. Thompson (eds.) *Powers of desire: The politics of sexuality.* New York: Monthly Review Press. pp. 280–299.

Ehrenreich, B., Hess, E., & Jacobs, G. (1987). *Remaking love: The feminization of sex.* Garden City, New York: Anchor Books.

Heinman, J., LoPiccolo, L. and LoPiccolo, J. (1976). *Becoming orgasmic: A sexual and personal growth program for women.* New York: Prentice Hall Press.

James, J. and Meyerding, J. (1977). Early sexual experience as a factor in prostitution. *Archives of Sexual Behavior,* 7:1.

Johnson, A. (1980). On the prevalence of rape in the United States. *Signs,* 6:1. pp. 136–146.

Koss, M., Gidycz, C. & Wisniewski, N. (1987). The scope of rape: Incidence and prevalence of sexual aggression and victimization in a national sample of higher education students. *Journal of Consulting and Clinical Psychology,* 55:2. pp. 162–170.

MacKinnon, Catharine A. (1982). Feminism, Marxism, method, and the state: An agenda for theory. *Signs: Journal of Women in Culture and Society,* 5:3. pp. 515–544.

Maltz, W. and Holman, B. (1987). *Incest and sexuality: A guide to understanding and healing.* Lexington, MA: Lexington Books.

Rubin, Gayle. (1984). Thinking sex: Notes for a radical theory of the politics of sexuality. In Carol Vance (ed.) *Pleasure and danger: Exploring female sexuality.* Boston: Routledge & Kegan Paul. pp. 267–320.

Russell, Diana E. H. (1986). *The secret trauma: Incest in the lives of girls and women.* New York: Basic Books.

Safran, C. (1976, November). What men do to women on the job: A shocking look at sexual harassment. *Redbook,* 148:149. pp. 217–223.

Southern Women's Writing Collective, Women Against Sex. (1987a). Sex resistance in heterosexual arrangements. Paper presented at the New York Conference "Sexual Liberals and the Attack on Feminism."

Southern Women's Writing Collective, Women Against Sex. (1987b). W.A.S. speaks out: Dismantling the practice of sexuality. ASWWC.

Stoller, R. (1979). *Sexual excitement: Dynamics of erotic life*. New York: Simon & Schuster.

Walker, L. (1979). *The battered woman*. New York: Harper & Row.

Willis, Ellen. (1983). Feminism, moralism, and pornography. In A. Snitow, C. Stansell & S. Thompson (eds.) *Powers of desire: The politics of sexuality*. New York: Monthly Review Press. pp. 460–467.

Sexual Liberalism and Survivors of Sexual Abuse*

Valerie Heller

The sexual liberals create myths to disguise and distort the effect of exploitative, abusive behavior on the victims of incest and child sexual abuse. These myths serve to absolve both the society and the abuser from accountability, placing the responsibility for the continued oppression of the victim on the victim herself. These myths distort our perception of reality, so that those being harmed do not know they are being hurt, and those perpetrating the harms do not believe they are hurting others.

As a feminist and as a survivor of incest, which includes child-rape and the making of child pornography, I am naming the criminal acts that liberals distort and deny. Incest and the sexual use of any child by an adult, whether the adult is the parent, the parent figure, or a pedophile, is a crime. The crimes are many in a single act of sexual violation. There are always assault and battery. There are weapons—tangible and intangible. For the child, the intangible weapon is emotional extortion. Another weapon is the threat of death, seldom articulated by the child rapist, yet feared by the victim.

Since 1980, as a leader in the anti-incest movement, and as a therapist working specifically with victims, I have heard the pain of thousands of adult women survivors of incest, of child sexual abuse, and of battering. I've experienced tremendous sadness as I learned of the sexual self-mutilation that some female sex abuse victims ritualize, trying to make it right. This behavior, an actual or symbolic reenactment of what was done to the child victim, is often an abortive attempt to heal the adult. I am infuriated when I think of the thousands of women and children who attempt suicide as the only way to end their sexual abuse.

---

*Dedicated to Linda Marchiano.

Attempting suicide is another way of expressing the hurt that is going on in their lives. The fact is that in most of these cases the victims were either not heard or not believed.

Consider the harms a child sustains during the development of her sexuality when she has been sexually abused. Remember that I am not speaking of a single rape. I am speaking about the hundreds of rapes and sexual violations that many sexually abused children endure while growing up. I am speaking about multiple acts of sexual violation, lasting many years and some of the times involving more than one abuser. I am speaking about a form of social conditioning experienced by 25 percent of all women.

Many women who, like myself, have been repeatedly sexually assaulted, believe that their sexuality has been robbed from them as a result of the sexual abuse. I don't believe that. I think that our sexuality cannot and has not been taken from us. It has without a doubt been thwarted. Sex was one weapon, one of the tools my abusers used against the development of my autonomy. In the past, I measured my self-esteem through my sexual performance, which had nothing to do with my sexuality. My sexual performance had to do with how excited he got, how satisfied he was, how full of lust I appeared to be for him. My sexuality—the inner experience of my sexual energy—is, in actuality, something that I am becoming aware of and experiencing for the first time.

The inability to distinguish between what is abusive and painful and what is desired and pleasurable is central to the self-hate of most adult survivors of childhood sexual abuse. In a conversation I had with a survivor, she said, "Because I didn't like the sexual abuse that was happening to me, I believed I was a prude and uptight. I thought there was something wrong with me because I didn't enjoy the pain during sex." She went on to say,

> When men exposed themselves to me on the street, I thought they couldn't help themselves because I was an attractive women. As a child I had been taught to be attractive and to want to elicit these responses. Eliciting them meant that I was a success as a women. When I was sexually abused as a child, I was taught that the way to become a women was to have sex and therefore as an adult I believed that the better I performed sexually for a man and the more pleasure he got out of it the better a woman I was. It had nothing to do with my pleasure. It had to do with how well I could perform for a man.

Myths are not just untrue facts. They are unproved collective beliefs that are accepted uncritically and used to justify a social institution. The social institution, in this case, is the oppression of women through sexual subordination. This includes the practice of incest and child sex-

ual abuse; pornography, as a reinforcer of the process of dehumaniza-
tion; prostitution; and wife battery.

The myths I speak about are believed by abused and nonabused
alike. It was painful for me, a woman who has experienced much sexual abuse, to realize that I have accepted these lies. I understand now
that this acceptance helped me to defend myself emotionally against
the painful reality I was living. It probably also kept me alive. When I
was very young, I learned to distort my perceptions to accommodate
the myths about what I was supposed to be as a girl and woman. I
have no doubt that if I had taken in the reality of my childlife, I would
have risked insanity. The question is why those who were not abused
believe and perpetuate these myths.

One answer may be another myth specifically designed to invalidate
the realities of the adult survivors of child sexual abuse. The myth is
that adults who were sexually abused see sexual abuse everywhere.
Therefore when victims and survivors say no to the sexual abuse of
themselves or others, the response they receive is that they are just
"too sensitive" because of what happened to them. They are just imagining it. The result is that the survivor's no is not respected; abusive
situations are dismissed as innocuous; and the survivor's reality is seen
as fantasy. The truth is not that sexual abuse survivors are "too sensitive." It simply is that we know what abuse looks like, what it feels
like, and what effect it will have on the abused.

Another myth is that some women need pain in order to feel during
sex. This is translated, mostly by men, into "she likes it, she wants it,
she needs it." This is said, like a mantra, to excuse the abuser's behavior: it is acceptable to inflict pain when the pain is seen as wanted.
Which means that no one has to acknowledge that a woman or child
is being abused or snuffed out. The rational question to ask is—who
likes to be repeatedly beaten, raped, cut up, drugged, or starved? The
answer is no one, no animal or human. Yet there exist those who believe we like it, we want it, we need it.

When this myth is internalized by survivors, the end result is women
who make statements like, "It's healing for us to act out our child sexual abuse experiences in adulthood through sadomasochism." I totally
disagree. Acting out sadomasochism reinforces the survivor's conditioning of self-hate; that is all that it does. Sadomasochism is nothing
less than assault and battery. Healing begins with the accurate identification of that abuse.

The belief that females exist to be unconditionally sexually available
to males is central to the perpetuation of child sexual abuse. Abusers
rationalize their behavior by believing that the child is their sexual
property; foster fathers believe the abused child is damaged sexual goods

and can therefore be abused again. Some adult survivors of incest and child sexual abuse internalize this myth. As if on automatic, these women act as though the protocol for any interpersonal interaction requires sex, which they will obsessively pursue if others do not initiate it.

Another liberal myth is that the victim of sexual abuse really wants it because she just lies there and takes it. This is a justification of the condition of the sexually abused child, who is taught to lie still and take it. In adulthood, this myth reinforces learned patterns of submission: survivors think they can't say no to the sexual needs or advances of a person they think they like or care about. To say no means not being believed, facing the devastating fear of annihilation and rejection by another person. To say no requires that the survivor have confidence in what she perceives reality to be and what she knows her needs to be.

As adults, some survivors think that they are resisting abuse by lying still and taking it; it isn't true. The internalization of this myth in sexually abused adult women is demonstrated by the masochist who contends that the "bottoms" have power and the prostitute who believes that she has control over her tricks. These women are not resisting; instead, their conditioning of abuse is being reinforced. The fears and feelings from childhood are being reactivated. Our oppression continues each time we lie still and take it.

The traditional myth applied specifically to survivors is that they abstain from sexual interaction because there is something wrong with them. The truth is that for some survivors, abstaining from sex is part of the recovery process. The decision to abstain is not usually a deliberate one; the survivor does not one day sit down and decide no longer to be sexually active. Instead, it is an intrapsychic decision that emerges from the survivor's realization that as a child, she or he was sexually violated. This often sudden awareness and acceptance of the truth jolts the survivor's reality. To be sexual at that time could activate deep conflicting feelings, disturbing memories, and fears. The adult may reexperience the earlier trauma in the form of flashbacks, with periods of confusion, and sometimes in regressed states. At the time of self-disclosure, a great amount of working through must occur. It is appropriate for survivors to abstain, for the period of time they choose, as part of their healing. Remember that some survivors have been "on call" to service someone sexually ever since they were little children. To abstain from sexual activity may be the first time in a survivor's life that she is able to explore her own sexuality.

This last myth pertains only to survivors. Some of the time we believe that by experiencing the intensity of our sexual energy, in the present day, it will destroy us. That it will make us disappear. This is something that we had a tremendous fear of as sexually abused children. The heightened states of arousal, foreign to a child's body and mind, the terror, the indescribable pain, and the absolute devastation at our abandonment by adults we loved and trusted are all attached to our experience of our sexuality. In adulthood as we experience our sexual energy, and when the intensity increases during arousal, many of us leave our bodies, just as we did when we were children.

To stay as the adults that we are in the present during sexual arousal and orgasm means for many of us to experience our sexuality for the first time. We begin to take control of our sexuality, choosing when to continue sexual stimulation and when to end it. We separate ourselves from the pattern of harmful sexual experiences from childhood. We learn to associate our adult sexual experiences with self-empowerment and autonomy. We tell the truth about our experience—first to ourselves, then to others. Each step of the way we are replenished with renewed strength. When we challenge all the myths—those we have internalized, those that have been imposed on us—we begin to free ourselves from the prison our sexual abuse constructed for us and reclaim our sexuality.

Part V

THE MALE
BACKLASH

The Many Faces of Backlash

Florence Rush

Suffer women once to arrive at equality with you, and they will at that moment become your superiors.

Cato, Roman Statesman, 195 B.C.

The second wave of the women's liberation movement was born a brief twenty-two years ago. A large segment of this movement was generated by left-wing women who painfully discovered that their male comrades dismissed their struggle as trivial compared to the "larger issues" of classism, racism, capitalism, and imperialism. The male mentality could not, or would not, grasp the premise that women, as a sex, suffered from discrimination, rape, and battering, whether located in the gilded cages of suburbia or the slums of the inner city. After many bitter confrontations, these women came to understand that men, whether Marxists or reactionary warmongers, were equally reluctant to forego their male prerogatives. So they struck out for themselves, and created the radical arm of the women's liberation movement.

When the sit-ins, street theater, antiwar demonstrations, and student rebellions dissipated in a conservative climate no longer conducive to their protests, the revolutionaries of the 1960s and early 1970s exchanged Karl Marx, Mao, and Che Guevera for the teachings of Eastern gurus, Werner Ehrhart (EST founder), the American Civil Liberties Union, and the Human Potential Movement. They moved from collective freedom to freedom of the spirit, from group action to self-assertiveness, from the rights of the oppressed to the individual right of Nazis and pornographers, and from radical change to superficial reform. The radicals of the 1960s became the liberals of the 1970s and 1980s and in the process undermined the work of the women's movement.

For a while "women's liberation" was a household word and it was no longer fashionable to belittle its impact. The simultaneous emergence of the "sexual revolution," however, became a convenient, though erroneous, synonym for "feminist revolution." It offered some free thinkers the comfortable illusion of tolerating feminism without depriving men of their legacy of sexual privilege. They could support issues favoring birth control and abortion; these issues eased sexual access to women without the responsibility for unwanted pregnancy. They could, with good conscience, enjoy *Playboy* and *Penthouse* as women-loving feminist publications and still retain the identification of women as sexually available playthings. Others, who wanted in on the then-exciting attention-getting women's movement, adapted the principles of feminism to a masculine cause. The "feminine mystique" was replicated by the "masculine mystique"; women as "sex objects" were matched by men as "achiever objects," and the stifling sex roles which socialized women to be passive and dependent were equated with stifling sex roles which conditioned men to be brave, strong, domineering, and independent. Just as women sought to free themselves from the constraints of sex roles, so men wanted to break the bonds of machismo (Joseph Pleck and Jack Sawyer, 1974). From the rib of the women's liberation movement, the men's liberation movement was born.

Men's meetings and consciousness-raising groups were organized. Books and articles appeared announcing that men's emotional lives were stunted. Being a master was a burden. Men no longer wanted the strain of competition or of living up to a masculine image of strength, success, and sexual performance. Warren Farrell, prime organizer and founder of this movement, said in his book *The Liberated Man:* "This is the only revolution (women's) in which the alleged oppressed is in love with and sharing children with the oppressor. . . . Therefore this makes it possible for the growth of one person to benefit from the growth of the other" (Warren Farrell, 1975: p. 5). This struck a chord in many women. He offered the possibility that these newly sensitive men understood the plight of women and wanted to change and grow by embracing and integrating the precepts of feminism.

On the surface, the pleas of the men's liberationists were very appealing; but closer examination and personal experience revealed a self-serving program and a disarming strategy to defuse the threat to male hegemony posed by our movement. Male liberationists overlooked the fact that, no matter how much women tried, their association with "feminist" men was opportunistically exploited in the work place, the home, the family, and in bed. This oversight was the logical consequence of misinterpreting female emancipation as a boon to men. The financially independent woman, Farrell claimed, will share the breadwinning burden, will no longer use men as "security objects," and will give men more time to spend with the children. The woman in control of her life will not feel the need to control her husband and, in case of divorce, will relieve him of alimony and child support. And, most important, since men traditionally make "the pass" and expose their "fragile egos" to the "emotional hurt" of refusal, the sexually free women will do the asking and men will have the opportunity to do the rejecting. But, Farrell warned, "Men cannot be expected to participate in these changes unless women's liberation is redefined as a two-sex movement which provides enough benefits for men to make the change worthwhile" (Warren Farrell, 1975: p. 161).

What changes is Farrell talking about? Farrell and his followers managed not to notice that working women have always shared the breadwinning burden and, in today's standard two-income home, they do so more than ever. They ignored the fact that men have always availed themselves of women's income and labor as much for their own security as the reverse; that men have always had the greater need to exercise control over either financially dependent or independent women; that they rarely use leisure time with children, rarely meet alimony and child-support obligations and that men, traditionally in the driver's seat, more often than not humiliate and reject women sexually and otherwise. Farrell's platform for a two-sex movement was carried a step further by the Berkeley Men's Center Manifesto. It proposed that "human liberation" is the only ultimate goal because "all liberation movements are equally important; there is no hierarchy in oppression" (Joseph Pleck & Jack Sawyer, 1974: p. 174). Clearly, these men had not the slightest understanding of what the women's movement was all about. Had they bothered to learn, they might know that movement women never sought to entice men with rewards nor make compromises in exchange for their support. Had they bothered to investigate sexist history, they might know that, vis-a-vis men and women, there has always existed a hierarchy of oppression, that even the most subjugated and enslaved men have always kept women in a state of subordination.

The concept of male liberation has no basis in history because men, as a sex, were never oppressed within age-old established patriarchal ideology, which still controls our social structure and its institutions. Consequently, male liberationists invented their own agenda, which would allow them to continue to enjoy their existing advantages at the expense of women's existing disadvantages. And their goals for human liberation—more cooptation than a mutually beneficial alliance—could only dull the sharp edges of sexist politics to nonthreatening ineffectiveness. Their platform merely reinforced the entrenched sexist status quo. And when women would not buy their proposals, would not accept them as our benefactors nor allow them to piggy-back off our movement, male liberationists did not retreat graciously; they became angrier and nastier.

BACKLASH: REVERSE SEXISM

In his zeal for male/female unity, Warren Farrell became an active member of the National Organization for Women and was three times on the board of NOW–NYC. But the seeds of his resentment and forthcoming backlash had already been planted. As he meandered through the women's movement he found that

> consciousness raising takes women out of the security of subservience before it offers the security of the self. It creates a vacuum of insecurity. It is during this period of insecurity that I have felt that some women do try to downgrade men even beyond the point where it appears justified . . . and by doing so they are building themselves up. (Warren Farrell, 1975: p. 223)

It should come as no surprise that when Farrell's efforts failed, when women were not impressed by the feeble attempts by "sensitive" men at emotional expression or communication, or when they did not burst into grateful applause each time daddy made a bed or changed a diaper, Farrell concluded that movement women "downgrade" men and are motivated by superiority rather than equality.

I have not read Farrell's last book, *Why Men Are The Way They Are,* but his recent article "Gender: A Noted Author Warns of Reverse Sexism" sufficiently summarizes his position. "Why is it," he asks, "that the more independent-oriented the women's magazine, the greater the attack on men?" With the film *Fatal Attraction,* he finds

> millions of women identifying with Glen Close's attempt to murder the man who would not leave his family for her once she had sex with him: the same "Death Wish" that makes millions of movie goers cheer as Charles Bronson killed his muggers. . . . The "new sexism" is the new death wish. (Warren Farrell, 1987)

Farrell reiterates his concern for "emotionally hurt" men and adds that sexual rejection compels them "to turn women into sex-objects," hence to pornography, which "offers men access to women without rejection." He also joined the countless attacks on Shere Hite's *Women and Love,* a book which identifies women's general dissatisfaction with the men in their lives, because it presents "no category for female abuse of men." In short, it is unyielding women who harbor a death wish toward men, force them to turn to pornography, downgrade them in their publications, and refuse to recognize that women abuse men, who are guilty of reverse sexism.

Farrell's discovery of the "new sexism" falls neatly in step with broader antiwomen attacks by the mushrooming "men's rights" groups. Sidney Siller, organizer of the National Organization for Men, publishes his brand of reverse sexism each month in his *Penthouse* "Men's Rights" column. He finds discrimination against men in matrimonial and child custody disputes. He insists that men are victims of false accusations by disgruntled, angry women in cases of sexual harassment, rape, and child molestation, and that women's struggle for pay equity and their programs for affirmative action deprive men of employment and their livelihoods. Reverse sexism has come to mean that not only individual women, but also our institutions, our justice system, and our limited hard-won legislation to protect women's civil rights, discriminate against and oppress men. The Farrells and the Sillers are now frequently exhibited in the print and electronic media and their misogynist reverse sexism is presented as a legitimate, bona fide protest.[1]

BACKLASH: GENDER-NEUTRAL

About two years ago I was notified of the formation of a committee of male rape survivors. Its purpose was to raise public awareness of the problems of the rape of males which, the notice said, is far more common than people realize, citing statistics which indicated that a quarter or more of all rape victims in New York City are males. The committee hoped it would not be dominated by one gender. This appeared to be an invitation for women to join because the problem of rape is a concern for both men and women. The stated goal of the committee is to work for "gender-neutral" assault statutes.

Was this group simply looking for equal protection under the law or was it telling us that male rape is not an issue of sexism because women also rape men? We know and they know, of course, that it is gay and heterosexual men, not women, who rape men. This fact, however, does not make male rape gender-neutral. Men rape other men because they feminize their victims within heterosexual patterns of dominance and

---

[1] I do not wish to include Men Against Pornography or Northeast Men's Emerging Network (NEMEN) in the Farrell category. These groups, and perhaps others, support and contribute to women's efforts and try to solve their own problems without looking for benefits or compromises.

subordination. When men treat other men as women, humiliate and shame them in the same way, then male rape is indeed rooted in sexism. If gay men could understand this, they would certainly have a commonality with feminists; but since so many choose the heterosexual formula as their preference for sexual expression, their problem is hardly gender-neutral. Gender neutrality is rooted in the idea that both genders, male and female, are equally oppressed and that any attempt to hold men and male institutions accountable for transgressions against women is no longer fashionable nor acceptable.

This concept has become a useful tool in an attempt to establish that women are as guilty as men for the offenses attributed to them. Professionals and experts tell us that women are also rapists and child molesters, that women batter and sexually harass men and are also the producers and consumers of pornography. And just as men sexually objectify women, so women have their male strippers, *Playgirl* (in reality, enjoyed mostly by gay men), and their beefcakes and hunks. And if one should conclude that it is only women who are trapped by an obsession with youth, well, damn it, men are also getting face lifts and tummy tucks, using anti-aging formulas and cosmetics, going on diets, and becoming anorexic.

True, some small percentage of women sexually abuse children and sexually harass men, but I can safely assure you that if women were the rapists, child molesters, and sexual harassers, the problem of sexual assault would barely exist. If women were the only producers and consumers of pornography, the industry would go bankrupt. And if men were the only sex supporting cosmetic surgeons and the cosmetic industry both would go out of business. As for the occasional new terminology "beefcake" and "hunk," the definition of women as "cunt," "piece of ass," and "whore" has existed within our culture from Biblical times to this very day. The current Webster's *Collegiate Thesaurus* still defines "man" as human, husband, lover, and master whereas "woman" is wife, ball-and-chain, doxy, mistress, and paramour. The continued treatment of women as inferior sex-objects is not gender-neutral.

BACKLASH:
THE POSTFEMINIST ERA

The myth that in this postfeminist era women have achieved their desired goals has gained credibility with the public. Women, we are told, now compete with men on equal terms for status, power, and material rewards, and the previous conditions which suppressed their full human development no longer prevail. I will not bother to list the prevailing conditions which remain as obstacles to women's equal status with men and continue to suppress women's full development. We can, however, surmise that if women have not availed themselves of the options and opportunities now open to them, it's their own fault. This assumption has become the theme of pop psychology, talk show experts, the human potential movement, programs for individual and group therapy, and "how-to" self-improvement books written by and for women.

These widely publicized and promoted how-to books are blockbuster best sellers. Under the guise of advancing female autonomy, they fall into the "it's your fault" category and succeed in convincing us of women's insufficiency. The authors identify themselves as feminists and sister sufferers who discovered that, with the "marriage crunch," the essential root of women's discontent is their inability to get and hold a man. While it is true, they say, that our male chauvinist culture has produced some very difficult men, an emotionally healthy woman can make adjustments within the parameters of the established male standard. Any attempt to relieve her distress by external or social remedies is futile. Her only answer is to dig out and discard neurotic self-destructive tendencies.

The women who write these books are usually therapists who shrink the larger problems of male chauvinism to a more manageable size that can fit the already self-doubting female psyche. In my neighborhood bookstore, I found endless volumes telling women what is wrong with them and how to overcome the emotional disorders that prevent them from getting and keeping a mate. During this past decade *The Cinderella Complex* gave us the phobic female whose fear of independence puts men off because she is too needy and dependent. *Too Smart for Her Own Good* prefers the overly independent career type who, afflicted with delusions of superiority, is just too picky and fussy to find a suitable man, while *Women who Love Too Much* offers the love-addicted variety who masochistically entangle themselves with abusive males. These, plus their numerous counterparts, such as *Men who Hate Women and the Women Who Love Them*, *How to Have an Affair with Your Husband (Before Someone Else Does)*, *How to Marry the Man of Your Choice*, *Women Men Love/Women Men Leave*, ignore the fact that the essential problem facing women today is not the lack of a male partner but the persistent and prevailing social system which relegates the uncoupled female to poverty and stigmatizes her as a social and economic liability. Columnist Ellen Goodman appropriately said:

I worry about the mental "help" professionals who take every public problem and wash it into a private one. I worry, too, about lay people who spin-dry each social illness until it looks like an emotional disease. I worry about the rest of us who wring every fear into a phobia. (Ellen Goodman, 1981: p. 13)

The most recent within this genre is Dr. Toni Grant's *Being a Woman*, subtitled "Fulfilling Your Femininity and Finding Love." Dr. Grant, a clinical psychologist and adviser on her nationally syndicated radio talk show, "The Toni Grant Program," moves the source of the problem from the female psyche directly to the damaging influence of the women's movement—or, as she puts it, "the big lies of women's liberation." What are these big lies? They are the notions that women professionals can "have it all," that "accomplishment and education" are advantages, and there is merit in the "grandiose" idea of women's "unrealized potential." In the world according to Grant, these myths have produced misguided Amazons who delight in man bashing and dominating men. Women's strength, she goes on, must be tempered with qualities attributed to the mother, madonna, and courtesan archetypes. Mother is for caring and nurturing, madonna is for virtue and morality, and courtesan is for sexual allure. She advises that "the integrated women must assimilate all these aspects of womanhood into her personality to experience herself as a full woman" (Toni Grant, 1988). Men, however, who are just fine the way they are, are exempt from any responsibility in their relationships with women. It strikes me that any woman who accepts this double standard and attempts to assimilate these impossibly contradictory aspects, would wind up a tragically unbalanced, splintered, fractured, schizophrenic personality. The previously mentioned how-to, self-improvement books progressed from keeping women "barefoot and pregnant" to keeping them "neurotic and miserable." But Toni Grant's *Being a Woman* (1988) is the most virulent, in its attempt to return us to the dark ages of submission and acceptance of our socially imposed inferiority.

BACKLASH: A REACTION TO STRENGTH AND DETERMINATION

Retaliation from right-wing elements against the women's movement is neither sudden nor surprising. It is an extension of the traditional designation of women as inferiors; it is the result of the continued assertion that subordination, ordained by God and biology, is women's destiny. It is straightforward, unabashed misogyny; it is obvious, to be expected, and we can challenge it. The reaction by liberals, who come as friends offering support, is deceptive and far more insidious, and has taken an enormous toll. Many women find it hard to resist the promise of a caring, equal relationship with a sympathetic man. Others have been moved by the possibility that men also suffer from their brand of sex-role conditioning, and some have come to believe that males and females offend and are victimized equally. The myth of equal opportunity in this so-called postfeminist era is particularly harmful to younger women who, led to believe that they have been born into a free society, blame themselves for what they must endure in this real, sex-biased world. In addition, each day we are inundated with media messages from talk-show experts, news reporters, advertisers, pop psychologists, and sociologists; all write us off as a passing trend. Yet we exist and we persist.

Throughout the cities of this country, pockets of feminist activity can be found in centers for victims of rape, incest, child sexual abuse, and family violence. Women are organized to deal with birth control, abortion, teen-age pregnancy, child care, sex education, pornography, the media, legislation, women's poverty, and women's health. They fight discrimination against lesbians and women athletes; they fight in the work place, in the courts, in prisons, in schools and in universities. Just because the media have chosen to promote the liberal backlash does not mean that we are defeated; just because they choose to ignore feminist activism does not mean that we have been erased. We need to explain this backlash in terms of its defensive reaction against women's strength and determination. A more positive definition is needed to validate our undefeated existence.

According to *Roget's Thesaurus*, the synonyms for backlash are "counteraction" and "recoil." Some alternative usages for counteraction are opposing causes, action and reaction, antipathy, antagonism, defense, neutralizing, cancelling out, repression, and suppression. Synonyms for recoil are to spring back in revulsion, shrink, and flinch, but also listed are backlash and retaliate (Robert Dutch, 1962). Funk and Wagnall's *Modern Guide to Synonyms* tells us that recoil can imply "the subject has gone along with a situation as long as possible but stops short, calling a halt out of . . . anger" (S. Hayakawa, 1968: p. 152). Yes: The subject (the liberals) have gone along with the situation (the women's movement) but stopped short in anger when staunch women did not comply with the subject's (the liberals') program to render us ineffective. The *Random House Dictionary of English Language* says that recoil can mean "to fly back as a consequence of force and impact" (Jess Stern and Lawrence Urdang, 1973). Yes. Uncompromised women have triggered the lashing out against the steadfast force and impact of the women's movement. Why not then select a combination of these usages to formulate our own definition? For example: (a) Liberal backlash: The hostile counteraction resulting from frustrated liberal attempts to neutralize the force and impact of a particular radical group or movement. (b) Reaction: behavior of male liberationists who balk and become openly antagonistic when female liberationists reject them as allies. (c) Action: Acrimonious backlash against the women's movement resulting from failed attempts by progressives to neutralize women's demands for radical change.

The survival of women's movements is founded on periodic revolts by women over the centuries. Their persistent demand for liberation has given us a history, an identity as full human beings, and hope for a nonbiased future. Our history, identity, and hope consolidate us as an ongoing force. The many faces of backlash substantiate the truth that feminism is not dead, cannot be ignored, is effective, has a steady impact, and that, one way or another, it will win.

REFERENCES

Dutch, Robert A., ed. (1962). *Roget's thesaurus,* Rev. ed. New York: St. Martin's Press.

Farrell, Warren. (1975). *The liberated man.* New York: Bantam Books.

Farrell, Warren. "Gender." *Los Angeles Times.* (November, 1987).

Goodman, Ellen, (1981). *At large.* New York: Fawcett Crest.

Grant, Toni. (1988). *Being a woman.* New York: Random House.

Hayakawa, S. (1968). *Modern guide to synonyms.* New York: Funk and Wagnall.

Pleck, Joseph H. and Jack Sawyer, eds. (1974). *Men and masculinity.* Englewood Cliffs, New Jersey: Prentice-Hall.

Stern, Jess and Lawrence Urdang, eds. (1973). *The Random House dictionary of English language.* New York: Random House.

Liberals, Libertarianism, and the Liberal Arts Establishment

Susanne Kappeler

There has been a very interesting shift in the use of the words *liberal* and *libertarian* in recent sexual politics. In my experience, a shift in the usage of words, names, and labels is never insignificant. I consider it significant, for instance, that in public usage and in the media, our movement has become the *women's movement* or *feminism*, where we originally called it the women's liberation movement. And this change in name has accompanied an attempt to obliterate the political aims of the WLM, namely the liberation of women from oppression, so that now the terms *woman* and *feminist* have apparently become interchangeable and have replaced the term *women's libber*.

While the terms *liberal*, *libertarian* and *libertine* all have something to do with *liberty*, they have acquired different connotations and of course have different histories. While a libertine was originally a free thinker on religion, the so-called free thinking of the Marquis de Sade has given the word a new meaning, which the *Oxford English Dictionary* (OED) lists as *licentious (man)*. Similarly, the term libertarian, defined by the *Oxford English Dictionary* as a "believer . . . in free will (opp. *necessitarian*); advocate of liberty," has acquired the taint of a somewhat excessive demand for liberty, which might account for the change in contemporary sexual politics from sexual *libertarian* to sexual *liberal:* signaling a more moderate and measured commitment to liberty. By contrast, the term *liberal* still has a pretty nice ring about it, of generosity (as in a liberal dose of brandy), of open-mindedness, absence of prejudice, and devotion to democratic reforms. Few remember the meaning which my *OED* lists as the *first and original* sense of liberal: "fit for a gentleman." It adds that this use is now rare, *except* in liberal education—

which thus means an education fit for gentlemen, further specified as "directed to general enlargement of mind, *not professional or technical,*" and also *"not rigorous or literal"* (my emphases).

In radical political culture, liberal—or usually "wishy-washy liberalism"—has the negative connotation of lack of rigor and sitting on the metaphorical fence made famous by liberal intellectuals and politicians. As feminists, we would do well to remember and highlight the fact that the history of liberalism, of libertarianism, and libertinism has been a history of gentlemen advocating liberty and license for gentlemen—liberties to which the rights and liberty of women have habitually and routinely been sacrificed. As with anything else in the history of men and ideas, liberalism contains and hides an issue of sexual politics.

But there is more to political liberalism that concerns us as feminists than the licentiousness of libertinism. Traditionally, political liberalism has seen itself as defending the interests of "the individual" as against the state. As such, it is a profoundly masculinist, oedipal conception, at the heart of western thinking, which structures the self in opposition to a greater authority: the self, like Oedipus, faced not only by the power of his father, the king, but also by the absolute power of the gods who have determined his fate in advance, who have organized the cosmos and history. It is a perfect image (as Freud found) for the self-conception of a child under the authority and at the mercy of parents and a powerful patriarchal father, a conception in which the parental adult is seen to hold not only the power of restriction, but also of fulfillment. It is, in other words, a perfect symbol for the state of a human infant not yet fully socialized, who has not yet matured toward an understanding and an acceptance of the fact that there is a *reality* (rather than a caretaker) which sets boundaries for his infantile egotism, gratification, and fantasy. It is a conception developed under the rule of the pleasure principle and with an insufficient grasp of the meaning of the reality principle, which the male infant, as Freud has demonstrated, confuses with the gendered power of the father from the perspective of an infantile castration anxiety. What Freud has not sufficiently analyzed are the consequences of this failure to deconstruct the fantasy of the all-powerful father, especially the consequence so crucial, for women, of the male infant's realization that as a male, he will himself grow into such absolute power.

Male political theory bears strong traces of this memory of the (male) child-father relationship, the oedipal connection: on the one hand, conservatism or right-wing philosophy assumes the paternalistic role of the "fathers of the nation" who arrogate to themselves the responsibility for their "children," the people they mean to govern. On the other, liberalism defends the interest, as it were, of those children of the nation, on the model of the adolescent boy who attempts to free himself from parental control and to reduce that authority in favor of increased personal liberty and self-determination. Both political philosophies accept the parent-child relationship as an appropriate model for the relationship of the individual to society and government.

In the context of the so-called sexual liberals, or sexual libertarians, we have the same schema of the individual claiming greater personal liberty from a repressive social, moral, or legal authority. In the 1960s, this was conceived of simply in (male) heterosexual terms, as a greater *permissiveness* in response to a past of moral and religious constraint. In the 1980s in Britain, the spokes*men* for sexual liberty are most predominantly theoreticians of gay (male) sexuality, who plead for a greater tolerance of minority forms of sexual practice and orientation. What is significant is that both share a common concept of a social authority from which permission is sought and tolerance asked. In the very act of demanding or asking for greater personal (sexual) liberty, that authority is being acknowledged and thereby validated. This might of course be seen as simply a feature of *realpolitik,* i.e., recognition of the reality of state power over sexuality in a campaign for a change in legislation (e.g., the decriminalization of male homosexuality; reduction of the age of consent for male homosexuals). However, I am concerned with a theoretical discourse on sexuality whose polemic is directed not so much against state and legislation, as against conventional sexual morality and increasingly—as this conference highlights—against feminist politics and its critique of male sexuality. In this discourse, which relies heavily on Foucault, the concept of *transgression* is central to the theorization of desire and pleasure, as central as "taboo" has been (and still is) for the sexual libertarians of the 1960s: a reflection of the concern with authority and law, and the adolescent or oedipal desire to rebel against the former and break the latter.

Feminist political theory constitutes a radical intervention in the male conceptions of the political, based as it is on the fundamental principle that the personal is political and, in contrast to the conventional political, that it is the interpersonal, not just the relationship of the individual to the state, which constitutes the domain of the political. The concept of sexual politics encapsulates this, and is made explicit in Andrea Dworkin's formulation that

> intercourse both presumes and requires *a society of at least two persons* before it can occur at all; and the state is concerned about the nature of that society—how it is constructed, that it be hierarchical, that it be male-dominant. (Andrea Dworkin, 1987: p. 148) (my emphasis)

From the point of view of feminist politics, the relationship between women and men, and that between women and the state are part of a common framework of patriarchal politics, where any question of the "individual," if she is a woman, is mediated by her gender relationship to men, and where the relationship of the state to women expresses the collective interests of men. While for the "individual" man there is, on the one hand, a relationship to the state which is· public and social, and on the other, a relationship to women which is considered part of his privacy, feminist politics, based on the experience and viewpoint of women, recognizes that a relationship of two is a "society," is public, and is regulated by the state: not as an exempt sphere of personal liberty, but as a political structuring of the personal.

But the recognition by feminist theory that the personal is political also brings concepts of (social) responsibility to the person, who is thought of as a fully emancipated, socialized, and adult member of a society of equals. The boundaries to personal liberty are seen to derive from an equal interest on the part of the individual in the existence of that society as in her own existence as an individual person. Male liberalism, by contrast, sees every other as a member of that abstract society which is intent on curbing the liberty or license of the (male) individual; in other words, it perceives every other as a potential enemy. Underlying feminism is a fundamental wish to live *in* society (not despite, against, or in competition with it), to live life as a member of a human collectivity and to maximize the mutual benefits of community, friendship, and relationship, of work, cooperation, and communication, to gain and contribute by sharing, rather than to accumulate privately by taking what you can from others, i.e., publicly.

The fundamental misconception at the heart of sexual liberalism is of course the "sexual" construed as a dimension of the individual: the individual wanting more sexual freedom, or more freedom of expression. There is no space in this conception for the sexual other, the sexual partner or, as it is usually put in libertarian discourse, the sexual object. The freedom which is being demanded from the paternal state or social authority is in fact the license to continue to regard the other *as* sexual object, vehicle for the individual's sexual pleasure, and not to have to recognize that other as also an individual subject. Although questions of sexual consent—i.e., the consent of the other—are increasingly having to be muted due to the technical, legal emancipation of black people from slavery, of women from male custody, of peoples from colonial subjugation, conceptually the emancipation of the other has not yet impinged on the ideological structures of western thought, structures shaped by slavemasters, custodians of women, and colonial imperialists.

The sexual, or sexuality, continues to be constructed as pertaining to the individual—sexuality rather than sexual relations or sexual politics—and the theories of contemporary sexual libertarians in Britain are significantly formulated around "object-choice." In a contribution to a volume on *Sexual Difference,* significantly titled "The Banality of Gender," Simon Watney directly argues for a redefinition of the concept of sexual difference as no longer signifying the male/female difference, but a difference in *masculine* sexuality predicated on object-choice. He dismisses a notion of sexual difference which "involves a taken-for-granted distinction between male and female" in favor of "the other major axis of sexual difference—that which Freud explores in the name of the object-choice, and to which Foucault gives the word "sexuality" (Simon Watney, 1986: p. 14). In a nutshell, we can see the significance of the recent shift in British usage which has tended to replace "gender" with "sexual difference" (e.g., what used to be "race, class, and gender" has become "race, class, and sexual difference"). The sexual politics of gender gives way to a politics of sex around object-choice; the sexual difference at the root of gender gives way to a difference in the sexuality of the male gender; and the oppression of women, central to the analysis of gender, is replaced by what in Watney's view is the "actual sexual oppression," namely gay oppression (Simon Watney, 1986: p. 16).

Watney is too preoccupied with "a given individual's identification," "the issue of desire" (Simon Watney, 1986: p. 15) and a "theory of sexual pleasure" to be bothered either with a concept of class or one of gender, both of which share, in his view, "the same sense of a single all-determining factor." (Simon Watney, 1986: p. 17) Or, as we might note, both describe collectivities or factors of collectivity rather than a "given individual," social groups in relations of power and struggle with other social groups rather than an individual subject in relation with a personal "object-choice."

What masquerades as a (male) challenge to compulsory heterosexuality is in fact a demand for increased choice on the part of the sexual subject, the individual, the gentleman, choice from a wider range of desirable objects: not just women-objects, but also men-objects, and children-objects. Along with the liberal sexual consumerism of object-choice comes a wider choice also of sexual practice: sadistic, masochistic, fetishistic; a wider choice of forms of relationships than the heterosexual model of monogamy: bath houses, international sex tourism, and prostitution (with a variety of object-choices), and entertainment sex or pornography, also in all variants of object-choice: heterosexual, homosexual, lesbian; with the mainly heterosexual sub-genres of child, disabled, pregnant, old age pornography that are already on the shelves

(Harold Offerdal, 1986; Mazer Mahmood, 1986). And along with all this comes a liberal invitation to all, including women, children and minorities, to share this sexual feast, to become sexual consumers — at least in (the) theory.

In practice, this liberal generosity, this open-minded and unprejudiced democratic reform to extend what is fit for a gentleman to commoners and women and blacks, is liberal in a different sense, too: not rigorous or literal. For this pleasure so rigorously structured around object-choice, where the chosen object is a demoted subject, could not exist in a democracy of equals where everyone was fit to be a subject and consumer: there would be no one left to be chosen and consumed as object.

What enables this discourse around object-choice and desire is far more than gay liberation politics. It is the orthodox structures of western patriarchal thinking, centered around the individual and *his* freedom. The same structure is visible in our economic and cultural entrepreneurism and consumerism, and of course in what is so appropriately called the "liberal arts." It is the arts establishment which conducts the most vigorous defense of a "principle" of freedom of expression which gives license to the enormous industry of culture and pornography, without ever so much as referring to the *industrialized and commercial* form of the expression which it defends. Freedom of expression, like all the human rights formulated by nations and united nations, concerns the rights of the (male) individual vis-a-vis the state and safeguards against the state's encroachment upon individual personal freedom. It does not, as women the world over know, safeguard the rights of the individual against the individual. And while the latter is protected by the law of the nation in the case of men, the law, as we have seen, also regulates the "rights" of men to "privacy," i.e., to women, and thus encroaches directly on the freedom and rights of women themselves (Andrea Dworkin, 1987; Catharine MacKinnon, 1983).

The freedom of expression defended by the arts establishment, by FACT, and by other defenders of pornography is the freedom to produce and market "expression" industrially and commercially, not the right of the individual to hold and express views and opinions and to seek information. Indeed, the capitalist production of "expression" can be said to militate directly against the individual's right to express and seek to obtain a diversity of information and opinion. In Britain at this moment, the government itself is launching an attack on the freedom of expression and access to information, by a proposed clause, Clause 28, which would prohibit local government from

(a) promot[ing] homosexuality or publish[ing] material for the promotion of homosexuality;
(b) promot[ing] the teaching in any maintained school of the acceptability

of homosexuality as a pretended family relationship by the publication of
such material or otherwise;
(c) giv[ing] financial or other assistance to any person for either of the
purposes referred to in paragraphs (a) or (b).[1]

What is interesting in this context is that the government proposes no
interference in the promotion of homosexuality, be it as a pretended
family relationship or a superior object-choice, much less the promotion of (male) heterosexual hatred, the acceptability of violence against
women, and the pretended pleasure of women in that violence, where
that promotion is a commercially viable business, i.e., pornography,
not requiring public subsidy. What looks simply like a moral concern
with sexual "normalcy" according to heterosexist tradition, is in fact a
careful suppression of information produced for the sake of information rather than profit.

It is also interesting that it is the opposition of the arts establishment
to this clause, rather than the opposition of lesbians and gays, which
has had some lobbying influence in the House of Lords. Since especially the performing arts are a notoriously unviable commercial business and rely on public subsidy, the interests of the liberal arts (and
hence the lords and gentlemen) are seen to be affected by the clause,
although the arguments turn mostly around freedom of expression rather
than the financial arrangement with the public sector which supports
it.

The notion of the artist in fact is kept conceptually untarnished by
any commercial considerations: he is our model of the great and free
individualist who expresses himself for the sake of self-expression. There
is no explicit acknowledgment of the fact that any artist who qualifies
for the term is a *published* artist—an artist who sells and exhibits his
products through the channels of commercial establishments such as
publishers, galleries, cinemas, record companies, and the entertainment industry generally. The term artist no longer denotes "creativ-
ity," but public fame. Nor is there very much acknowledgment, even
less, criticism, of the immense egotism involved in a commitment to
self-expression, where expression, like sexuality, is conceived as the
dimension of an individual's right (or rather, privilege). There is very
little sense that the artist wants to reach *you* in a process of communication where you, of course, might want to express yourself in turn:
all the artist wants from you is your receptive attention, your money
and your acclaim.

---

[1]Quoted in "Outlawing the lesbian community: A briefing paper," Rights of Women
Policy Group and Lesbian Custody Group, London, January 1988. Now become law as
Section 28 of the Local Authorities Act, in slightly revised form.

It does not even matter what is the political orientation of those who practice in the arts establishment: the very conception of the arts ensures the continuation of its fundamental liberal individualism, the maintenance of a principle founded on what is fit for a gentleman. Thus, one of the major Marxist critics in Britain tells us that

> artists need a guaranteed freedom to communicate what, in terms of *their own* understanding of their work, needs to be communicated. This sounds like, and is, a definition of individual freedom. (Raymond Williams, 1982: pp. 124–125)

It also sounds like, and is, a definition of who *is* an individual who merits freedom, namely artists. For you, or we, are those who must guarantee *their* freedom, and we also need to be available for them to communicate to what in their own terms they feel they need to communicate. We need to be communicationally available to them as we need to be sexually available to the sexual liberals: we are their expression objects as we are their sex objects. The artist, like the liberal, and like the adolescent, *demands* what he deems is his need, and the arts establishment, like indulgent liberal parents, justifies his needs and his diminished responsibility. In the received notion of the artist we defend the fundamental infantilism of the individualist; we celebrate artists as the *enfants terribles* of the body politic who are naughty but clever, and whose daring self-interest we envy. We model on the artist not only our conception of the self, but on his work our desired relationship to work, which is becoming institutionalized in the ethic of professionalism. As professionals we demand, like artists, satisfaction from our work and the opportunity, or the freedom, to exercise our talents for the sake of self-expression.

Feminism, therefore, is under attack not only for its critique of male sexuality, which is seen to curb the absolute license of heterosexual men. It is also under attack for its radical critique of patriarchal thinking, which is centered on the infantile individual, for positing the political at the personal level, and for demanding of the adult member of society not just the pursuit of self-interest, but responsibility toward the other and toward the community. Feminist practice—of work and services, relationships and sexuality, knowledge and research as collective undertakings and social contributions rather than as personal fulfillment of career ambition—posits a threat to liberal individualism far greater than any conventional political opposition. Which is why, with the sexual liberals at the forefront, they are declaring this the era of postfeminism.

REFERENCES

Dworkin, Andrea. (1987). *Intercourse.* London: Secker and Warburg.

MacKinnon, Catharine A. (1983, Summer). Feminism, Marxism, method and the state: Toward feminist jurisprudence. *Signs* 8, no. 4, 635–58.

Mahmood, Mazher. (1986 August 3). Scandal of Britons who buy young boys for £3/ night. *The Sunday Times.* p. 3.

Offerdal, Harold, (1986, August 24). The child victims of porn. *The Observer.* p. 6.

Rights of Women Policy Group and Lesbian Custody Group. (1988, January). "Outlawing the lesbian community: A briefing paper." London.

Watney, Simon. (1986). The banality of gender. In Robert Young (Ed.). *Sexual difference* The Oxford Literary Review (special issue) 8, nos. 1–2. p. 4.

Williams, Raymond. (1982). *Communications.* 3rd ed. Harmondsworth: Pelican.

You Can't Fight Homophobia and Protect the Pornographers at the Same Time—An Analysis of What Went Wrong in *Hardwick*

John Stoltenberg

Like a lot of activists in the radical-feminist antipornography movement, I've been trying to figure out the hysterical animosity that has come at us from the gay community. I want to sketch briefly what I think is going on—and why.

The situation we're dealing with goes back many years, of course, almost to the beginning of the modern gay liberation movement in the late 1960s and early 1970s. Though gay liberation emerged soon after women's liberation, the male-dominated gay liberation movement never really grasped how homophobia is rooted in the woman hating that is a fixture of male supremacy. Quite simply, the male homosexual is stigmatized because he is perceived to participate in the degraded status of the female—and if he doesn't understand that, he'll never have a radical political analysis.

I use the words "male supremacy" on purpose, because they imply an angry point of view about the sex-class hierarchy, the political system of discrimination based on sex. Those of us who are queer have a fairly obvious special interest in ending sex discrimination, because homophobia is both a consequence of sex discrimination and an enforcer of sex discrimination. The system of male supremacy requires gender polarity—with real men as different from real women as they can be, and with men's social superiority to women expressed in public and in private in every way imaginable. Homophobia is, in part, how the system punishes those who deviate and seem to dissent from it. The threat of homophobic insult or attack not only keeps men aimed at women as their appropriate sexual prey; it also keeps men "real men."

The system of gender polarity requires that people with penises treat people without as objects, as things, as empty gaping vessels waiting to be filled with turgid maleness, if necessary by force. Homophobia is, in part, how the system punishes those whose object-choice is deviant. Homophobia is a kind of sexualized contempt for someone whose mere existence—because he is smeared with female status—threatens to melt down the coat of armor by which men protect themselves from other men. Homophobia keeps women the targets. And to men who sexually objectify correctly, this homophobic setup assures a level of safety, selfhood, self-respect, and social power.

Most men internalize cultural homophobia whomever they are attracted to. Inside men's bodies, homophobia becomes an ongoing dread and loathing of anything about themselves that even hints at gender ambiguity; it means a constant quest "to be the man there," whatever that takes.

The political reality of the gender hierarchy in male supremacy requires that we make it resonate through our nerves, flesh, and vascular system just as often as we can. We are *supposed* to respond orgasmically to power and powerlessness, to violence and violatedness; our sexuality is *supposed* to be inhabited by a reverence for supremacy, for unjust power over and against other human life. We are not supposed to experience any other erotic possibility; we are not supposed to glimpse eroticized justice. Our bodies are not supposed to abandon their sensory imprint of what male dominance and female subordination are supposed to be to each other—even if we are the same sex. Perhaps *especially* if we are the same sex. Because if you and your sex partners are not genitally different but you are emotionally and erotically attached to gender hierarchy, then you come to the point where you have to impose hierarchy on every sex act you attempt—otherwise it doesn't feel like sex.

Erotically and politically, those who are queer live inside a bizarre double bind. Sex discrimination and sex inequality require homophobia in order to continue. The homophobia that results is what stigmatizes our eroticism, makes us hateful for how we would love. Yet living inside this system of sex discrimination and sex inequality, we too have sexualized it; we have become sexually addicted to gender polarity; we have learned how hate and hostility can become sexual stimulants; we have learned sexualized antagonism toward the other in order to seem to be able to stand ourselves—and in order to get off. Sex discrimination has ritualized a homosexuality that dares not deviate from allegiance to gender polarity and gender hierarchy; sex discrimination has constructed a homosexuality that must stay erotically attached to the very male-supremacist social structures that produce homophobia. It's a little like having a crush on one's own worst enemy—and then moving in for life.

If what I've said is true—if in fact male supremacy simultaneously produces both a homophobia that is erotically committed to the hatred of homosexuality *and* a homosexuality that is erotically committed to sex discrimination—then it becomes easier to understand why the gay community, taken as a whole, has become almost hysterically hostile to radical-feminist antipornography activism. One might have thought that gay people—who are harassed, stigmatized, and jeopardized on account of prejudice against their preference for same-sex sex—would want to make common cause with any radical challenge to systematized sex discrimination. One might have thought that gay people, realizing that their self-interest lies in the obliteration of homophobia, would be among the first to endorse a political movement attempting to root out sex inequality. One might have thought that gay people would be among the first to recognize that so long as society tolerates and actually celebrates the "pornographizing" of women—so long as there is an enormous economic incentive to traffic in the sexualized subordination of women—then the same terrorism that enforces the sex-class system will surely continue to bludgeon faggots as well. One might have thought, for that matter, that gay men would not require the sexualized inequality of women in order to get a charge out of sex —or that a gay man walking through a porn store would stop and take a look at the racks and racks of pictures of women gagged and splayed and trussed up and ask himself exactly why this particular context of woman hate is so damned important to him.

Sex discrimination: being put down or treated in a second-class or subhuman way on account of the social meaning of one's anatomy. That is what the bulk of pornography is *for*, and that is what the radical-feminist antipornography movement is *against*.

But in many ways over the past decade, most gay and lesbian publications, most gay advocacy organizations, and most gay leaders and spokespeople have been rather obviously committed to a course of defending the rights of pornographers. Despite the presence of many lesbians and some gay men in the radical-feminist antipornography movement, most gay people seem now to believe—some cynically but some very sincerely—that if our nation does not impede its thriving pornography industry, it will someday recognize the civil rights of gay people; but if in any way you encroach on the rights of pornographers, you will surely jeopardize gay liberation. People frame this point of view in many different ways, of course, but it all basically comes down to an equation between the future of gay civil rights and the free-enterprise rights of pornographers.

And this is not merely a philosophical meeting of minds between gay-rights advocates and pornographers; there have been countless actual coalitions and political convergences: substantial money contributions to gay-rights organizations from pornographers, lawsuits brought jointly by gay activists and pornographers, campaign support from pornographers for pro-gay-rights politicians, page upon page in pornography magazines offered to gay writers to trash the radical-feminist antipornography movement, and so on. I don't think anyone needs convincing that the gay community, taken as a whole, tends to view its naked political self-interest as lying somewhere in bed with the likes of Al Goldstein, Hugh and Christie Hefner, Bob Guccione, and Larry Flynt—to say nothing of various notables in organized crime.

An ideological huddle between gay-rights activists and the pro-pornography movement has also been at the very center of game plans for getting homosexual sex acts decriminalized. Let me tell you what really happened, for instance, in the recent *Hardwick* case.

In 1985 the Supreme Court agreed for the first time to hear a case, *Bowers v. Hardwick*, that would bear on the constitutionality of broad state laws against sodomy.[1] Arguments put forth in the case from the gay-rights camp turned primarily on the so-called right of privacy—a dim legal doctrine that exists only through constitutional inference. Justice William O. Douglas first spelled out this privacy right in *Griswold v. Connecticut* in 1965, where it was applied to "the sacred precincts of marital bedrooms."[2] But the privacy principle really blazed into the libertarian limelight with *Stanley v. Georgia* in 1969, in which the Supreme Court ruled that a man may legally possess obscenity in his home, even though the stuff is criminally banned everywhere else. Basically, the Supreme Court declared, "A man's home is his castle," at least where obscenity is concerned;[3] and this was the narrow crack through which gay-rights advocates hoped the esteemed justices would also want to slip when it came to consensual sodomy. The pro-sodomy legal argument in *Hardwick* was written and choreographed mostly by

---

[1] *Michael J. Bowers, Attorney General of Georgia, v. Michael Hardwick* 478 U.S., October term, 1985.
[2] See *The Douglas Opinions*, edited by Vern Countryman (New York: Random House, 1977), 234–36.
[3] In *Paris Adult Theatre I v. Slaton* 413 U.S. 49 (1973), paraphrasing *Stanley*, in an opinion written by Chief Justice Warren Burger.

Laurence H. Tribe of Harvard; he made quite explicit that gay sex in private should be defended on the same grounds as the private possession of obscenity:

> It would be ironic indeed if government were constitutionally barred, whatever its justification, from entering a man's home to stop him from obtaining sexual gratification by viewing an obscene film—but were free, without any burden of special justification, to enter the same dwelling to interrupt his sexual acts with a willing adult partner. The home surely protects more than our fantasies alone.[4]

In case you missed it, that ignoble equating of same-sex sex acts with the "liberal" position.

Tribe's single-minded privacy tactic might have seemed expedient and pragmatic given the Supreme Court's historic hostility to homosexuality.[5] Legally, however, the tactic was sheer sophistry, claiming a shield for criminal sodomy only "in the most private of enclaves," the home (motel rooms, presumably, did not qualify), but completely conceding the state's power to delegitimatize homosexuality however and wherever else it pleases: "There is thus no cause for worry," argued Tribe, that a favorable ruling from the Supreme Court "would cast doubt on any administrative programs that states might fashion to encourage traditional heterosexual unions."[6] That could only be reassuring if one is a heterosexual man—to whom women are invisible. And in the age of AIDS, what exactly did he mean by "any administrative programs"?

Politically, Tribe's argument gets even worse. Consider, for instance, the fact that for women in heterosexual unions the home is the most dangerous place on earth; it's where women get raped most, assaulted most, and killed most. Moreover, Tribe's privacy-based argument embarked on a slippery slope that could seriously erode the state's ability to protect individuals from injury such as incest. Essentially, by appealing narrowly to the privacy right, Tribe's line of argument paid tribute to some linchpin precepts of male supremacy (among them, men's right to sexual release, in fantasy and in fact, no matter at what cost to anyone else) and opened not a single area of jurisprudential discourse that might conceivably defy the forces that keep homophobia alive and well.

One does not need a great legal mind to grasp that if your claim to legal entitlement rests on a self-interested sellout of others who are powerless, you've got a craven and shabby case.

---

[4]Laurence H. Tribe, et al., "Brief for Respondent," *Bowers v. Hardwick* 478 U.S., 16.
[5]In a 1976 case called *Doe v. Commonwealth's Attorney* 425 U.S. 901 (1976), the high court flatly rejected a challenge to Virginia's sodomy law.
[6]Tribe, et al., p. 24.

The Supreme Court released its decision in *Hardwick* June in 1986, and by a 5–4 majority it rejected the argument that "prior cases have construed the Constitution to confer a right of privacy that extends to homosexual sodomy."[7] Therefore, the court ruled, a state's antisodomy laws are not intrinsically unconstitutional.

Across the country there were angry protests against the Supreme Court's decision in *Hardwick;* and in the aftermath of outrage I was approached, often sympathetically, by friends who assumed I was heartbroken. But my response was not what they'd expected. I pointed out that if the Supreme Court *had* struck down all state antisodomy laws because it had *accepted* the privacy argument as put forth by Tribe et al., it would have done so for wretchedly wrongheaded reasons. So though my feelings about the *Hardwick* decision were very mixed, I was hopeful that a more honorable argument might eventually come before the court.

For instance, a braver strategy would be to argue from the state's interest in eliminating sex discrimination. The argument might go like this:

1. Because social homophobia perpetuates and reinforces sex discrimination, and
2. because laws against sodomy perpetuate and reinforce social homophobia,
3. it would be in the interest of the state to decriminalize homosexual sex acts—in order to diminish sex discrimination.

An important corollary of that argument might go like this:

1. Because social homophobia perpetuates a social climate in which overt acts of homophobic personal violence are more likely to occur, and
2. because laws against sodomy, even if not enforced, actively contribute to that climate of personal violence by legitimatizing social prejudice and hatred,
3. it would be in the interest of the state to decriminalize homosexual sex acts—in order to more completely guarantee "ordered liberty."

Even to argue that laws against sodomy deny homosexuals Fourteenth Amendment equal-protection rights would be to say something that is self-evidently true and also something that would strengthen the body of sex-discrimination law—rather than undermine it by appealing to the right of privacy.

Of course such a strategy might not work at first, and it might need

---

[7]Justice Byron R. White, delivering the opinion of the court. *The United States Law Week*, June 24, 1986, 4920.

buttressing by some years of activism and education before the Supreme Court would "get it" (segregation, for instance, took them a *very* long time), but at least it would have a credible human-rights politics and the courage of a radical conviction: the nerve to reveal something true about the interrelationship between homophobia, violence, laws, and men's social power over and against women.

I have discussed the *Hardwick* case at some length, partly in order to demonstrate the reactionary ideological alliance between gays and the pro-pornography movement and partly to suggest what an antihomophobia agenda might look like if the gay-rights movement were ever to take seriously what radical feminists have taught us about the way male supremacy really works.

So long as the gay-rights movement is committed to dissociating itself from the radical-feminist project to uproot sex discrimination completely and to create sex equality, gay liberation is headed in a suicidal direction. You can't have a political movement trying to erode homophobia while leaving male supremacy and misogyny in place. It won't work. Gay rights without sexual justice is a male-supremacist reform.

So long as the gay community defends the rights of pornographers to exploit and eroticize sex discrimination, we who are queer do not stand a chance. So long as the pornographers get to own not only the Constitution but also our most intimate sexual connections with one another, we will have lost all hope. Sex discrimination is what we must oppose, even if it turns us on. It's what puts queers down because it's what puts women down, and ultimately it's what does us all in. You can't fight sex discrimination and protect the pornographers at the same time.

A View from Another Country

Susan G. Cole

Canadians, and Canadian women in particular, face a troubling situation. We live next to the richest, most powerful country in the world, a country that also produces more pornography than any other country in the world. We do feel threatened by American hegemony, so much so that we worry we will become the fifty-second state at any time. It is a problem particularly because we speak English like you do, well, sort of like you do. I am not convinced that you could waltz into Mexico and appropriate that country, its economy, and its culture with the same ease as you might swoop into Canada. Canadians are more susceptible. We are at a critical point in the delicate relationship between our two countries. Canadians are very concerned about the free-trade agreement negotiated by our Prime Minister and your President. To me personally, free trade means pornography and always did. It means that Americans are going to take the trees out of our country and sell them back to us in the form of pornography.

We are worried about two things. One, how to avoid importing your pornography, and two, how to avoid importing your liberalism.

First, let me deal with the pornography. In my work I've discovered that pornography has the same effects on Canadian women that it has on American women. When women are around pornography, they expect it to be used against them, and they experience it as a form of abuse. I should say that not many Canadian women are used in the pornography itself. That is because, like many cultural products, the economics of the situation are such that it is cheaper for Canadian distributors to import American pornography and sell it (just the way it is cheaper to import American television programs to give another example) than it is to develop a home-grown product. But although there is not a Canadian pornography industry built on Canadian women's subordination, the pornography sure as hell is coming into the country.

To find out what that has meant to women, I have undertaken a research project in conjunction with shelters for assaulted women. In it I ask shelter residents five questions: (a) Does your spouse use pornography and what kind? (b) Does he ask, expect, or force you to buy it? (We asked this question so that we could respond to video retailers who keep telling us that 53 percent of their clients for pornography are women. We suspected that many of these women are purchasing or renting these materials under conditions of inequality and coercion.) (c) Does he ask, expect, or force you to look at it? (d) Does he ask, expect, or force you to do the things in the pictures? (e) How do you feel when these things happen?

Since 10 percent of Diana Russell's random sample reported being upset by pornography,[1] we guessed that as many as 20 percent of our sample of assaulted women would report similar abuses. In fact, a full 30 percent in our survey answered yes to the first question. All those women described some kind of abuse in association with pornography. This research continues.

I wanted to do the research because I thought that with the exception of the Russell study I just mentioned and Wendy Stock's (1983) and Carole Knafka's (1985) work, women's voices were breathtakingly silent in the laboratory. I realized that these men, and they are mostly men, were showing tons of violent pornography to their subjects, looking at it, and looking at it, and still they were unable to see the harm there, even though it was right there on the screen. They were wiring up their male subjects' penises, and their hearts and their brains and their sweat glands to see what they were thinking and feeling, never wondering what women thought about the pornography that is forced on them so often. So we decided to ask women. My research methodology begins with the premise that women matter and that we should believe them when they speak.

We found that the presence of pornography in our lives makes a difference. I don't know if you are aware that in the United States there is a high value placed on a particular kind of pornography. The pornographers in Hong Kong—they are the Americans' chief competitors —produce two different kinds of pornography for the world market: one that is sexually explicit and one that is explicitly violent, tailor-made for the American market. Did you know that Americans consume more violent pornography than any other country? The problem

---

[1] Diana E. H. Russell, 1982. Russell's study was the first to canvass a random sample of women on the sexual violence they experience.

for us in Canada is that the sexually violent pornography is the material that crosses our border.

Now surely you have detected a note of nationalism in my approach, but I don't want you to get the wrong impression. I've certainly tried to imagine it, but I don't think there is such a thing as a Canadian sexuality. The sexuality of male dominance crosses the 49th parallel and other borders quite easily, and it is probably a global phenomenon. What I mean is that there are some patriarchal phenomena we nurture in Canada without the help of Americans. But I do value my Canadian identity, and I do know that pornography hurts Canadians. So, what are we going to do about the pornography?

This brings me to the big C-word: censorship. We have an obscenity law that, like American obscenity doctrine, does not do much. But we do have one law that has been particularly useful, to us anyway, and that is our Customs Tariff. It says to the pornographers, "Keep it out." It's not a perfect law. The main problem with it is that it was constructed in the terms of decency and morality, which are not words feminists use when we discuss pornography because we see it as a political problem having to do with power, not morality.[2] Recently, a court decision compelled Parliament to reframe the law with clearer guidelines, and at this time we could probably design a tariff regulation that used a feminist definition of pornography to create a law that would do a great deal to keep pornography out of the country.

Now if that sounds like censorship to you, you can call it that. But I would say that when a cultural product from one country threatens the cultural integrity of another country, to say nothing of the sexual lives of its people, especially women, then that product has to be dealt with. I get the sense that this is hard for many of you to accept. In fact, I have been amazed at the intensity of the anticensorship feelings, even at this conference. I sat at lunch with some wonderful women who warned that if the United States allowed any kind of censorship, Americans would never hear anything about Central America or South Africa. I thought this rather bizarre, for in reading your newspapers, (frankly I have found readable ones only in Los Angeles, Chicago, Boston and New York, and even in those, foreign news seems to be anathema) I find very little about what is going on in those countries and other areas of struggle. In Canada, we had been reading reports of Contra activity in Nicaragua for a full year before revelations of Contra activity shocked Americans, and we are farther away from that action than you are. What has surprised me is that even radical feminists

---

[2]The best explanation of this distinction between the moralist and feminist views of pornography can be found in C. A. MacKinnon (1984).

have bought the notion that a liberal democracy and its companion, a "free" press, actually thrive here in the United States.

Please understand that I am aware there can be and have been abuses of censorship. You've no doubt heard the argument. If we allow censorship, it will get us first. And the Customs Tariff has been used against the wrong materials. But sometimes liberals and their partners, anti-censorship feminists, can be misleading about how dangerous these abuses are. For example, many of you have probably read or heard that the Canadian antipornography documentary, *Not a Love Story*, has been banned by the Ontario Film Review Board. That is not true. The censor board did decide that the film should not get a license for public screenings, but that anybody could see the film, provided they agreed to have a discussion period afterward. Not a bad idea, actually. So all of you who think *Not a Love Story* has been banned have been lied to by pornography apologists who want you to believe that censorship is the worst thing on earth. Look at women's lives and think about how ridiculous that claim is. I want to add that *Not a Love Story* is one of the most widely viewed National Film Board movies ever made in my country. Some ban.

I will agree that the Customs Tariff has been administered, shall we say, unevenly. After the court decision I described earlier, the Customs Tariff was supplanted by a customs memorandum that offers what I call a laundry list of all the depictions that are not allowed in the country. Among the proscribed depictions are the celebration of incest, the sexualization of rape—those are inspired by feminist antipornography activity—as well as other depictions that have fallen under our obscenity law, which, in our country, tends to target erect penises and penetration. Some call obscenity anti-sex. If you define sex as the penis, I guess it is.

Anyway, included in the list is depictions of anal sex. This element of the tariff has been used against gay male sex education about AIDS. I'll give you an amazing example, just to show how laws sometimes miss the point that what we are after is subordination. The customs officials perused one gay male magazine and read a description of a spectacularly subordinating experience one man had on his hands and knees sucking a man off. The description didn't bother the customs officials. What did vex their standard was a letter to the editor that asked how to have anal sex without getting AIDS. After Customs was through with the magazine, the description of fellatio was intact while the letter to the editor, and the editor's valuable response was deleted. Very bad.

Fortunately, this case was taken to court, and eventually, anal sex was removed from Customs' list of undesirables. But my point is this.

Anticensorship activists report that something like 1,700 pro-lesbian and pro-gay sex materials (which, by the way, are not necessarily **not** pornography) have been kept out of Canada. But what do we do with the fact that another 8,000 samples of bona fide pornography have been kept out as well? What do we do with this fact? How do you balance out the harms? Gay and lesbian identity gets set back by keeping gay-positive sexual materials out of the country but fewer women are harmed when we keep the pornography out. Abstract discussions of freedom will not make these questions go away.

I am still in favor of some kind of customs tariff. I am also involved with a group pursuing civil remedies, something like ordinances passed in this country that identify pornography as a violation of women's civil rights. But what I want to say is this. Yes, there are abuses in censorship. Yes, censors make mistakes. Yes, I could live with the removal of the Film Review Boards in Canada. But it is also true that we live with film censorship in Canada and some of us still have sex. When I hear Americans talk about censorship, they get that glazed look of fear that betokens what I call future-tense panic. Is there really anything that could happen to us that is worse than what is happening to women already? Or, let me try this question for antipornography feminists who espouse the anticensorship line: Don't you think that perhaps you haven't totally exorcised the liberal in you?

Which brings me to the importing of liberalism. I live in a country that tends to be quite comfortable with authoritarianism. Canadians really don't have that freedom-loving individualistic liberal streak. For example, our RCMP (Royal Canadian Mounted Police, the equivalent of your FBI) illegally bugged phones in 1973, and Canadians couldn't have given a damn. The typical Canadian just said, "Go ahead, tap my phone. I'm not doing anything wrong." We just don't have that civil libertarian impulse. It all hails back to the fact that we shook hands with the British instead of throwing them out. We had a very polite revolution. This tendency is, by the way, not always positive, for it has paved the way for other government excesses. However, it does create a healthy psychological block against U.S.-styled liberalism.

Canada just got a brand new Charter of Rights, something like your Constitution. With any luck we may be able to avoid importing into Canada the liberalism that has been carved into the legal tradition of your country for the past 200 years. So far, almost all the charter challenges based on a freedom of speech claim have failed in our courts. The Customs Tariff was brought before the courts and though the law was judged to be too vague, the ruling made it clear that a Canadian democracy would tolerate restrictions on freedom of expression.

We have been able to stem the tide of freedom of speech absolutism.

But we are having a harder time with another liberal value: freedom of sex. You will have heard these values espoused in the pornography debate in that wishy-washy claim that it is not the sex in pornography we mind; it's the violence. You've heard this, haven't you? We love sex. We hate violence. Well, all of that doesn't take into account that the violence is there for sex, and it completely avoids the conditions of women used in that so-called "just sex" type of pornography.

We found out how dangerous that avoidance can be in a recent obscenity decision made in Canada. We had a judge who had obviously been listening to those feminists who tout the "give us sex but spare us the violence" line. He had been listening to all those liberal platitudes about consent, and in a mad moment decided that he would look at a picture and decide on its face whether it was obscene. And he looked at the pornography and said, "This is not obscene because I see consent on the screen. I see it in the woman smiling." Guess what movie he was looking at? *Deep Throat.*

So we have a case in Canada in which *Deep Throat* has been judged not to be obscene. Why? For a number of reasons: Because the judge was looking only at the images on the screen instead of considering the practice of subordination on which pornography thrives. [Linda "Lovelace" Marchiano's book *Ordeal* tells the brutal truth about *Deep Throat.*] Because he was listening to pseudofeminists who were refusing to analyze sexuality. Because he was listening to pseudofeminists who consider prostitution a profession freely chosen instead of an institution of sexual abuse. Because in some cases in Canada, these pseudofeminists have actually gone to court to defend pornography against obscenity charges.

It strikes me that our movement has to confront these tendencies. We have to be able to say that speech is not more important than women's lives. We have to stop celebrating "consent" when we address prostitution and start noticing the gender breakdown in the so-called sex trade, especially the painfully obvious questions about who is buying and who is being sold. And we have to avoid the easy liberal path to pro-sex politics and be sex-critical instead. These views may not be especially popular in our hypersexualized culture, but they are the wave of feminism's future.

REFERENCES

Knafka, C. L. (1985). Sexually explicit, sexually violent and violent media: The effects of multiple naturalistic exposure and debriefing on female viewers. Unpublished Ph.D. dissertation, University of Madison, Wisconsin.

Lovelace, Linda. (1980). *Ordeal,* New York: Citadel.

MacKinnon, Catharine A. (1984). Not a moral issue. *Yale Law and Policy Review,* 2.

Russell, Diana E. H. (1982). *Rape in marriage.* New York: Macmillan.

Stock, Wendy. (1983). The effects of violent pornography on women. Paper presented at the American Psychological Association meeting.

Women and Civil Liberties

Kathleen A. Lahey

The American Civil Liberties Union (ACLU) and the Canadian Civil Liberties Association (CCLA) have long been considered the defenders of civil liberties in North America. Siding with disadvantaged groups and supporting unpopular positions, civil libertarians (CLers) attracted their share of hostility as they struggled to carve out a sphere for political and social protest during the great struggles for liberty of the last century. Several of these struggles directly involved feminist issues, such as Margaret Sanger's fight for birth control in the 1910s and 1920s, or issues important to women, such as the right to organize in labor unions.

But the traditional male domination of the ACLU and the CCLA has led them, in recent years, to make political choices that primarily serve men, and, as a corollary, big business. A quick rundown of the current ACLU-CCLA client list reveals that CLers now represent rapists and pornographers as well as Nazis and the tobacco industry. These choices have generated huge and painful splits between the women who have decided to stay with the CLers and those who have felt that they could not work within such organizations. These splits have been all the more painful because many of the women who have made the decision to withdraw have defined feminism as a matter of women's civil liberties, and have always felt strongly about the defense of civil liberties—of both women and men. Indeed, some of these women have decided that the present CL positions on issues relating to women are a perversion of the meaning of civil liberties, and having left the CLers reluctantly, are now deciding that it is time to reclaim this part of their movement.

There are probably many reasons for the emerging antifeminism of the CLers. One explanation is purely structural: the Skokie marches split the ACLU (and to a lesser extent, the CCLA), and one of the results of this split was that many members resigned in outrage or simply became less active. The people who were left in leadership positions were people who had not been outraged or demoralized by the ACLU's support of the Nazis, and these people, one could imagine, would not be any more upset by rape or pornography than they were by the Nazi march on Skokie. It may be significant that the remaining CLers are indeed split over women's issues, but I think it is also significant that the remaining CLers are, by now, hardened by the Skokie split.

I am one of those feminists who have very little faith that the ACLU-CCLA, in the absence of structural changes, is genuinely able to serve any interests other than those of men. My reasons for this position are both theoretical and empirical. On a theoretical level, it is clear to me that the civil liberties movement is a direct outgrowth of the larger western liberal political movement, and that liberal theory to a great extent depends on the continuing instrumentalization and exploitation of women in order to make liberal politics "pay off" for men. On an empirical level, it is increasingly evident that as women's claims move more fully into the political and legal arenas—the forums in which the CLers are most active—local and national chapters are increasingly taking positions that are directly damaging to women, whether those women consider themselves feminists or not. To the extent that any CL chapters have self-consciously aligned themselves with the interests of women, it is almost always because feminists (or lesbian-feminists, as opposed to "gay" women) have obtained positions on those boards and have used those positions to influence policy, which is what happened with the Southern California chapter of the ACLU in the CalFed case.

"LIBERTY" AND LIBERAL
THEORY

On the level of political theory, it is my contention that so long as "liberty" claims remain central to the political agenda of western liberalism, feminists and civil libertarians will remain locked in conflict. This contention has two aspects. First, I contend that not only do women presently have less "liberty" than do men in the liberal state, but that men have never been able to imagine "liberty" without assuming the oppression of women. If there were no women (socially or sexually), then men could not experience that state or condition they call liberty. Second, contemporary attempts to achieve the liberal ideal—the perfection of "liberty"—cannot be accomplished without the continued subjugation of women, and in particular, without such subjugating practices as rape, so-called surrogacy arrangements, pornography, and prostitution.

The concept of liberty was originally devised by men during the bourgeois revolution that began in Europe in the 1600s. The purpose of the bourgeois revolution was to promote wider distribution of political and economic power among male members of the state: in effect, "liberty" was a theory of affirmative action for nonaristocratic men (Kathleen Lahey, 1983). Early liberal theory is sometimes described as antipatriarchal, since it rejected feudal patriarchy as the organizing basis of the social order. However, this antipatriarchalism did not extend to the organization of the family or to the status of women, either within the family or within the larger social context (Zillah Eisenstein, 1981). Although newly formulated liberty claims legitimated egalitarianism among males, these liberty claims depended upon the continuing inequality of women to make liberty meaningful for men.

Support for this reading of early liberal theory is not difficult to find. The practices of the Marquis de Sade, which continue to define the essence of liberty for contemporary civil libertarians ranging from Susan Sontag to Larry Flynt, included rape, sexual torture, pornography, and prostitution.[1] Sexual practices and preferences of libertarians aside, political economists such as John Locke conceptualized property and liberty in a way that assumed the continuing male appropriation of women's productive and reproductive energies, and treated as *reductio ad absurdum* any suggestion that women should be treated as equals or as self-determining persons in the emerging liberal state (Kathleen Lahey, 1983).

Indeed, if the ability to engage in economic and sexual exploitation is the essence of the liberal bourgeois revolution, then women can only now be said to be emerging from feudalism.[2] And not surprisingly, our bourgeois revolution looks a lot like the last one. Women now can—

---

[1] Andrea Dworkin (1979) has the best analysis of the political content of the Marquis de Sade's actions.

[2] The essence of feudalism is nonpersonhood. As men freed themselves from feudalism and took on the legal status of persons, they acquired the basic civil liberties that are now taken for granted: the right to own property, the right to work for money, custody of children, the right to enter into contracts, the right to vote. As Blacks who were liberated in the United States in the 1860s discovered, however, the de jure acquisition of civil rights does not necessarily ensure de facto exercise or enjoyment of those rights. One of the fundamental political issues of our time is whether liberal and bourgeois revolution is the only way out of feudalism, or whether there is another route. Before the Russian Revolution, socialist theory assumed that it was necessary to go through capitalism en route to socialism; women generally reject that necessity, but the alternative is not yet clear.

and do—play the Marquis to our sisters, whether we are lesbian or heterosexual women, inflicting pain on others for our own (and allegedly for their) sexual gratification, all in the name of sexual freedom.[3] Women now can—and do—purchase the reproductive capacities of other women, in the name of freedom of contract.[4] Women now can—and do—defend our rights to serve (or even to become) pimps and johns, in the name of freedom of choice.[5] Women now can—and do—define equality as men's rights to everything that women have—including pregnancy leave, child custody, and mother's allowances—at the same time that they define women's equality claims—such as the claim that pornography harms women—as infringements on the principle of freedom of speech or expression.[6]

In our liberal moments, we women—along with all other civil libertarians—are busily engaged in justifying the continuing inequality of some women on the basis of sex; romanticizing emotional independence as the defining core of individualism; eroticizing instrumental rationality as the way to get off sexually; and identifying "the state," rather than male supremacy in its entirety, as the source of our oppression.[7]

THE PRACTICES OF CIVIL LIBERTARIANS

Some argue that liberalism has long since exceeded its male-centered origins, transcended its narrow antipatriarchalism, been transformed in the dialectic of contemporary discourse, and it now forms a viable theoretical basis for feminist practice as well as for the more traditional civil liberties movement. Any tension around specific issues, the argument continues, is merely due to random and uncomfortable lurches

---

[3]See generally publications such as *On Our Backs*, which are published for the sexual gratification of lesbians.

[4]The paradigmatic case in point is the Baby S case, in which Elizabeth and William Stern attempted to purchase a child from Mary Beth Whitehead (referred to in the media as the "Baby M" case) and have used the legal process to enforce their claims. Many feminists have supported the Sterns' claims, even though they have had to admit that Mary Beth Whitehead and her daughter have been injured by the transaction.

[5]See, for example, COYOTE and other pro-prostitution groups.

[6]See, for example, Judge Sarah Barker's decision in the Indiana district court in the American Booksellers' challenge to the Indianapolis anti-pornography ordinance. *American Booksellers Association v. Hudnut*, 598 F. Supp. 1316 (S.D. Ind 1984), aff'd 771 F. 2d 323 (CCA 7 1985), summ. aff. 54 U.S.L.W. 3560 (USSC Feb. 24, 1986) (No. 85–1090).

[7]Kathleen Lahey. (1984–85). I originally developed this criticism of liberalism as a result of reading male liberals; I now see that it also applies to liberal feminists.

of the dialectic, not to fundamental differences between modern-day feminists and civil libertarians.

Unfortunately for women, uncritical acceptance of this analysis undercuts the fragile gains that women have made in the last twenty years. I can offer three recent cases in point. In the first case, the CCLA and ACLU have been complicitous in the media campaign against the Fraser Report, *Pornography and Prostitution in Canada,* and the Attorney General's Commission's report on pornography in the United States. In the second case, the CCLA has led the attack on the Canadian ERA (the sex equality guarantees in the Charter of Rights) in the form of constitutional challenges to the rape shield laws that Canadian feminists struggled to enact in the 1970s and the 1980s. In the third case, the CCLA supported a male professor who used a defamation suit to silence a woman who had brought a claim of sexual harassment, contending that she had infringed upon his academic freedom.

Pornography

As the controversy over pornography intensifies, civil libertarians are finding it more difficult to conceal their essential antifeminism as well as their conservative alliances. The 1986 media campaign against the antipornography movement illustrates these alliances.

In 1985, the Fraser Committee on Pornography and Prostitution (constituted by the federal Liberal government, which lost power shortly afterward) reported on its deliberations (Fraser Committee, 1985). Its findings and recommendations were dramatically different from those of the United States Report on Obscenity and Pornography in 1971: in its recommendations the Fraser Committee recognized the harms of pornography. It advocated a range of legal methods of addressing that harm, including the enactment of various kinds of civil remedies and the revision of administrative guidelines (including the customs tariff and the film board guidelines) in order to combat the importation of pornography (Fraser Committee, 1985). Canada imports 97 percent of all pornography that is consumed domestically; 85 percent comes from the United States (Fraser Committee, 1985). In 1986, the report of the United States Attorney General's Commission on Pornography came to many of the same findings and recommendations as the Fraser Committee: pornography harms women in a variety of ways, and a range of legal remedies—including civil remedies—should be adopted to deal with that harm (Fraser Committee, 1985).

Although civil libertarians in Canada had remained fairly silent in the face of the Fraser report, they were alarmed by the United States report, doubtless because they knew that the United States report would have much more influence than the Canadian report in both the United States and Canada: such is the nature of cultural domination. Even before the United States report was released, however, it was clear that it would attract considerable public and government attention in Canada, and therefore Canadian pornographers—led by Ray Argyle—developed a major pro-pornography media campaign.

Ray Argyle is the chair of Argyle Communications, Inc., a Toronto public relations firm. Early in 1986, he contacted his United States affiliate, Gray and Company of Washington, D.C., to propose a major media campaign to "educate" North Americans about the threat to free speech posed by the antipornography movement. As a result of this proposal, Gray and Company entered into a contract for $900,000 with the Council for Periodical Distributors Associations. According to the contract proposal, the project would have the following purposes:

1. to discredit the Commission on Pornography and antipornography workers;

2. to create a major coalition of individuals and organizations opposed to the Commission's findings and recommendations, including "academicians, civil libertarians" and others; and

3. to "launch a series of preemptive strikes against the Commission's report, using 'advertorials' in major national newspapers and magazines, placing spokespersons on national and local television and radio news, public affairs, and talk shows, holding a series of news conferences in major cities," and lobbying. (Gray and Company, 1986)

Overall, this campaign has been designed to defend the publishers and distributors of pornography by enabling them to hide behind rhetoric about freedom of speech, since even the principals of Gray and Company recognized that public attitudes toward pornography were negative and it would not be easy for pornographers to get public support if they made free speech claims on their own behalf. And part of the strategy was to recruit civil libertarians as spokespersons in order to legitimize the campaign — especially feminist civil libertarians, who would give this campaign credibility among feminists.

The Council for Periodical Distributors is a member of the Media Coalition, along with the American Booksellers Association, the Association of American Publishers, and the National Association of College Stores. Most of these groups, joined by the ACLU and others to make their interests appear to be local, filed an amicus brief written by Michael Bamberger supporting Paul Ferber in the Supreme Court case testing the New York child pornography law. (Michael Bamberger is the lawyer for the Media Coalition.) Most of these groups, with a few local ones added, again represented by Michael Bamberger with the

ACLU as amicus, brought the Indianapolis action testing the civil rights ordinance against pornography (Catharine MacKinnon, 1986).

As far as anyone knows, this is the first time that antifeminists and conservatives have engaged in such "major, concerted, intentional, and funded" opposition to the feminist antipornography movement (Catharine MacKinnon, 1986). Not only was the contract executed, but Gray and Company has been very active on its clients' behalf: the list of "themes" in the memorandum describes precisely the substance of press stories and television shows (Catharine MacKinnon, 1986).

And there is more to this story. In the wake of the media smear campaign, the Ontario Liberal government announced that its film review board might have to be dismantled in order to "adjust" the Canadian legal regime to the dictates of an impending free-trade agreement with the United States. This announcement was made despite repeated assurances that Canada will be allowed to retain its cultural self-determination even if such a free-trade agreement is executed (Kathleen Lahey, 1986). To the list of essential liberal freedoms, then, feminists learned that we must also add free trade. And feminists daring to question the effect that a free-trade agreement will have on the availability of pornography in Canada have been accused of media hype and hysteria, with politicians insisting that Canada's self-determination on this issue will be protected by Article 20 of the GATT, which protects local sovereignty from imperialist trade conduct in matters of "public morality and safety."

Rape

Civil libertarians have also actively opposed feminist efforts to reform rape laws. In the 1970s, Canadian feminists, like feminists everywhere, engaged in detailed studies of the operation of rape laws in an attempt to figure out why this crime against women went largely unreported, and, even when it was reported, why it usually went unpunished. Feminists discovered that the nature of the evidence that was considered to be admissible in rape investigations and trials had a lot to do with whether women even wanted to report having been raped, let alone go through a trial: women could be examined in detail about their past sexual history by police, judges, and defense lawyers. The abuses that women suffered under those evidentiary rules are now legendary, and in some jurisdictions, legal history. Until recently, Canada has been one such jurisdiction, for the federal government enacted a series of reform measures in the 1970s and 1980s to make this kind of evidence inadmissible.

Then Canada adopted its ERA, a set of constitutional equality guarantees which not only give sex equality explicit constitutional status, but which also expressly state that any measure designed to ameliorate the condition of any disadvantaged group—including groups disadvantaged by sex—are not to be considered as constituting sex discrimination. Ever since the ERA came into effect (in 1985) the largest number of cases which have raised charter defenses have been rape cases, with rapists arguing that the past sexual history rules of the reformed rape laws violate their rights to a fair trial.[8] (To my knowledge, no rapist has yet argued that rape is also protected by freedom of expression.) In recent appeals to the Ontario Court of Appeal in two of these cases, the CCLA was an intervenor, making the constitutional argument for the rapist. In a letter explaining why she did not think that she was acting against the interests of women, Louise Arbour, the feminist lawyer who acted for the CCLA on the appeal, contended that she understood the importance of civil liberties in Canada because she had been in Quebec when the War Measures Act had been invoked (Louise Arbour, 1987).

Sexual Harassment

At one North American university (which cannot be named here because the professor involved has said that he will sue for defamation), the very first person to be accused of sexual harassment under the new guidelines threatened to sue the complainant for defamation unless the accusation was withdrawn. After being informed that the local civil liberties association had endorsed the professor's position (on the grounds of academic freedom), the complainant withdrew her complaint, and she still cannot publicly air the dispute without fear of a defamation suit.

As if this tactic were not enough to silence the actual complaints that women have made under these procedures, male academics have now organized themselves to oppose even the existence of sexual harassment procedures. In a recent academic newspaper (which cannot be named here because the professor involved in the unnameable case will sue for defamation), the very professor who had been the subject

---

[8]See *R. v. Gayme and Seaboyer*, No. 7 C.R.D. 725.330–05 (Ont. Sup. Ct., Nov. 22, 1985) (sections 246 and 246.7, limiting defense counsel's scope of permissible cross-examination, held inoperative and violative of Charter); *R. v. LeGallant*, No. 6 C.R.D. 725.330–03 (B.C. Sup. Ct., June 10, 1985) (sections 246.6 and 246.7 violate the principles of fundamental justice set out in the Charter); cf. *R. v. Wiseman*, No. 6 C.R.D. 725.300–02 (Ont. Dist. Ct., June 25, 1985) (section 246.7 is reasonable and noncapricious provision and it does not violate Charter). As of 1989, *Gayme and Seboyer* was on appeal to the Supreme Court of Canada.

of the unnameable complaint at the unnameable university wrote an "academic" and "objective" critique of the sexual harassment procedures at the unnameable university to show why they offend principles of fairness and due process: (a) Sexual harassment is not a problem; everyone knows that statistics can be manipulated to support any position. (b) There are no men (or faculty members) on the five-person panel that is to hear the complaints. (c) There are no men (or faculty) on the standing advisory committee that screens the complaints. (d) A verdict is reached by majority vote, which means that if there is even one prejudiced person on the panel, she can affect the outcome. (e) The rules imply that a plaintiff's mere allegation that she felt uncomfortable in a situation is some evidence that the accused sexually harassed her. (f) The university, in essence, pays for the complainant's lawyer. (g) The long and drawn-out proceedings are not worth the time and effort. (h) The whole procedure amounts to ideological "thought policing." And who has supported the male professor throughout this entire process? Yes, it has been one of the civil liberties organizations in North America, but I have been requested by the complainant not to disclose which one because she does not have the resources to defend against a defamation suit.

CONCLUSION

As these examples indicate, the differences between the CLers and feminists are scarcely superficial or trivial; on the contrary, they go to the core of the feminist agenda, and, if one is interested in analyzing them from the perspective of CLers, they also go to the core of the western liberal agenda. These differences are fundamental, and, I submit, they are fundamental because feminism challenges male prerogative on all points across the male political spectrum—including the point of liberalism's greatest aspirations and activism.

As a political movement, western liberalism is dedicated to improving the quality of life for men and for those who share their psychological styles, aesthetic tastes, and economic goals. Access to and exploitation of women is basic to maintaining and optimizing the male quality of life. As a political movement, feminism is dedicated to improving women's quality of life, and particularly to combatting oppressions that women experience at the hands of men. This means that so long as women experience male domination and exploitation as oppressive, feminists and liberals will continue to differ. And these differences will not be resolved until the men—and the women—who run the ACLU and the CCLA admit that this is all true.

REFERENCES

Arbour, Louise. (1987, January 27). Letter. (Copy on file with Kathleen A. Lahey, Faculty of Law, Queens University of Kingston, Ontario.) [Note: Louise Arbour was appointed to sit as a trial judge in the Supreme Court of Ontario in December 1987.]

Dworkin, Andrea. (1979). *Pornography: Men possessing women.* New York: Perigee Books.

Eisenstein, Zillah. (1981). *The radical future of liberal feminism.* New York: Longman.

Fraser Committee, Minister of Justice and Attorney General of Canada. (1985). *Pornography and prostitution in Canada, Report of the special committee on pornography and prostitution.* Ottawa: Minister of Supply and Services in Canada.

Gray and Company. (1986, June 5). Memorandum. (Copy on file with Kathleen A. Lahey, Faculty of Law, Queens University of Kingston, Ontario.)

Lahey, Kathleen A. (1983). Notes on equality. Unpublished.

Lahey, Kathleen A. (1984–1985). The Canadian charter of rights and pornography: Toward a theory of actual gender equality. *New England Law Review* 20:4, 649, 652–61.

Lahey, Kathleen A. (1986). Free trade and pornography: A discussion paper. Toronto: METRAC. (Available from Metro Toronto Action Committee on Violence Against Women and Children, 158 Spadina Road, Toronto, Ontario Canada. Telephone: (416) 392-3135.)

MacKinnon, Catharine A. (1986, July 27). Letter. (Copy on file with Kathleen A. Lahey, Faculty of Law, Queens University of Kingston, Ontario.)

Minister of Justice and Attorney General of Canada. (1985). *Pornography and prostitution, Report of the special committee on pornography and prostitution.* Ottawa: Minister of Supply and Services Canada.

Part VI

POLITICS AND POSSIBILITIES

Be-Witching: Re-Calling
the Archimagical Powers
of Women

Mary Daly

This is an invitation to myself and to you, my sisters, to an Otherworld journey. And by "Otherworld" I don't mean spacing out, although at times I am a sort of space cadet. But an Otherworld journey which is very much thisworldly and very much grounded in be-ing in this world.

And that invitation is to the country of the Strange. And since, as Wild Women, we are Strange, it is to our homeland.

I also would like to conjure our sisters, the elements—the earth, the air, the fire, the water—the Archimagical powers of words which have been muted by the mind and word mutilators. I would like to conjure our sisters—the planets, the stars, the moon, the farthest galaxies— and our Foresisters—past, present, and future.

In the past, there were, oh, so many: Sojourner Truth, Matilda Joslyn Gage, Virginia Woolf, Sappho. In the future, there are our blossoming Selves, and Others to come. And in the present, I would like to mention Robin Morgan, who gave us, years ago, you know, this wonderful kind of mantra. And it's about Lust. You remember? "I want a women's revolution like a lover. I lust for it, I want so much this freedom, this end to struggle and fear and lies we all exhale, that I could die just with the passionate uttering of that desire" from "Monster," in *Monster* (New York: Vintage, 1972, p. 82).

There is, of course, a battle going on. Pornography is one major part of it. It is also a symptom. I see the battle as a Battle of Principalities and Powers. It is a deeply psychic/spiritual, as well as physical, battle. It is a battle about life and death. It is about Biophilia, or love of life— which I hope we represent, which I choose with every breath to be, to have—and necrophilia, you know, the hatred of life, the love of what is decaying, dead.

And I think that the way we fight this battle most essentially is not on the men's terms, on the boys' terms, but by expanding our auras, our O-zones, our be-ing, by turning, as Sonia Johnson says, our eyes away from the guys, very frequently, even though on another level we may be watching them.

This means opening our Third Eye, and opening our Inner Ear, our Third Ear. It means, also, making a crucial distinction which every one of us can understand very deeply, and maintaining that distinction. That is between the foreground, which is the fathers' flatland, the plastic world that they have manufactured, and the deep Background, Named by Denise Connors, which is the Wild Realm of women's Selves.

In the 1980s, as I hardly need to tell you, we have been facing a time in which all the earth's creatures, including ourselves, are targeted by the maniacal fathers, sons, and holy ghosts for extinction by nuclear holocaust or, failing that, by chemical contamination, by escalated ordinary violence, by manmade hunger and disease that proliferate in a climate of deception and mind-rot.

Within the general context of this decade's horrors, women face in our daily lives forces whose intent is to mangle, strangle, tame, and turn us against our own purposes. And yet at this very time—somehow, living, longing, through, above, before and beyond it—thousands, hundreds of thousands, hopefully millions of women struggle to Re-member ourselves and our history, to sustain and intensify the life-loving that is a Biophilic consciousness.

I would like to say something about lust. I would like to talk to you about the very word *lust*, and the expression "pure lust." The very title of my book, *Pure Lust*, is double edged, and the word *lust* is double-edged.

On the one side, *lust* and *pure lust* Name the deadly dispassion that prevails in patriarchy, the life-hating lechery that rapes and kills the objects of its obsession/aggression. Indeed, the usual meaning of *lust* within the lecherous state of patriarchy is well-known. It means sexual desire of a violent, self-indulgent character, lechery, lasciviousness. Phallic lust, violent and self-indulgent, levels all life, dismembering spirit/matter, attempting annihilation.

Its refined cultural products, from the sadistic pornography of the Marquis de Sade to the sadomasochistic theology of a Karl Barth are on a continuum. They are the same. This lust is pure, in the sense that it is characterized by unmitigated malevolence.

The word *Lust*, however, has utterly other meanings than this. It means vigor, fertility, as the increasing Lust of the earth, or of the planet. It means an intense longing, craving. It means eagerness, enthusiasm. The word, then — drawn from the Latin *lascivus*, meaning playful, wanton — is double edged.

Wise women wield our wits, making this word our Wand, our Labrys, our double-ax. As Amazons, going on our horses, we swing this double-ax, cutting down the demons that block our way. For it Names not only the "thrust of the argument" that assails women and nature on all sides, but also the way out. *Lust* Names the vigor, eagerness, and intense longing that launches Wild Women on Journeys beyond the State of Lechery. Primarily, then, "Pure Lust" Names the high humor, hope, and cosmic accord, harmony, of those women who choose to escape, to follow our hearts' deepest desire, and bound out of the State of Bondage, Wanderlusting and Wonderlusting with the elements, connecting with auras of animals and plants, moving in planetary communion with the farthest stars.

This Lust is in its essence astral. It is pure passion, unadulterated, absolute, simple, sheer striving for abundance of be-ing. It is unlimited, unlimiting desire, fire. One moved by its magic is Musing, Remembering her Self. Choosing to leave the dismembered state, she casts her lot, life, with the trees and the winds, the sands and the tides, the mountains and moors.

She is Outcast, casting herSelf outward, inward, breaking out of the casts of phallocracy's fabrications, moving out of the maze of mediated experience. As she lurches, leaps into starlight, her tears become tidal, her cackles cosmic, her laughter Lusty.

As we move on the Journey of Pure Lust, we encounter some obstacles. All right. I will give some names for the more concrete of those obstacles in a moment. But let me first characterize the world that they make as the sadosociety, legitimated by sadospirituality, characterized by a flight from phallic lust. For indeed they are "snools"—*snool* is a wonderful word; it's in the dictionary. *Snool* rhymes with drool, fool. You know? It means a cringing, cowering person. They are so obsessed with their lust that they must always flee from it into phallic asceticism. Here is an example from St. Jerome:

> I sat alone, the companion of scorpions and wild beasts, and yet was in the midst of dancing girls. My face was white with fasting, but the mind in my cold body was hot with desires. The fires of lust burned up a body that was already dead.

Jerome was a typical saint.

And it goes on, you know. St. Symeon Stylites was a famous pillar ascetic. Despairing of escaping the world horizontally, he mounted his pillar to escape it vertically. It was about sixty feet tall, and he stayed there for many years. Emperors and kings crouched at the foot of the pillar to catch the precious turds that dropped, while Symeon touched his feet with his forehead 1,244 times in succession.

If this seems bizarre, it is because the sadoworld is bizarre. Another ascetic was Robert Oppenheimer, the manufacturer of the first atomic bomb, the great scientist, who declared that he needed war, that it was necessary for discipline. He said: "Study, and our duties to men and to the commonwealth, war and personal hardship, and even the need for subsistence, ought to be greeted by us with profound gratitude. For only through them . . . can we know peace."

Now we could leave them to it, except that they impose this asceticism upon the rest of us, you know, in the form of all kinds of deprivation. And among these, physical deprivation. Yes, millions, millions, millions are starving. Sensory deprivation: these buildings. Mental deprivation in the form of Biggest Lies.

If you are a graduate of the catholic church, you are aware of the doctrine of the Eucharist. What does that mean? It means that this isn't bread and wine; it's the body and blood of Christ. It looks like bread; it tastes like wine. But it's really flesh and blood.

And when you've been trained in Biggest Lies, you can believe anything.

In that same tradition is pornography. Just think about it. Andrea Dworkin has pointed out that the pornographic conceit is the lie that women want it. That women want to be raped, maimed, murdered, tortured, and finally dismembered.

If they create Biggest Lies, then we're so grateful for a modicum of truth that we grovel, grovel, grovel for something from the boys, these ascetics who are depriving us of our fullness of life force.

One of the strategies that they use is reversal. George Orwell talked about "doublethink." Doublethink is the internal mechanism by which the doublethinker forgets what he or she is doing, and at the same time, on some level, knows.

Reversal is the external manifestation of doublethink. For example, Reagan is called the "Great Communicator." The MX missile—these are obvious—is called "Peacekeeper." Animal rights activists are called "terrorists." The "natural look" is the name for makeup, and women who won't wear it are called "unnatural." Those who do not want women to have free choice about abortion are called "pro-lifers."

And then there is another type of convoluted reversal. For example, the expression "forcible rape" implies that there's another kind of rape, which is benign. And indeed, there are psychologists who do proclaim that there's such a thing as "benign rape." So what they do is they make this big category, "rape," and then you have two types, forcible and benign. Ugh.

So reversal and doublethink permeate the atmosphere of the sado-society.

Among the obstacles are embedded needs. Embedded in women is a false need for belonging. There's this box, this need to belong: to belong to a man; to belong to some organization; to belong to a movement which isn't moving; to belong to some little community; to belong to a therapy group.

And the more women try to belong, the more they forget about Be-Longing. And if I separate, if I capitalize and make it *Be-Longing*, then I'm Naming the Lust for Happiness. Our real Lust is not to belong; it's Be-Longing, ontological longing.

Another box which is a trap, which they've embedded into women, is the possessed need for befriending. The need to be befriended, dead-ended. This makes me think of therapy, you know, all of this need to be befriended by this person that you're paying a fortune to because you don't have friends, or whatever.

So, the need to be befriended is a shrunken caricature of the desire for Be-Friending, which is the sharing of Happiness. Be-Friending is the Lust to share Happiness.

And bewitching is another box which is a trap. You know, the need to be bewitching: "Feminization 101." Femininity. Feminization.

And what is really underneath that captivated, warped desire is the desire for Be-Witching, which is the Lust for Metamorphosis. So we have to spring free from that box. That means that we have to dislodge from our psyches those plastic passions which have been embedded by the mind-manipulators, the mind-binders. I would admit that plastic passions are "real," the way plastic is real. I mean, they're blobs in inner space that just roll around, roll around. They have no nameable agent or object.

They're therapeutic. By therapeutic I mean this kind of mentality: "How can I deal with the way you feel about how I deal with the way you deal with how I deal?" "Oh, that lecture was very therapeutic." Writing is "therapeutic." Speaking is "therapeutic." *Not* writing is "therapeutic." *Not* speaking is "therapeutic." Whereas I would suggest that writing is writing, speaking is speaking, acting is acting, doing is doing.

The plastic passions, then, are embedded through their therapy, their media, their religion, their gunk, their pseudo-feminism, their FACT, their man-made plastic feminism. These plastic passions are guilt, anxiety, depression, hostility, bitterness. "Oh, she's so bitter. It must be that Catholic background." There are also resentment, frustration, boredom, and saddest of all—as Simone de Beauvoir once pointed out —resignation. And yet sadder than the saddest of all, I think, is "fulfillment." Fulfillment. I don't want to be full-filled. I don't want to be a full-filled woman. Where do I go when I'm full-filled? Can you imagine a passionate song, a poem, about fulfillment?

And so, leaping out of this junk, these plastic passions, I suggest that we need new Virtues—which are Vices—like the Courage to Be, the Courage to See through it all, the Courage to Leave all that and turn our minds to our own be-ing, and stop just reacting, reacting, reacting. Women need the Courage to Live, the Courage to Sin. Sin, by the way, has the same etymological root as the verb "to be." To be is to Sin. For a woman to be is to Sin. To Sin is to be.

We need the Virtue of Rage, and the Virtue of Disgust. They're so disgusting, and we don't seem to be disgusted enough. How disgusting can they be? I'm talking about the rulers of the snooldom, of the sadosociety, and we need the Virtue of Laughing Out Loud. Okay? And the Virtue of Lust.

To exercise these Virtues, which are Vices, we need to overcome illusions. And this requires the creating of Other vibrations. And laughing in particular, I think, creates a crack in the cosmos. It breaks the house of mirrors. When women laugh at snooldom and its rulers, something happens. And the light comes in, and the air comes in, and it cracks open.

Now before proceeding to the *Wickedary*, I'd like to say something about what it means when we put these Virtues together, and we say: "Okay. I'm trying for these Virtues, these Vices, these new habits. And I proclaim myself, in doing so, a Radical Feminist."

I've thought of four criteria that should be applied when judging the truth of the assertion: "I am a Radical Feminist." Is it really true—that assertion: "I am a Radical Feminist"—or is it just jargon? I suggest these criteria:

First, if it's really true that I am a Radical Feminist, I will have a sense of radical, awesome Otherness from what patriarchy wants me to be, from what the patriarchs want me to be. And I mean "Other" not only in the sense that de Beauvoir writes "other," as the lower case "other." You know, the oppressed. I mean big capital "O" "Other." It's an Otherness that I choose. I choose with my whole being. It is my integrity. It is my broom. It is my Nightmare.

And then the second criterion is that when I say I am a Radical Feminist, I have clear and certain knowledge of the sanctions that will come down from the patriarchy, and I proceed anyway, knowing that

I'll be punished just as much for being a little bit of a feminist as for going the whole way. So we might as well go the whole way.

The third criterion for the truth of that enunciation, that statement, is that I have the feeling, the experience, of moral outrage on behalf of women as women. Not just on behalf of women as this class, this race, this group, this age, this particular physical ability or disability, but on behalf of women as women. That means that in every cell of my being, I feel outrage on behalf of the women burned as witches; on behalf of the women burned as widows in India; on behalf of the clitoridectom- ized women of Africa; on behalf of those raped, battered, tortured in and on the model of pornography; on behalf of incest victims. I feel outrage for all women because I am a woman, and if I were the last one to affirm this, I still would be a Radical Feminist. Because, don't you see, I *am* a woman. And if I love myself, then I am a Radical Feminist.

The fourth criterion is constancy or persistence. And that means that I'm a Radical Feminist even when it's not cool, even when it's not rewarded. And it never really is rewarded. It just appears to be at cer- tain points, when the boys have let out a few pseudo-rewards. Even when there are no apparent rewards, I am constant to that vision. If this is true of me, or of you, or of anyone, then perhaps we have the right to say: "I am a Radical Feminist."

On the Journey there are many travelers.

I think I see quite a few here: the Hags, the Nags, the Crones, the Furies. There are also Augurs, Brewsters, Dikes, Dragons, Dryads, Fates, Phoenixes, Prudes.

Prude. I like the word "Prude." *Prude* is from the French *prude- femme*, meaning a wise, good, proud woman. Prudes, then, are proud women. And we are Shrewd. And we are Shrews. Prudes are Shrews. A Shrew, according to the *Oxford English Dictionary*, is a person—es- pecially a woman—given to railing, or scolding, or other perverse or malignant behavior.

And we are Scolds. A Scold is a woman addicted to abusive lan- guage. Given the usual language in patriarchy, this is thought provok- ing.

And some of us are Websters. A Webster, as Judy Grahn first pointed out, is—according to *Webster's*—a female weaver. And we are Weirds. A Weird is a Fate, a Norn. And, of course, we are Dikes—some of us. A *dike* is, according to *Webster's*, a barrier preventing passage, espe- cially excluding something undesirable.

There are obstacles. Women are called "mysterious," and that's a very convoluted ideology, isn't it? I would like briefly to comment on the mystery of man. Men are mysterious. The patriarchal male is the most mysterious creature there is. Notice that it's really not a very nice word. If you look up *mystery*, you'll find that it is derived from a word meaning to close, used of the eyes and lips. I don't want to close my eyes and my lips, but that's what it means to be bound by mystery.

Each definition of *mystery* is more unappetizing than the next. According to *Webster's* it means "a religious truth revealed by God that man cannot know by reason alone, and that once it has been revealed cannot be completely understood." It sounds like something they would think up.

It is Crone-logical to point out that one possible reason a "religious truth" said to be revealed by God continues to be unintelligible is simply that it makes no sense. Mystified believers are, of course, commanded to deny their own intellectual integrity, and blindly believe the babbling of men to whom God purportedly has revealed the nonsensical mystery.

A Bitchy, Bewitching woman—a Soothsayer—is compelled to Notice and Denounce the universal lack of sense masked by the mysterious men. Such Formal Denouncements by Furies could be grouped under several nonclassifications, such as "The Failure of Man"; "Flopocracy: A History of Man's Disasters"; "The Mysterical Man: A Critical Study in Male Psychology"; "The Eternal Mystery/Mistery/Misery of Man."

Many women, having frequently peeked behind the male veils and Gossiped out the facts, are able to Hear such Denouncements. Sensing and dreading the imminent possibility of such exposure, man cloaks himself in ever murkier mysteries. He is constantly having mysterics/misterics. In his religious "revelations," especially, he mysterically reveals/re-veils himself. He withdraws into all-male clubs and secret societies—those manifold priesthoods of cockocracy marked by mumbo-jumbo, ridiculous rituals, and cockaludicrous costumes. Hoping to distract from his own stupendous senselessness and to prevent women from Seeing through and Naming his illusions/delusions, he requires/prescribes female "mysteriousness," pompously proclaiming that women's eyes and lips must be sealed.

And so, opening our eyes and lips further, what can we think and what can we say? What we can say is sometimes blocked by the fact that our vocabulary to Name the snools is limited. We can say prick, prick, prick; here a prick, there a prick, everywhere a prick, prick. And whereas there's a multiplicity of precise pejoratives, these have not been accessible, and so I devised the "Glossary of Snools" in *Pure Lust*, and then in the *Wickedary* I went further off the edge.

Among the snools are the fixers, the jocks, the plug-uglies. Plug-uglies are among the grosser forms of snoolish incarnations.

I would like to fly ahead here to speaking about the doomsday clock. You know, the doomsday clock is an image that occurs in the "Bulletin of the Atomic Scientists." And they have had this little logo for many years. Actually, for forty years—since about 1947.

The hands of the doomsday clock have been moved from various positions such as twelve minutes to midnight (midnight representing nuclear holocaust) to seven minutes to midnight, to three minutes to midnight. In 1984, for the second time the hands were moved to three minutes to midnight.

And when we think of the various atrocities of pornography, of incest, of sexual abuse, of all of this, we must think also most profoundly of the rape and holocaust of our Sister the Earth, which is the rape and holocaust of all of us, and which they intend.

Jumping off the doomsday clock requires opening our Third Eye and flying—no longer reacting to them; there is no time for that. Don't you see? It requires moving into our own Time/Space, so that yes, we may act, we may demonstrate, we may be very, very active on the boundary of their institutions, but only in so far as our Vision tells us that it is the correct expenditure of energy, which is so precious: our Gynergy.

So I'd like to come to a conclusion here with briefly speaking to you about "Jumping Off the doomsday clock . . . Eleven, Twelve, Thirteen." You know that "Widdershins" is the direction which is the "left-hand path" of pagan dances. And it's the direction of the moon. Spinsters Spinning Widdershins—turning about-face—feel/find an Other Sense of Time.

We begin by asking clock-whys and then move on to counter these clock-whys with Counterclock Whys—Questions that whirl the Questioners beyond the boundaries of Boredom, into the flow of Tidal Time/Elemental Time.

The man-dated world is clockocracy—the society that is dead set by the clocks and calendars of fathered time. It is marked by measurements that tick off women's Lifetimes/Lifelines in tidy tidbits. Clockocracy is marked by male-ordered monotony that breaks Biorhythms, preparing the way for the fullness of fathered time, that is, doomsday. The fathers' clocks are all doomsday clocks, meting out archetypal deadtime, marking the beat of the patriarchal death march. They are measures of the untime of the State of Possession—tidy time, nuclear time, doomed time.

Spinsters Spinning about-face face the fact that clockocracy's clocks are elementary moons. Whirling Witches Announce that the subject of clocks and calendars is about Face. Will we Face down the faceless "face-saving" fools who are the fathers of phallocracy/foolocracy? Lusty women, in tune with the Moon, pose the poignant Question: Is the Moon's Face the Face that can stop the doomsday clock?

The Moon in her various aspects awakens our knowledge of Gorgons, of Weirds, of Fates, of Norns. In the face of impending disaster, these Sidereal Sisters draw us onward, sharing their Powers.

Empowered by this Company, women as Gorgons look toward the madmen and turn them to stone—the doomsday men with their doomsday clocks whose tick-tocks mimic the rhythms of Lunar Time. Gorgons glare outward, refusing to serve the masters' commands to peer into mirrors. We tear off the blindfold from captive Justice, crying that the Time has come to Activize, to see with Active Eyes. We actualize Archimagical Powers, Beaming through the archetypal images that block Vision. We say that Eye-Beams/I-Beams can stop the doomsday clock—that Moonward-turning Eyes can break the spells of twelves, Spelling *Thirteen*.

Twelve is the measure of the master-minded monotony of the foreground. Nags need only think of the twelve apostles, the twelve days of christmas, twelve men on a jury, twelve hours on clock, twelve months on a cockocratic calendar.

Thirteen represents the Other Hour, beyond the direction of disaster. It signals the Presence of the Otherworld—Metamorphospheres—true Homeland of all Hags, Crones, Furies, Furries, and Other Friends. It represents the Realm of Wild Reality, the Background, the Time/Space when/where the auras of plants, planets, stars, animals, and all truly animate be-ing connect. It Spells awakening of Metamemory.

The awakening of Metamemory is crucial to the Eyebiting Power of the Crone. Since Metamemory is Deep Ecstatic Memory of participation in Be-ing, it is also the Broom of the Crone, enabling her to jump off the doomsday clock of doomdom, to hop into the Hour of Hope, the Be-Witching Hour of *Thirteen*.

To Crone-logically Leaping Intelligence, *Thirteen* Spells the hitherto/ as yet Unknown, the Elemental Forces/Sources that can save even planets doomed to destruction. It signals events that are not measurable, controllable, predictable—the Call of the Wild, the ever-recurring Spring of New Creation.

This is our context, not these tiny pinhole cubbyholes that they have given us, but the expansion of our spirits that is endless possibility. This celestial context is real. We have only to Name it and act on it; to believe in it and to be.

Thirteen Re-Calls Hope. It Spells Hope. It Re-Calls possibilities of

Metamorphosis to those who will to shift the shapes of words, of worlds. It points to spaces, times of new beginnings, of whirling whirls.

Thirteen, then, is the Time of synchronicities, of Syn-Crone-icities, of "coincidences" experienced by Crones as Strangely significant. It is the Time of Realizing Star-Lust—the longing for knowledge of Astral connections, for scintillating cosmic conversations.

What holds us back? For one thing, the archetypes, the deadly archetypes. For example, of the family, the family, the family. Why is everyone desperate to have a baby, a baby, a baby? Where is this coming from? Have a baby! All lesbians have to have a baby?! Everyone has to have a baby. If you're 69½, you'd better hurry up and have a baby.

And marriage, and marriage. And belonging, and belonging, and belonging. Where are all these archetypes coming from? *Archetype* is an interesting word. It's from the Greek *arche*, meaning "original," and *typtein*, meaning "to beat," as well as from the Sanskrit *tumpati*, meaning "he hurts."

Well, armed with its archetypes, the patriarchy beats down our originality, our original sunrise, our power to create, our Elemental sources, forces, which alone can save us.

So I see us as smashers of these archetypes, as Realizing the Great, Original Witch within, who calls to us, always, from deep inside, who is calling now through our Foresisters: past, present, and future; from the Elements that are groaning under phallic control; from the stars; from everything that would free us from the mindbindings that keep us tied to little, little—you know—teensy pinoramic views.

This Witch, you know, she is within, and she howls, and howls. And sometimes she whispers. Sometimes she even speaks in an academic way, and sometimes in a very raucous way, always in a Wild way. And what she is always saying, I think, is "Rush with my waters. Fly with my winds. Hug my earth. Light my fire!"

Not a Sentimental Journey: Women's Friendships

Janice G. Raymond

Over the past several weeks, I have been interviewed by many publications, specifically about the Baby M case and more generally about the issue of surrogacy.[1] With few exceptions, each of these interviews has raised the specter of women having a go at each other—Mary Beth Whitehead competing against Betsy Stern. The media depicts surrogacy as something that has been created by women for women out of one woman's desperate need for a child, and the other's so-called altruistic "drive" to give the "gift" of a child. The failure of the surrogate arrangement is portrayed as the failure of women, women who ultimately come into conflict with each other; the failure of females who, fickle as we are, change our minds. Then the cat fight begins. Unfortunately this perception often gets replicated at a personal level. For example, most of Mary Beth Whitehead's anger is directed at Betsy Stern, not Bill Stern.

What the media does not present is *how* women get pitted against each other, and how surrogacy is really about two women doing for one man, fulfilling his need for a genetic link to a child and for reproductive continuity. Both women in the surrogate package provide merely the maternal environment for a new brand of father-right—a reproductive ménage à trois with the man's needs once more at the center of the triangle. Nancy Reame, a nurse who worked in Noel Keane's surrogate agency and counseled many women who served as so-called surrogates, said she'd come to see surrogacy as a male transaction. The

---

[1] The conference, at which this paper was originally given, was held shortly after the first New Jersey Court decision rendered on the "Baby M" case. Commonly referred to as the Sorkow decision, it was promulgated on March 31, 1987. The interviews I mention took place prior to and after that decision.

real interaction, she said, is between the sperm donor and the male psychiatrist who ultimately adjudicates the fitness of the supposed surrogate mother (Gena Corea, 1987). This does not make the news.

The left-wing media has a more subtle take on women's supposed cat fights. I was called several weeks ago by a writer from the Chicago-based democratic socialist weekly, *In These Times*. He told me, near the middle of the interview, that his "angle" on the Baby M story, for which I was being interviewed, was dissension among feminists over surrogacy. (He believed class to be the essence of this case and wanted to highlight how feminists were divided over surrogacy because of their class consciousness.)

When the left-wing *New Statesman*, a major socialist journal in Britain, wanted to excerpt for publication a section of my book, *A Passion for Friends*, I was surprised, because much of my work has been critical of the left's antifeminism. The section that was excerpted was part of my chapter on "The Obstacles to Female Friendship." The way this excerpt was headlined, wrenched from its context and introduced, made it sound as if the book was a testament of women's inability to sustain friendships because of the various obstacles, and that this was the essence and substance of the entire book.

We witnessed the same highlighting of dissension among women in the so-called pornography debates, this time with *women* writing the copy. The headline in the June, 1986, issue of *Off Our Backs* read: "Coming Apart: Feminists and the Conflict Over Pornography." Barbara Ehrenreich, in her review of two books on pornography in the *New York Times Book Review*, contended that "the level of intrafeminist invective on one issue [pornography] has sometimes threatened to surpass the antifeminist invective from the far right." Writing in *Sojourner*, during the campaign for the antipornography ordinance in Cambridge, Boston FACT members accused "ardent" ordinance supporters of dividing the women's movement by name calling and discrediting dedicated feminists (*Sojourner*, 1985). Even a radical feminist journal, in an editorial that basically supported the ordinance, chastised defenders of the ordinance for their "extremism" and "intolerance" which supposedly presents a "dire threat" to the women's movement and which promotes tension, fear, and mistrust among women (Lise Weil, 1985).

There was one thing that was terribly lopsided about all these charges and warnings. Most of them put the blame for this dissension squarely on the shoulders of those women who supported the ordinance and who reacted with creative rage to the FACT brief, because they found in it a real betrayal of women. But there is another thing that is very wrong about all these charges and warnings. They sentimentalize dissension, and they sentimentalize unity among women. It is as if to hold a strong position on feminist issues any more is tantamount to dividing women. If you're not a moral relativist, you're an extremist or, in some circles, a fascist. Enter the liberal notion of unity—a unity that is achieved only by ceding the capacity for making moral and political judgments.

Let us not sentimentalize dissension as we should not sentimentalize unity in the women's movement, and from whence it comes. What kind of unity can be built on an unwillingness to make judgments about what is pornography, about sadomasochism, about incest? More recently, what kind of unity can be built on a perception of surrogacy as reproductive choice, enhancing the liberation of women? What kind of unity can be built on an unwillingness to create a politics of resistance to this violence against women? It was easy in the early days of this particular wave of feminism to assert judgments that were in opposition to clearly accepted male-dominant values. Sentimentalism set in when judgments and action came into conflict with those of other women, especially women from within the ranks of those supposedly committed to the same cause. In the name of some amorphously defined feminist unity, value judgments and the will to enact them in opposition to other women is now seen as divisive.

What truly divides women is a legal brief that supports women's victimization in pornography by equating the defenders of the victims with the pornographers. What truly divides women is a call for model legislation which defends surrogacy as reproductive freedom while reinforcing the reality of a breeder class of women which has vast implications for the reproductive traffic in women worldwide. What truly divides women is trying to take real legal power out of the hands of women before women even have that power. What truly divides women is using the real ways that women have been abused in pornography, as well as the ways that women have been committed to motherhood at any cost to themselves, as simple harmless stereotypes that reinforce women's victimization. What truly divides women is claiming that women need pornography for sexual freedom, and the whole gamut of the new reproductive technologies for reproductive freedom. What truly divides women is doing nothing for women while doing everything to support the pornographers and a burgeoning medical and legal empire that makes its money and its reputation off the bodies of women.

We fight for these things, not to divide women, but because we care about women, and most of us fight for them because we love women. But love, too, is real. It is not sentimental. What often passes for a loving unity among women may actually make us passive and uncritical, because this kind of unity is sustained only at the cost of ignoring what causes the real divisiveness among women. Love for women cannot only *appear* to be sensitive and respectful of other women's opinions. It must *be* a love that takes action, even in the face of other women's opposition to that action. A sentimental love for women fosters a tyranny of tolerance. We do not have to be tolerant of any opinion or action that other women express in the name of unity, especially when that tolerance becomes repressive. Women have the right and the authority to say no, pornography is wrong, surrogacy is wrong, and to persuade others, to make judgments, and to make those judgments real in the political world.

During six years, in the course of writing a book on female friendship, I have been preoccupied with the obstacles to female friendship (Janice Raymond, 1986). One of the most horrendous obstacles is the state of violation, subordination, and atrocity in which many women live their lives. And one of the most devastating consequences of this state is to make women *not lovable* to their own selves and to other women. When a woman sees a sister dehumanized and brutalized throughout history, throughout her own life, in almost every culture; when a woman sees the endless variations of this abuse and brutality, and how few women really survive; when a woman sees this graphically depicted all around her, female friendship is erased from memory, and women are not affected by other women. The state of pornography, incest, and surrogacy (among others) reinforces the absence of women to each other. Violence against women is not only *central* to women's oppression. It is central to the lack of female friendship.

The forces of sexual liberalism tell all of us who have a vision of female freedom and female friendship not to make that vision *real*. They tell us to settle for a superficial unity that is built upon the apolitical and sentimental notion that anything that divides us is not worth the price of the conflict.

Female friendship is much more than the private face of feminist politics. We need an ideal and reality of friendship that invests women with power. Radical feminism befriends women because it empowers women to act on behalf of ourselves and each other.

Working for women is a profound act of friendship for women. It makes friendship political. Our work is based on the conviction that it is possible for women to be free, to struggle against those forces that are waged against us all, and to win, only if we have a real vision of what unites women; only if we are capable of translating that vision into a reality that makes our affection for women political; and only if affection for women translates into action for women.

REFERENCES

Corea, Gena. (1987, January). Quoted in a conversation with.

Raymond, Janice G. (1986). *A passion for friends: A philosophy of female affection.* Boston: Beacon Press.

Sojourner, September 1985.

Weil, Lise. (1985, Summer). "Imagining our freedom: Thoughts on the pornography debate." *Trivia: A Journal of Ideas* 7, pp. 4–10.

Author Index

Subject Index

Easterbrook, Judge Frank, 37
Economic dependence, of battered women, 63
Egg donation, 87–88
Electronic fetal monitoring, 87
Ellis, Havelock, 15, 18–21, 25, 126
Ellis, Kate, 130
Elmy, Elisabeth Wolstenholme, 17
Embryo evaluation, 87
Embryo flushing, 87, 89
Embryo freezing, 89
Emerson, Professor Thomas I., 114, 118–19, 121
Emma magazine, 93
Enthusiasm, in sexual intercourse, 23, 24
Equality, "gotchas" of, 114–22
Equality-as-sameness model, 10
Erotophobia, 128
Exploitation, 29, 200
  by pimps, 71
  by pornographers, 78

FACT, see Feminist Anti-Censorship Task Force
Family structure:
  battering of women, 63 66
  incest, 43–55
  as prison, 61–66
  prostitution and, 67–81
  women in patriarchy, 56–60
  see also Patriarchy
Feminism:
  nuanced view of, 103, 109
  opposition to women-hating, 39
  as political practice of fighting male supremacy, 31
Feminist Anti-Censorship Task Force (FACT), 9, 104–8, 112, 125, 148–55
  brief, 9–11
Feminist political theory, 178–79
Feminist pro-pornography, 106
Feminists, as socialization failures, 154
Ferber, Paul, 203
Fetal monitoring, 87

Fetishism, 126, 127
First Amendment, pornography and, 36–37
Flynt, Larry, 187, 200
For Yourself (Barbach), 153
Fraser Committee on Pornography and Prostitution, 202–4
Freedom, criticism of, 5
Freud, Sigmund, 18, 61
Friedan, Betty, 96
Friendships, women's, 222–26
Frigidity:
  as "hostility," 24
  origin of term, 22–23
  see also Sexuality
Frigidity in Woman in Relation to Her Lovelife (Stekel), 23–24

Gay-rights advocates, pornographers and, 187
"Gender: A Noted Author Warns of Reverse Sexism" (Farrell), 168
Gender neutrality, 169–70
  definition of, 12
Genetic testing/counseling, 87
"Gotchas" of equality, 114–22
  pornography gotcha, 119–22
  pregnancy gotcha, 115–17
  privacy gotcha, 117–19
  "women will be harmed by equality" gotchas, 115
Griswold v. Connecticut, 117–19, 187
Giobbe, Evelina, 67–81
Guccione, Bob, 137, 187

Harassment, see Sexual harassment/assault
Harrison, Garnett, 45–47
Harris, Seale, 85
Harris v. McRay, 7
Hefner, Christie, 187
Hefner, Hugh, 107, 126, 187
Heller, Valerie, 157–61, 222–26
High Society pornographic computer service, 77
Hite, Shere, 168
Homophobia, 184–90

About the Editors and Contributors

Louise Armstrong
Louise Armstrong is the author of *Kiss Daddy Goodnight* and *Solomon Says: A Speakout on Foster Care*.

Pauline B. Bart
Pauline B. Bart has written extensively in areas of women's health and in violence against women. Together with graduate students she has written *The Student Sociologist's Handbook* and *Stopping Rape: Successful Survival Strategies*.

Twiss Butler
Twiss Butler is on the staff of the National Organization for Women with responsibility for analyzing institutional promotion of sex discrimination in the areas of pregnancy, insurance, pornography, and communications and education media.

Phyllis Chesler
Phyllis Chesler is the author of six books, including *Women and Madness, About Men, Mothers on Trial: The Battle for Children and Custody*, and most recently *Sacred Bond: The Legacy of Baby M*. She is currently active in assisting mothers who are involved in custody battles.

Susan G. Cole
Susan G. Cole is a co-founder of the Canadian feminist review *Broadside* and the author of *Pornography and the Sex Crisis*.

Gena Corea
Gena Corea, and investigative journalist, is author of *The Hidden Malpractice* and *The Mother Machine*. An editor of *Reproductive and Genetic Engineering: Journal of International Feminist Analysis*, she is also associate director of the Institute of Women and Technology.

Mary Daly

Mary Daly teaches Feminist Ethics in the Department of Theology at Boston College. She is the author of *The Church and the Second Sex, Beyond God the Father, Gyn/Ecology, Pure Lust,* and *Webster's First New Intergalactic Wickedary of the English Language* (In cahoots with Jane Caputi).

Andrea Dworkin

Andrea Dworkin is a radical feminist theorist, activist, and writer. She led protests against the Women's House of Detention in the later 1960s that resulted in its closing, and protested against the "snuff" films in the early 1970s; the protests raised the consciousness of the entire nation. The books she has authored include *Women-Hating, Intercourse, Pornography: Men Possessing Women, Right-wing Women,* and the novel *Ice and Fire.* With Catharine MacKinnon, she drafted the Minneapolis and Indianapolis ordinances that made the practice of pornography a civil rights violation of women.

Evelina Giobbe

Evelina Giobbe is the founder and current Director of WHISPER. WHISPER is a Minnesota-based national organization of survivors of prostitution working with other women's advocates in the larger feminist community to educate the public about the reality of prostitution and to work for services for survivors.

Valerie Heller

Valerie Heller is a graduate student in criminal justice at the City University of New York (CUNY), and a past acting president, and president-elect of VOICES (Victims of Incest Can Emerge Survivors). She is currently writing her doctoral dissertation on dissociative states resulting from longtime sexual victimization. She is also a psychotherapist specializing in sexual victims' recovery.

Sheila Jeffreys

Sheila Jeffreys is a lesbian and revolutionary feminist who has been active in the Women's Liberation Movement since 1973, mainly in campaigns against male violence and pornography. She is the author of *The Spinster and Her Enemies: Feminism and Sexuality 1880–1930* and *Anticlimax: A Feminist Perspective on the Sexual Revolution.*

Sonia Johnson

Sonia Johnson is a professional speaker and the author of *From House-wife to Heretic, Going Out of Our Minds: The Metaphysics of Liberation*, and *Wildfire: Igniting the She/volution*.

Ann Jones

Ann Jones is the author of *Women Who Kill*, and *Everyday Death: The Case of Bernadette Powell*. She has contributed to *Take Back the Night*, *Women's Worlds* and many other periodicals.

Susanne Kappeler

Susanne Kappeler teaches at the University of East Anglia in Norwich, England. She is the author of *The Pornography of Representation* and one of the editors of *Trouble and Strife*, a British radical feminist magazine.

Kathleen A. Lahey

Kathleen Lahey is a Professor at Queens University faculty of law in Kingston, Ontario. She has been involved in feminist and lesbian theory and activism for many years.

Dorchen Leidholdt

Dorchen Leidholdt is a founding member of Women Against Pornography and the Coalition on Trafficking in Women. She is currently a staff attorney with the Legal Aid Society in New York City.

Catharine A. MacKinnon

Catharine MacKinnon is a lawyer, teacher, writer, and activist. With Andrea Dworkin, she conceived ordinances recognizing pornography as a violation of civil rights. She has written *Sexual Harassment of Working Women*, *Feminism Unmodified*, and *Toward a Feminist Theory of the State*.

Janice G. Raymond

Janice Raymond is a professor of Women's Studies and Medical Ethics at the University of Massachusetts. She is the author of *The Transsexual Empire* and *A Passion for Frienas* and is currently writing a book on *Reproductive Gifts, Contracts and Technologies*.

Florence Rush

Florence Rush is the author of *The Best Kept Secret: Sexual Abuse of Children* and many published articles on women and children. She lectures nationwide on the sexual abuse of children and women's issues.

Wendy Stock
Wendy Stock teaches in the Department of Psychology at Texas A&M University.

John Stoltenberg
John Stoltenberg is a writer and magazine editor. He is chair of the Task Group on Pornography of the National Organization for Changing Men and co-founder of Men Against Pornography in New York City.

THE ATHENE SERIES
An International Collection of Feminist Books
General Editors: Gloria Bowles, Renate Klein, and Janice Raymond
Consulting Editor: Dale Spender